Family Bonds

Studies in Feminist Philosophy is designed to showcase cutting-edge monographs and collections that display the full range of feminist approaches to philosophy, that push feminist thought in important new directions, and that display the outstanding quality of feminist philosophical thought.

STUDIES IN FEMINIST PHILOSOPHY
Cheshire Calhoun, *Series Editor*

Advisory Board
Harry Brod, University of Northern Iowa
Claudia Card, University of Wisconsin
Lorraine Code, York University, Toronto
Kimberlé Crenshaw, Columbia Law School/UCLA School of Law
Jane Flax, Howard University
Ann Garry, California State University, Los Angeles
Sally Haslanger, Massachusetts Institute of Technology
Alison Jaggar, University of Colorado, Boulder
Helen Longino, Stanford University
Maria Lugones, SUNY Binghamton
Uma Narayan, Vassar College
James Sterba, University of Notre Dame
Rosemarie Tong, University of North Carolina, Charlotte
Nancy Tuana, Penn State University
Karen Warren, Macalester College

Published in the series:
Abortion and Social Responsibility: Depolarizing the Debate
Laurie Shrage

Gender in the Mirror: Confounding Imagery
Diana Tietjens Meyers

Autonomy, Gender, Politics
Marilyn Friedman

Setting the Moral Compass: Essays by Women Philosophers
Edited by Cheshire Calhoun

Burdened Virtues: Virtue Ethics for Liberatory Struggles
Lisa Tessman

On Female Body Experience: "Throwing Like a Girl" and Other Essays
Iris Marion Young

Visible Identities: Race, Gender, and the Self
Linda Martín Alcoff

Women and Citizenship
Edited by Marilyn Friedman

Women's Liberation and the Sublime: Feminism, Postmodernism, Environment
Bonnie Mann

Analyzing Oppression
Ann E. Cudd

Ecological Thinking: The Politics of Epistemic Location
Lorraine Code

Self Transformations: Foucault, Ethics, and Normalized Bodies
Cressida J. Heyes

Family Bonds: Genealogies of Race and Gender
Ellen K. Feder

Family Bonds

Genealogies of Race and Gender

Ellen K. Feder

OXFORD

UNIVERSITY PRESS

2007

OXFORD
UNIVERSITY PRESS

Oxford University Press, Inc., publishes works that further
Oxford University's objective of excellence
in research, scholarship, and education.

Oxford   New York
Auckland   Cape Town   Dar es Salaam   Hong Kong   Karachi
Kuala Lumpur   Madrid   Melbourne   Mexico City   Nairobi
New Delhi   Shanghai   Taipei   Toronto

With offices in
Argentina   Austria   Brazil   Chile   Czech Republic   France   Greece
Guatemala   Hungary   Italy   Japan   Poland   Portugal   Singapore
South Korea   Switzerland   Thailand   Turkey   Ukraine   Vietnam

Copyright © 2007 by Oxford University Press, Inc.

Published by Oxford University Press, Inc.
198 Madison Avenue, New York, New York 10016

www.oup.com

Oxford is a registered trademark of Oxford University Press

Library of Congress Cataloging-in-Publication Data
Feder, Ellen K.
Family bonds : genealogies of race and gender / Ellen K. Feder.
    p.   cm.—(Studies in feminist philosophy)
Includes bibliographical references and index.
ISBN 978-0-19-531474-8; 978-0-19-531475-5 (pbk.)
1. Race—Philosophy.   2. Race awareness.   3. Sex role—Philosophy.
4. Foucault, Michel, 1926–1984—Political and social views.   I. Title.
HT1523.F43 2007
305.8001—dc22   2006052466

9 8 7 6 5 4 3 2 1

Printed in the United States of America
on acid-free paper

For Jen, again.
And now for Nic.

To interpret is a way of reacting to enunciative poverty, and to compensate for it by a multiplication of meaning; a way of speaking on the basis of that poverty, and yet despite it. But to analyse a discursive formation is to seek the law of that poverty, it is to weigh it up, and to determine its specific form. In one sense, therefore, it is to weigh the "value" of statements. A value that is not defined by their truth, that is not gauged by the presence of a secret content; but which characterizes their place, their capacity for circulation and exchange, their possibility for transformation, not only in the economy of discourse, but more generally, in the administration of scarce resources. In one sense, discourse ceases to be what it is for the exegetic attitude: an inexhaustible treasure from which one can always draw new, and always unpredictable riches; a providence that has always spoken in advance, and which enables one to hear, when one knows how to listen, retrospective oracles: it appears as an asset—finite, limited, desirable, useful—that has its own rules of appearance, but also its own conditions of appropriation and operation; an asset that consequently, from the moment of its existence (and not only in its "practical applications"), poses the question of power; an asset that is, by nature, the object of struggle, a political struggle.

—*Michel Foucault,* The Archaeology of Knowledge

Acknowledgments

From the beginning, this project has been about telling stories. It seeks to tell stories in different ways and to ask questions about the meanings of these different tellings. I have been fortunate that so many people have taken an interest in the stories I tell here about gender and race, and especially gratified that many have shared their own stories along the way. Sometimes they told stories of childhood experiences on the gender border and what *they* most enjoyed doing with Barbie or Ken. More often, they recounted stories of their own children and the different sorts of gendered behavior they manifested, speculating on the effects of gender variance with respect to their own status as parents.

Some years ago, I spoke to an old friend about the founding of Levittown, the subject of chapter 2. My friend had grown up in a mostly Jewish and Irish development on Long Island that had been built by William Levitt's company in the early 1960s. I told her what I'd learned about the "Homeowner's Manual" that all new residents of Levittown received. These manuals had all sorts of "do's and don'ts" that would be "strictly enforced." These included lawn-mowing guidelines, the requirement of permission to change the color of the house, and the prohibition of fences and clotheslines.

Yes, she nodded, she remembered that they couldn't have clotheslines. And she remembered something else: Her parents' annoyance every summer when their next-door neighbors placed lounge chairs on their *front* lawn. "What do they think this is, a stoop?" To their children, on the phone to other neighbors and extended family, they would exclaim, "A stoop! They must think this is some kind of stoop!" For my friend, reflecting on the story of Levittown, it became clear that it was the conviction that her parents had left "the stoop" behind in Brooklyn that provoked these seasonal fits of pique. She also had the sense that there was some connection between "the stoop thing" and the threat in her mother's voice when she told my friend and her younger sister to be home at such-and-such an hour and "don't make me yell out for you." "Yelling out," like passing hot days on the stoop among neighbors, was something that happened in the ethnic "neighbor-hood," not on the tidy streets of "the development."

My friend's story gripped me for many reasons. It offered a vivid illustra-tion of the success of European assimilation and the internalization of the discipline that made that assimilation possible. But it was something more than another example of the kind of power I examine here. Despite the fact that her parents' frustration over the neighbors' behavior was for her a vivid memory, the story was a new one—a result of knowledge she had just acquired about rulebooks and marketing practices employed by Levitt's company (including financial inducements to European Americans to leave the city and the exclusion of people of color). Where it had first been another illustration of how nutty her parents could be as she was growing up, the story of "the slippery slope to the stoop," as she now told it, was a depiction of the requirements a middle-class "whiteness" entailed and that her parents vigor-ously assumed, requirements she had unconsciously embraced, informing her own aspirations and judgments.

My friend's reflections were a genuine gift to me, for they attested to the possibilities for new stories that Foucault's method offers. I was moved, too, by my friend's engagement with the project. I have been fortunate throughout the development of *Family Bonds* to have had many people offer the generous attention that has made its completion possible. It is a privilege to acknowl-edge their contribution.

I am grateful to two women who shared stories that appear in these pages. First I must thank the mother I call "Mary," who candidly recounted her experience as a mother of a child with an intersex condition. I also thank Daisy Myers, who, with her family, integrated Levittown, Pennsylvania, in 1947. After reading her remarkable memoir—composed in the early 1960s at the urging of Pearl Buck but not published until 2005—I was honored to meet with her just as I was completing the final draft of this manuscript.

I owe thanks to those who encouraged my project in its earliest stages, including Mary Rawlinson, Eva Feder Kittay, Ed Casey, Irene Klaver, and Sharon Meagher. Repeated thanks are owed Eva Kittay. Though our shared surname does not mark a biological tie, her sustained attention to this and other projects gives meaning to the term "family bonds." The debt I owe her is immeasurable. My former colleagues at Vassar College, in particular Uma Narayan, Jennifer Church, Mitch Miller, and Angela Y. Davis, kindly read and commented on a first draft of chapter 3 one evening into the wee hours.

Many others have commented on various parts of this work that I have presented at conferences and invited talks over the years, including those at the Pacific Division of the American Philosophical Association, American University, the Society for Phenomenology and Existential Philosophy, the California Roundtable on Race, George Washington University's Human Sciences Seminar, and Feminist Ethics and Social Thought. My presentation at American came in my second year of teaching there, and I am fortunate to have enjoyed the collegiality of supportive colleagues ever since. A very early version of what is now chapter 3 first appeared in *Philosophical Studies* 85, nos. 2–3 (1997). Two articles that became chapter 4 appeared in *Radical Philosophy Review* 7, no. 1 (2004) and in *Hypatia* 22, no. 1 (2007). I thank Eduardo Mendieta, Alison Bailey, and Jacquelyn Zita for their comments on those essays.

I am indebted to those who offered careful readings of different chapters: Alia Al-Saji, Barbara Andrew, Marcos Bisticas-Cocoves, Edgardo Menvielle, Gail Weiss, Amy Oliver, Andrea Tschemplik, Shelley Harshe, and Michael Schmidt. All helped shape my arguments in critical ways. I am particularly indebted to those who read and commented on the entire manuscript at various stages, and I was truly fortunate to have in these readers just the variety of perspectives the project required. Carolyn Betensky always knew what I was really trying to say even when I couldn't quite get it out. Deborah Cohen and Eileen Findlay kindly and critically cast historians' eyes on the project. Falguni Sheth pushed me to achieve greater clarity. Alison Flaum brought an uncommon generosity and wit to a thorough reading of the final manuscript. With a similar generosity of spirit, Karmen MacKendrick read the book at "both ends"—from what she assured me were its "good bones" at the outset, to the final, fuller-bodied project. I am also grateful for the supportive and helpful comments offered by Andrew Cutrofello, Jane Flax, Charles Mills, and Dee Mortensen.

I owe thanks to many people for their work on the details of assembling this book. At American University, Shelley Harshe assisted me with all manner of manuscript preparation with remarkable good cheer. Lara Zoble at Oxford University Press has always been available with answers, advice, and reassurance, as has her successor, Brian Hurley. Carol Hoke provided a sensitive reading of the manuscript, Valerie Hazel gamely took on the preparation of the index, and Christine Dahlin expertly guided its production. Cheshire Calhoun and Peter Ohlin have been wonderfully supportive throughout the process. For their assistance with the collection of images that are reproduced here, I thank the librarians at Temple University's Urban Archives, particularly John Pettit, and Ann Glorioso at the Levittown, New York, public library. I also thank Elizabeth Connor, who prepared the line drawing in chapter 5, and Michael Wyetzner, whose beautiful watercolor appears on the cover of the paperback edition.

Finally, I thank my partner, Jennifer Di Toro, to whom I owe more than I can say, and our son, Dominic, who has brought such joyful noise to our days.

Contents

Family Bonds

1

Foucaultian Method

A New Tale to Tell

Feminist and critical race theorists alike have long acknowledged the "intersection" of gender and race difference; it is by now a truism that the ways that we become boys and girls, men and women cannot be disentangled from the ways in which we become white or black men and women, Asian or Latino boys and girls. Such theoretical analyses have contributed in important ways to discussions of how gender is "raced" and how race is "gendered." And yet, there has been little comparative analysis of the specific mechanisms that are at work in the "production" of each, that is, how they are intelligible as categories, together with the ways these categories come to make sense of us—as raced and gendered human beings. Recognizing important differences between the production of gender and race can help feminist and critical race theorists "think together" these categories without conflating and thus misunderstanding the specific mechanisms of each.

I propose that in Foucault's analytics of power we may find critical tools for understanding and addressing the gap between the reality, which is always a complex production of difference, and our analyses, which seem generally to focus on one sort of difference to the exclusion of another. Even as Foucault's failure to address the production of gender in a sustained way has been rightfully and frequently noted, feminist theorists have found Foucault's later (or "genealogical") work useful for understanding the production of gender and the specific expression of power that captures its operation.[1] In fact, as Susan Bordo has noted, Foucault's famous interest in the body and its "disciplining" coincided with feminist contentions that the " 'definition and shaping' of the [gendered] body is 'the focal point for struggles over the shape of power' " (Bordo 1993, 17). In Bordo's own feminist Foucaultian analysis in "The Body and the Reproduction of Femininity," for example, she observes that women's preoccupation with the "pursuit of an ever-changing, homogenizing, elusive ideal of femininity" effectively renders female bodies "docile bodies," "bodies whose forces and energies are habituated to external regulation, subjection, trans-formation, 'improvement' " (ibid., 166). The successful fashioning of the docile body thus relies ultimately on the internalization of standards, rules, and norms that are the focus of Foucault's analyses. In other words, even as women's active cultivation of femininity may be promoted by images in magazines or other media and reinforced by means of rewards and punishments via any number of social institutions, the real mark of what Foucault calls "disciplinary power" is its deployment by individual subjects who direct this power inward, applying it to their own bodies, their own selves.[2]

While feminist applications of Foucault's ideas are now commonplace, comparable applications of his analyses of power to questions concerning race have been more limited.[3] Foucault's work published before his death in 1984 reflects a virtual silence with respect to the deployment of race as a category of difference. Unlike gender, which, as Simone de Beauvoir famously noted, was not the result of some "occurrence"—that is, it has no clear beginning or "historical facts" that can explain the category or the subjection with which it is associated (Beauvoir [1949] 1989, xxiv)—the idea of "race" has origins traceable to the early modern period, from which time attributions of racial difference have entailed exploitation, enslavement, and even geno-cide.[4] It is for this reason that Foucault's conception of power as *pouvoir*, a concept that emphasizes "productiveness" over "repressiveness" and the pos-sibilities of "resistance" over "determination," fails to describe the operation of "power"—in the more conventional, encompassing sense—with respect to the history of racist oppression.[5]

Foucault in fact clarifies that the conception of power as *pouvoir* was not intended to describe these sorts of power relations. In "The Subject and Power," he writes that "slavery is not a power relationship when a man is in chains, only when he has some possible mobility, even a chance of escape. (In this case, it is a question of a physical relationship of constraint)" (Foucault [1982] 1983, 221).[6] Simple "constraint" is certainly too limiting a concept to describe the specific expression of power involved in the forms of racist exclusion prevalent today; "disciplinary power" inadequately captures the particular kind of power at work in the contemporary promotion of white supremacy. For example, de facto residential segregation—the racial homo-geneity that has generally marked neighborhoods in the United States since the Second World War (see, e.g., Massey and Denton 1993)—can no longer be attributed to an obvious sort of "constraint" as laws proscribing discrimi-nation have now been in place for decades. Nor, it appears, can an ascription of "disciplinary power" genuinely explain the great disparities in wealth and resources evident when comparing the status of white and nonwhite commu-nities. The multiplicity of measures denying black women reproductive free-dom relative to white women (see, e.g., Roberts 1997) are similarly difficult to characterize in these terms, as is the disproportionate number of black men involved in the criminal justice system (see, e.g., Maguire and Pastore 1998). Although it is compelling to describe the production of gender as a function of disciplinary power, then, we cannot simply extend that analysis to the production of race.

What these examples do suggest is that even if, as many have suggested, race and gender work in complementary ways, they do not work in the *same* way, which fact has presented a challenge to theorists who are trying to think the two categories together. The project of this book is to explore the nature of this difference and this difficulty. In this introduction I explain my effort to make use of Foucault's methods to understand the operation of gender and race. While, as so many feminist theorists have compellingly shown, the deployment of gender is best understood as a function of disciplinary power, I will argue that the deployment of race is primarily a function of what Foucault calls "biopower," an expression of power that is bound up with the state apparatus.

Foucault's "genealogical" work, particularly *Discipline and Punish* and the first volume of *The History of Sexuality*, has been prominently featured in feminist theory and frequently cited in work by critical race theorists. His earlier, "archaeological" works, up to and including *The Archaeology of Knowledge*, are more concerned with the examination of the discourses in and through which we think and act and have received comparatively less attention.[7] Nonetheless, Foucault's archaeological method significantly informs the genealogical work that follows it. This introduction demonstrates the important role that archaeological method—together with the genealogy that comes later—can play in thinking about the production of race and gender, illuminating the historical contingency of these categories of difference, which take shape and become meaningful at particular times and in specific geographic locations. As my present interest is in contemporary formations of race and gender in the United States, I take as the focus of my analysis cases that emerged here in the second half of the twentieth century.

To think about race and gender together, I ultimately contend, we must attend especially to a third figure, "the family," the critical site for the production of difference. By "the family" I mean both the social formation and the normative idea that shapes our understanding of what the family is or is supposed to be. I argue that disciplinary power—and the production of gender with which it is associated—may be located *within* the family, the privileged location of the internalization of social norms. By contrast, biopower—what Foucault sometimes characterizes as a "regulatory" power that he explicitly associates with the production of race—issues from outside and acts *upon* the family. While I contend that examination of the family should occupy a central place in examinations of the production of difference, I also note that the family has significantly receded in contemporary feminist theoretical analysis. This displacement of the family is an important development in the discipline; its examination provides us an opportunity to trace the deleterious effects of conceptions of gender that have come to dominance, as well as the possibilities for reconceiving these understandings, and is where I begin.

Toward an Archaeology of Gender

Feminist Theory: Privileging Gender, Obscuring Race

Thinking critically about the family constituted the focal point of feminist theoretical analysis at the beginning of the Second Wave. Redress of what Betty Friedan ten years earlier had called "the problem that has no name," that is, the suburban woman's confinement in the home (Friedan 1963), was taken in the burgeoning activism of the late 1960s and early 1970s to entail a much broader set of demands pertaining to woman's position in the family. These included the legal reforms that brought about reproductive choice, the recognition of marital rape, and the founding of battered women's shelters and day-care centers (Nicholson 1986; Echols 1989). Feminist theory and in particular Shulamith Firestone's *Dialectic of Sex* ([1970] 1979) and Gayle Rubin's "Traffic in Women" (1975) provided the most developed critiques of women's identification with the domestic sphere and foregrounded the figure of the family as the primary instrument of women's subjection. Despite the significant differences between Firestone and Rubin—differences that would come to characterize, for most of the rest of the century, principal and competing methodologies of feminist thinking—each places the institution of the family and women's position within it at the center of her analysis.[8] While feminist theory since that time can trace its focus on gender as the most salient object of analysis to Rubin's 1975 treatment, the work that emblematizes this shift in emphasis from the family to women's role is perhaps *The Reproduction of Mothering*, the book that came to be so closely identified with feminist theories of gender throughout the 1980s.[9]

In this 1978 classic Chodorow argues that gender identity is acquired in the family. To understand, as she writes, how women "are produced" as women, with the "social and economic location" (Chodorow 1978, 13) that production entails, we must examine the disparity between the positions men and women assume in the family. Both girls and boys will enjoy a primary emotional bond with their mothers, but the development of boys' and girls' identities (and the affective capacities with which these are associated) must then diverge at the oedipal stage to facilitate girls' assumption of the mother's position—generally restricted to the private sphere of the family—and boys' assumption of the father's, which occupies the public sphere beyond the family. This divergence in development is responsible, according to Chodorow, for the assignment of the different positions that characterize what she calls "the social organization and reproduction of gender" (ibid., 7).

Even as *The Reproduction of Mothering* came to occupy a prominent place in feminist theories of gender, it also came to stand, as Chodorow herself notes in the tenth-anniversary edition, as "the paradigmatic case of problematic feminist theorizing" (Chodorow 1999, vii). Among the most important and influential of the criticisms was Elizabeth Spelman's. Spelman takes Chodorow's analysis to be characteristic of a whole strain of feminist theorizing of this time, namely, that it attempts to understand gender "as a variable of human identity independent of other variables such as race or class" (Spelman 1988, 81). The problem with this approach, according to Spelman, is that gender cannot be distilled from other aspects of experience in this way. Gendered habits and behavioral codes, what is expected of a girl or woman, boy or man, and what each can hope for are shaped by a number of other sociocultural factors, saliently those associated with race, ethnicity, nationality, and economic status. As Spelman puts it, "it does not seem accurate to describe what my mother nurtured in me, and what I learned, as being simply a 'girl.' I was learning to be a white, middle-class, Christian and 'American' girl" (ibid., 85). Furthermore, she adds,

> I learn that my place in the established hierarchies of the social world is not determined simply by whether I am male or female but also by whether I am white or Black, rich or poor. In the society in which my mother and then I grew up, the differences between white and Black, middle and working class, Christian and Jew, were no less differences than the one between girl and boy. (ibid., 97)[10]

Joining a forceful and growing chorus of voices that began with the Combahee River Collective statement ([1979] 1982),[11] Spelman makes a convincing case that the many variables of our identities cannot be so readily parsed. Her larger point, that the methods characteristic of white feminist theorizing throughout the 1980s participated in the domination and exclusion they purported to challenge, was—and remains—similarly compelling.

I propose a different reading of the isolation of gender that gainsays Spelman's strong claim that "however... sound such inquiry seems, it obscures the ways in which race and class identity may be intertwined with gender identity" (Spelman 1988, 112). Spelman convincingly argues that in failing explicitly to reckon with racial difference, theorists like Chodorow cannot appreciate the way that race is functioning within their work: Their accounts—implicitly concerned with the gender development of white women—obscure the way that this (white) conception of gender relies on the exclusion of the racial other. While I grant that methods such as Chodorow's have had the effect of concealing what Kimberlé Crenshaw would later term the "intersectionality" of gender and race (Crenshaw 1991),[12] one of my aims in this book is to investigate whether or to what extent this isolation of gender from other categories of difference in fact reflects significant distinctions in the ways these differences are produced. I ask, in other words, whether the very difficulty, exemplified in Chodorow's work, of "thinking gender and race together" is owing to a challenge that inheres in the fact that these categories function in distinctive ways. Could it be that, even as an individual does not experience the different facets of her identity as separable in the way that an analysis like Chodorow's suggests, such separation could nevertheless be necessary to understanding the mechanics of the distinctive productions of the various facets of identity?

Hortense Spillers's Critique

This question concerning the distinctive operation of race and gender emerges from my reading of Foucault, together with feminist and critical race theorists' engagement with his work. Of special significance here is Hortense Spillers's essay "Mama's Baby, Papa's Maybe: An American Grammar Book" (1987), in which Spillers provides a Foucaultian analysis of the term "gender" that explores the peculiar history of this term.[13] I provide a detailed treatment of Spillers's work, for what she is doing in "Mama's Baby, Papa's Maybe" is also at the heart of my own project, namely, to make use of the tools Foucault offers to understand the distinctive operations of race and gender and the place the figure of "the family" occupies in their discursive production.

Spillers historicizes the discursive formation of the meaning of "gender," the privileged category of feminist analysis. "Strip[ping] down through layers of attenuated meanings" of what it means to be a black woman, Spillers begins with the opening of the Atlantic slave trade and continues through the publication of the Moynihan Report to the appearance of the "welfare queen." This discursive trajectory, Spillers provocatively argues, has excluded black women from the category of "woman," an exclusion that has been historically necessary for the construction of the (racialized) category of "woman." Spillers calls the symbolic order with which she is concerned an "American grammar" (ibid., 68), the rules of which restrict the application of the category of "woman" to white women. When she talks about these "rules," she does not mean formalized, explicit rules but the sort of rules that go unsaid because they go without saying.

Spillers's thematization of "grammar" works on several levels. Grammar prescribes formal rules of expression; it is a code, the violation of which can result in the production of speech that has no meaning, utterances that literally "make no sense." Whether one is schooled in these rules or not, grammar shapes our language by limiting the possibilities for speaking and thinking. We do not actively consult the rules of grammar in every sentence that we write or every phrase that we speak; once learned, these rules are internalized, "lived," as a phenomenologist might put it. One cannot "just say anything," and yet it is also this very limitation, or set of limitations, that makes language possible. By talking about an "American grammar," Spillers calls attention to how a specific history shapes the rules of thought. She also illuminates the ways in which gender—which operates implicitly in English, whereas it is explicitly in evidence in Romance languages, for instance—is concealed, even as it is shaping the language that gives gender its meaning.

The rules of this "American grammar" locate slaves exchanged as chattel outside the bounds of "the domestic," where, Spillers contends, the production of gender occurs. The refusal to recognize relations among blood kin of the enslaved requires an evacuation of the category of gender, which could not apply to bodies whose sexual difference was meaningful only in the calculation of a ship's maximum capacity (ibid., 67, 72). Spillers's claim that black females aren't "women" is a jarring one; after all, the special vulnerability to which a Harriet Jacobs is subject is obviously owing to the fact of her femaleness.[14] Spillers's challenging claim is that the category of woman itself is discursively restricted; that is, it is truly meaningful only when applied to white women; black women's exclusion from the category of woman was entailed by, and in turn hermeneutically entailed, the dehumanization of enslavement.[15]

Spillers's analysis suggests that the figure of the family functions as the privileged axis of this exclusion. If gendering takes place within the bounds of the domestic, it is the slaves' exclusion from that domain that defines their alterity. In the same way that black females are not granted the status of "women," social structures emerging from black kinship relations—those that come to be known as "the black family"—also fall outside the definition of family. "We might," Spillers says, "choose to call this connectedness [among black kin] 'family'... but that is a rather different case from the moves of a dominant symbolic order, pledged to maintain the supremacy of the race. It is that order that forces 'family' to modify itself [e.g. "the *black* family"] when it does not mean family of the 'master' or dominant enclave" (ibid., 75; emphasis in the original).

The discursive necessity to modify "family" when speaking of black families is owing to the historical meanings embedded in these terms. Spillers is thus engaged in precisely the kind of inquiry that concerns Foucault in *The Archaeology of Knowledge*: She is investigating, in other words, how a particular kind of implicit knowledge (the *savoir*) that permeates a historical period shapes the explicit knowledge (*connaissance*) that is institutionalized in the disciplines (Foucault [1969] 1972, 182–83). It is to this sedimented *savoir* that Spillers points when she identifies a continuity between the economies of exclusion shaping nineteenth-century laws determining slave "lineage" and the characterization of the black family found in Senator Daniel Patrick Moynihan's 1965 report, *The Negro Family: The Case for National Action*. The body of law that on the one hand designated the offspring of enslaved females as slaves and on the other guaranteed paternal authority in white families is present, Spillers argues, in Moynihan's discussion of the "fatherless" children of black women, whose "matriarchal" family structure is distinguished from that which engenders "legitimate" children. "Slave families" and "Negro families" alike are thereby positioned beyond the boundaries of "family," a concept legally drawn in terms of the proper vestiture of patriarchal authority and signified by the father's name.

This conception of "family," which is operating in the background of the Moynihan Report, this *savoir* from which the account issues, also conditions feminist thinking (*connaissance*) about "woman." With obvious reference to Chodorow's work and the body of analysis for which it has been so influential, Spillers writes, "One treads dangerous ground in suggesting an equation between female gender and mothering" (Spillers 1987, 78) since such an equation at once erases and enforces the interdiction of the "reproduction of mothering" for enslaved females. But where Elizabeth Spelman points out what is problematic about the (unmarked) category of gender and the way in which its exclusive focus obscures other kinds of differences, Spillers is more concerned with uncovering the historical conditions that shape theories about gender. She is interested, in other words, not in establishing the fact of exclusion but in tracing its development. In so doing, she comes to what might appear to be surprising conclusions concerning the production of gender and its implication with the production of race.

Even while Spillers highlights the danger in the equation of female gendering and mothering, there is nevertheless no suggestion that analyses of gender such as Chodorow's are *mistakenly* situated in the domestic; indeed, Spillers's analysis seems rather to substantiate Chodorow's positioning of the acquisition of gender identity—that is, a gender identity that is already understood as a *white* identity—in the family, as well as to underscore the imbrication of gender with the discursive production of subjectivity, likewise understood as white. If, as Spillers writes, " 'gendering' takes place within the confines of the domestic" (ibid., 72), where the mothers and sons and daughters that occupy Chodorow's account are produced, gender can be ascribed neither to the abjected black bodies circulating in the slave economy nor to the contemporary "welfare queens" to whom a legacy of slavery is attached. Instead, black bodies have historically taken meaning not through a familial system of kinship but through an economic system of property—an economy that circulates beyond the borders of the domestic, marking its limit.

If the very designation of what is outside the family is essential to the discursive production of gender, as Spillers contends, gender can be taken to occur within the domestic only by virtue of the limit constituted by the division between the different economies active on either side. We could say, then, that according to the rules of the "American grammar," the boundaries of the domestic are marked by the slave economy that is "beyond" it. The discursive configuration of the domestic sphere as self-contained or conceptually isolated (or isolable) from what is outside the space it demarcates maintains the putative separability of these economies. Yet, despite the division the grammar mandates, the signifying power of "the domestic" does not circulate solely within the bounds that have been constructed as proper to it but, as Spillers observes, also "spreads its tentacles for male and female subject over a wider ground of human and social purposes" (ibid.). The production of African Americans that occurs outside the domestic, then, while clearly not analogous to the production of familial subjects within it, can also not be conceived as wholly separable from it. The existence of this border between the two spheres accounts for the way in which both the slave economy and its relationship to the domestic sphere have been overlooked in examinations that appear specific to each. It is not simply a matter of "impropriety" that prevents discussions or treatments of the exchange of property from implicating "mothering"; economic matters appear to be irrelevant to our understandings of the maternal role, as "mothering" and "property" are terms cast as exclusive of one another.

Reading Spillers's discussion alongside Foucault's archaeology is thus extremely useful for understanding the dependence of the construction of gender on racial exclusion and, with it, the relationship between discursive and nondiscursive practices. Even if we take Spillers to overstate the case when she asserts that black bodies were "ungendered" in the middle passage, the claim brings into relief the untheorized set of associations present in Chodorow's treatment of gender and in the discourse that pathologizes black families still. Spillers poses the following question concerning feminist theory's repetition of the very "traditional symbolics of gender" that produce "women" within the domestic and the enslaved other outside:

> Because African-American women experienced uncertainty regarding their infants' lives in the historic situation, gendering, in its coeval reference to African-American women, *insinuates* an implicit and unresolved puzzle both within current feminist discourse *and* within those discursive communities that investigate the entire problematics of culture. Are we mistaken to suspect that history—at least in this instance—repeats itself yet again? (ibid., 78; emphasis in the original)

The puzzle, as I understand it, comprises an assemblage of contradictory propositions (e.g., that enslaved females are mothers but that within a slave economy their motherhood goes unrecognized and is unrecognizable). By emphasizing the conjunction of "current feminist discourse" with those other "discursive communities that investigate the entire problematics of culture," Spillers points to the ways in which the symbolic practices of feminist theories of gender such as Chodorow's participate in the dominant formation of twentieth-century discourse concerning "the family," such as that articulated in the Moynihan Report's attribution of poverty among African Americans to the "matriarchal structure" of the "Negro Family."[16]

Understood in one way, Spillers could be read simply to be making a claim similar to Spelman's concerning the problem of white feminist theorists' rein-scription of the relation between "the 'white' family, by implication, and the 'Negro Family' by outright assertion, in a constant opposition of binary meanings" (Spillers 1987, 66). In this structure, whiteness is cast as "the positive and the neutral," the discursive "man," as Beauvoir describes it, whose status as "the universal" depends on the construction of woman (or the racial other) as the particular (Beauvoir [1949] 1989, xxi). Spillers's work is so important, however, precisely because she does not stop at identifying the problematic endpoint; that is, she does not simply argue that race is excluded from thinking about gender. Instead, she traces the history of the production of the meaning of gender and the ways in which this history allows a restricted analysis such as Chodorow's to present itself as universal. Spillers provides a kind of primer in the grammar that dictates rules and possible meanings, as well as the restrictions of the meanings. What she offers, in other words, is an *archaeology* of the term "gender."

The Elements of Archaeology

The emergence of a "regularity" such as the historical continuity of the meaning of gender to which Spillers points signals the operation of what Foucault calls in *The Archaeology of Knowledge* a "discursive formation" (Foucault [1969] 1972, 38). The discursive formation does not refer to the discourse itself—that is, it does not concern the content of statements referring, for example, to "women" in the antebellum South or in late twentieth-century feminist theories—nor the "language," as Foucault writes, "used by discourse" (ibid., 46). Rather, the discursive formation refers to what Foucault calls the "rules" that constitute the conditions of the appearance of these terms—the rules, in other words, that govern what counts as a "woman."

These rules correspond to what Foucault identifies as the four interrelated "elements" that constitute a given discursive formation: "objects," "modes of statement" (or "enunciative modalities"), "concepts," and "thematic choices" (or "strategies").[17] The relations that obtain among the elements or rules can be described neither as self-contained ("internal to discourse") nor as imposed from without ("exterior to discourse") (ibid., 46, 73). They are, rather, complexly "established between institutions, economic and social processes, behavioral patterns, systems of norms, techniques, types of classification, [and] modes of characterization." Foucault draws a set of distinctions with which to identify the different levels of analysis at work within an archaeological study. These are "*real* or *primary relations*, a system of *reflexive* or *secondary* relations, and a system of relations that might properly be called [tertiary or] *discursive*" (ibid., 45; italics in the original).

"The system of primary relations" refers to those relations that can be examined "independently of all discourse." Primary relations are discernible within and among social groups, institutions, and techniques (i.e., among different "materialities"). Examples would include the relations involved in the commercial exchange of humans and the effects of the laws concerning this trade with respect to enslaved females and their offspring. Secondary relations entail an examination of the relationship between a body of knowledge or discipline (*connaissance*) and the materialities it studies. These would include the "disciplines" of psychology and feminist theory that Chodorow applies to her understanding of gender. Discursive, or tertiary, relations describe the historical conditions for the possibility of the primary and secondary relations. These might concern the "gestures by which, in a given society, [the category of 'woman'] is circumscribed, [juridically, socially, economically] invested, isolated, divided up into closed, privileged regions... arranged in the most favorable way" (Foucault [1963] 1975, 16). In his discussion of discursive relations in *The Birth of the Clinic*, where he introduces this concept of "spatialization," Foucault cautions that

> tertiary is not intended to imply a derivative, less essential structure than the preceding ones; it brings into play a system of options that reveals the way in which a group, in order to protect itself, practices exclusions, establishes

forms of assistance, and reacts to poverty and the fear of death. But to a greater extent than the other forms of spatialization, it is the locus of various dialectics: heterogeneous figures...political struggles, demands and utopias, economic constraints, social confrontations. (Foucault [1963] 1975, 16)[18]

While certain of these tertiary elements might properly be called "non-discursive," as Foucault indicates (Foucault [1969] 1972, 68), they do not fall outside the realm of a discursive formation; rather, it is in the interaction between discursive and non-discursive practices that meaningful statements are produced (Foucault [1963] 1975, 16), and this interaction is what a tertiary, or archaeological, analysis seeks to investigate. To analyze discursive relations, in other words, we must grasp discourse as everywhere "inter-twined," as Mary Rawlinson has put it, "with the technologies and the practices of the disciplines and professions in which it is spoken" (Rawlinson 1987, 375). Discursive relations involving a whole set of disciplinary demands and expectations, shot through with political limitations and possibilities, shape a text like *The Reproduction of Mothering* and account for the way in which an analysis such as Chodorow's can on the one hand wield feminist potential to elucidate the construction of gender and at the same time inexorably repeat the racist exclusions that limit the scope of that analysis.

A discursive formation, as Foucault conceives it, is not defined by the unity of the statements that compose it or by the "truth" of a single object, such as "mother," to which all sorts of discourses refer, but by the unity of the rules that produce "woman" in different ways at different historical moments. Foucault takes the example of madness, a central concern in his earliest work, as a case in point. Throughout the seventeenth and eighteenth centuries, he finds, the objects that emerge in "medical statements...psycho-pathological discourses...legal sentences or police action" are not identical; the statements concerning mental illness can in no way be said to refer "to a single object, formed once and for all...preserving it indefinitely as its horizon of inexhaustible ideality." In the same way that, as he writes, "we are not dealing with the same madmen," the mother (i.e., the "matriarch") who appears in the Moynihan Report differs from the woman in *The Reproduction of Mothering*. That "mother" can be conceived in vastly different or even incompatible ways is, in fact, the kind of matter that an analysis of discursive formations can helpfully address. The problem, as Foucault puts it, of "individualizing a group of statements" is "knowing whether the unity of a discourse is based not so much on the permanence and uniqueness of an object as on the space in which various objects emerge and are continuously transformed" (Foucault [1969] 1972, 32). It is the examination of the "interplay of rules" organizing this space that—paradoxically for Foucault—makes possible the individualization of a particular group of statements precisely by providing a way to describe the "dispersion" of the objects it produces, "to grasp all the interstices that separate [these objects], to measure the distances that reign between them—in other words, to formulate their law of division" (ibid., 33).

To say that the "law" of the discursive formation conditions the possibility of characterizing black females as mothers may help to clarify what Foucault means by "law" when he speaks of it with regard to the "interplay of rules" governing a discursive formation. He does not mean that this law would determine a given discursive formation in a totalizing fashion; one might well imagine that understanding a "black female" as "woman" would be unthinkable in that case. Rather, Foucault characterizes the law as the body of rules that determine the group of relations "necessary for the appearance of an object of discourse, the historical conditions required if one is to 'say anything' about it, and if several people are to say different things about it, the conditions necessary if it is to exist in relation to other objects" (ibid., 44).

Nevertheless, while different or even contradictory objects (or types of statements or concepts, for that matter) may be produced in a discursive formation (ibid., 65), it is not the case that at any given time simply any object can be produced (or that just anything can be said or unlimited concepts put into play) (ibid., 44). While "a field of possible options" is opened up by the rules organizing a discursive formation, Foucault writes, "all the possible alternatives are not in fact realized" (ibid., 66). What will and will not be realized is a critical matter not only for understanding the aim of an "archaeological" project but also for understanding the conception of power that emerges in Foucault's "genealogical" work, as well as the continuities between what has largely been taken as two distinctive methodologies. The studies that compose the central chapters of this book provide one way to grasp the multiple points of connection between the two analyses, attending to the elements of the discursive formation and making plain the relations of power that animate them.

From Archaeology to Genealogy: Bringing Power to the Fore

Making Difference: Disciplinary Internalization and Biopolitical Regulation

After *The Archaeology of Knowledge*, Foucault does not provide any truly extended treatment of his method; he does, nevertheless, claim that the archaeological and genealogical analyses are importantly joined, most directly in "The Discourse on Language," his inaugural lecture at the Collège de France. In this lecture Foucault outlines the way in which "critical and genealogical descriptions are to alternate, support, and complete each other" (Foucault [1971] 1972, 234). The thread that connects his earlier investigations to those that follow is accordingly an ongoing preoccupation with the complex operation of power and its multifarious effects. Indeed, while an analysis of power is explicit in the work that immediately follows *The Archaeology of Knowledge*, it was already present in the analyses leading up to that work. Reflecting on his archaeological analyses in a 1977 interview, Foucault says that, "When I think back now, I ask myself what else it was that

I was talking about, in *Madness and Civilisation* or *The Birth of the Clinic*, but power? Yet I'm perfectly aware that I scarcely ever used the word" (Foucault [1977] 1980b, 115).[19] Though Foucault clarifies that "discursive" relations are always already embedded in relations of power, it is in the work appearing after *The Archaeology of Knowledge* that the examination of power relations takes center stage.

The two texts that figure most prominently in this later period are *Discipline and Punish* and the first volume of *The History of Sexuality*. In *Discipline and Punish*, Foucault takes up the nature of what he calls "disciplinary" power. His account of disciplinary power is famously marked by his treatment of Jeremy Bentham's late eighteenth-century invention of the "Panopticon" prison. Bentham advanced a proposal for a new prison whose means of enforcement would be "internalization": A prisoner in his cell would be controlled by the understanding that he was at every moment subject to the watchful eye of an inspector whom he could not see. Compliance with authority in this prison would be premised neither on physical constraint nor on the principle of an objectified power outside the prisoner whose absence would mark a freedom from this power, but instead on the principle of *self*-enforcement, which would result in successful rehabilitation marked by continuous self-discipline.

Few images in contemporary philosophy have been so often cited as the Panopticon, together with the concept of "panopticism," coined by Foucault to encapsulate the nature of disciplinary power. As I noted at the outset, feminist theorists have remarked especially upon the particular resonance of this image with the specific expression of power associated with the production of gender. Reading Foucault's account of Bentham's machine for the first time, I, too, was struck by its resemblance to the more or less subtle regulation that is enforced "in the family." Parents' efforts to inculcate in their children any number of "behaviors"—keeping their mouths closed when they chew their food, looking both ways before crossing the street—are precisely the sorts of internalization that panopticism describes. This is the kind of power marked by the question "What would my parents think?" with regard to my considering that first cigarette or a particular boyfriend (or girlfriend). It should come as no surprise to learn that Bentham himself must have understood the workings of family in just this way: He himself recommended the installation of a warden *and his family* as the occupants of the Panopticon's central tower. But the effects of panopticism are marked not only in the internalization of the gaze of the "headkeeper" (or warden or parent); they are revealed, too, in the question "What will the neighbors think?" about the toys strewn around the yard or the "wild" daughter who comes home at all hours. Bentham himself understood, in other words, not only that the organization of the family as an institution was itself already constituted in terms of this different kind of power but also that its "anchor point," as Foucault puts it, lies outside the institution (Foucault [1982] 1983, 222) in, for example, the gaze of "other families."

While feminists have made use of Foucault's work on disciplinary power in thinking about the expression of power specific to the production of gender, however, Chodorow's account of the process of gender development—the development that occurs "in the family"—has played no role in these discussions. However, Chodorow's account of the process of gender development is strikingly congruent with Foucault's account of the disciplinary production of subjects. In the first part of this chapter I asked whether this understanding of gender as a function of disciplinary power could illuminate the ways that gender is implicated with race, precisely by pointing to the distinctive ways that these categories of difference are produced. If we understand gender as a function of the disciplinary power that is produced "within" the family, might we understand race as a function of the more familiar conception of power that acts "upon" the family? This power most closely resembles the kind of power Foucault takes up immediately after *Discipline and Punish*, namely, "biopower," which he discusses in the first volume of *The History of Sexuality* and then in the recently published lectures he delivered at the Collège de France in 1975 and 1976 ("Society Must Be Defended").[20] The work of these lectures is especially important, as Laura Ann Stoler has already demonstrated, for revealing Foucault's own preoccupation with power and the production of race; they also provide a more detailed treatment of Foucault's understanding of power more generally and clarify the many directions from which power must be studied (see Stoler 1995).

While Foucault's failure to think about gender has often been noted, race did occupy him, as the recent publication of his lectures makes clear (though the "race" under discussion in these lectures is not precisely the sense of race that is prevalent in the history of the United States). He associates this racial production with a distinctive kind of power, that is, a regulatory power associated with the state. While disciplinary power is applied to individual bodies (i.e., what Foucault characterizes in the lectures as "man-as-body"), biopower is applied "to the living man, to man-as-living-being; ultimately...to man-as-species" (Foucault [1999] 2003, 242). It is biopower, Foucault argues, that "inscribes [racism] in the mechanisms of the state" (ibid., 254). In the lectures he delivered the previous year,[21] Foucault traced the history of this "state racism" to what he described as an "older" ethnic racism identified with a concept of "degeneration." In this concept, he explained, illness or abnormalities of any kind are taken to be conditions that would be transmitted to one's offspring (ibid., 316); degeneration, in other words, is a family matter. But insofar as these matters become problems of public health, they become the responsibility of the state, and affected individuals—affected families—become the objects of state power.

It is not only the subject of race that interests Foucault, then, but also the figure of the family. Foucault himself makes frequent reference to the significance of the family in his published work, as well as in interviews, remarking on the family's dual roles—both object and agent—in the circulation of power (see, e.g., [1975] 1980, 56–58; [1976] 1980, 172–75). He even goes so far, in a parenthetical comment in *Discipline and Punish*, as to propose that "one day we should show how intra-familial relations, essentially in the parents-children cell, have become 'disciplined,' absorbing since the classical age external schemata, first educational and military, then medical, psychiatric, psychological, which have made the family the privileged locus of emergence for the disciplinary question of the normal and the abnormal" (Foucault [1975] 1979, 215–16). This analysis was never to materialize. Perhaps we may attribute the gap to the fact that Foucault was never specifically interested in the operation of gender, which, I have argued, is central to the operation of power in the family. However, we may still ask why feminist theorists themselves backed away from investigations of difference that made the family the central object of analysis. This is, as I point out in the first part of this chapter, the kind of inquiry to which an archaeological analysis may usefully be directed. The question also leads us to another important point of continuity between archaeology and genealogy, namely, the role of power in the production of knowledge.

Power/Knowledge

The explicit treatment of power in Foucault's genealogical work brings with it a different kind of emphasis on knowledge (*savoir*). Where one of the aims of Foucault's archaeological analyses is to objectify and investigate *savoir* as the kind of knowing that functions as the implicit ground of more recognizable forms of knowledge (*connaissance*) embodied in "disciplines," *savoir* in his genealogical works is expressly connected to power. Like his understanding of knowledge, however, Foucault's understanding of power is historicized, that is to say, it is itself a product of history; it changes form and shifts its objects over time. Power is thus for Foucault both a product and a producer of history. In a point Foucault develops from Nietzsche, historical accounts— the telling of stories—are themselves bound up with power: Power is operating in the telling and receiving of stories and is bound to the knowledge that our stories and histories give us.

In advancing this understanding, Foucault in this later work begins to make use of a composite term, "power/knowledge" (*pouvoir/savoir*). He does not mean to signal an equivalence of "power" and "knowledge," however; rather, power/knowledge indicates the way that the two can be implicated in one another both in everyday experience and in the institutionalized production of *connaissance*. Taking the first part of the term, "power," Gayatri Spivak advises English-speaking readers of Foucault to keep in mind the " 'can-do'-ness in '*pouvoir*,' if only because, in its various conjugations, it is the commonest way of saying 'can' in the French language." To capture some of the "homely verbiness of *savoir* in *savoir-faire, savoir-vivre* into *pouvoir*," Spivak suggests, "you might come up with something like this: if the lines of making sense of something are laid down in a certain way, then you are able to do only those things with that something which are possible within and by the arrangement of those lines. *Pouvoir-savoir*—being able to do something—only as you are able to make sense of it" (Spivak 1993, 34).

The kind of knowledge to which Foucault directs us here, then, is one that has no clear source but that a genealogical analysis—an examination of the historical conditions of possibility—illuminates. It is not the knowledge that is decreed, for example, by some authoritative body but is properly described in the passive voice: It is the kind of knowledge that "is recognized as true" or "known to be the case." For Foucault, this knowledge can exist only with the support of arrangements of power, arrangements that likewise have no clear origin, no person or body who can be said to "possess" it. Even the knower, the one who seeks knowledge and tries to understand history, is implicated in these webs of power/knowledge, which is part of what makes reading—and furthermore making use of—Foucault's work challenging.

Hortense Spillers's work already indicates some of the ways in which understanding the possibilities and limitations of feminist theories of gender in terms of power/knowledge can be illuminating. That is, even as feminist theory operates as a "reverse discourse" (Foucault [1976] 1990, 101) with respect to dominant discourse, it is both a product and producer of knowledge. Its persistent focus on white women subjects to the exclusion of racial others is a measure of the way in which feminist theory's own construction of knowledge remains bound to this dominant discourse. It is not, then, that theorists such as Chodorow intended to exclude women of color. On the contrary, their express aim was to provide an analysis that could be illuminating and beneficial to all women; rather, their limitations are a function and an illustration of power/knowledge in action.

If the appearance of Chodorow's theory of gender constitutes one chapter in the history of feminist theorizing, the shift in feminist theory away from thinking about gender in terms of "the family" in the wake of the critical response to *The Reproduction of Mothering* will count as a subsequent installment in the development of power/knowledge. Examining, as I have done here, one account of the development of feminist theory and its marginalization of the family opens up the possibility of telling different stories in which the family's role may figure more prominently. Returning the family to the center of feminist analysis will be instructive, moreover, in thinking about the production not only of gender but also of race. Thus while it may first appear that engagement with a work like Chodorow's leads us away from thinking about the intersection of race and gender, Spillers's work directs us instead to consider not only the way in which Chodorow's method provides only a partial view but also the way in which understanding the limitations of that view is nonetheless crucial for understanding the production of gender at this historical moment. Spillers's work suggests that the family is, as Foucault might have put it, a particularly "dense transfer point of power."[22] Spillers also indicates how a Foucaultian analysis can be useful in articulating the threads of the tangled discursive skein that make up the figure of the family.

Telling Stories

It is not only Foucault's conception of power that is useful for this detangling project but also his methods of archaeology and genealogy, his ways of telling stories. Reflecting on the increasing prominence of the use of stories in moral philosophy, Hilde Lindemann Nelson writes that narratives permit us "to work 'up close'—to put faces on faceless generalizations, to take the particulars of a given situation carefully into account" (Nelson 1997, viii). Narrative in this sense plays—and arguably should play—a prominent role in the discipline by providing concrete examples of theoretical points, illustrating how they work at a particular time and place, and offering opportunities to test theories and determine their limits. Philosophers not only make use of stories as tools of the trade but also take narrative itself as an object of analysis by postulating, for example, the narrative character of human life (see, e.g., Ricoeur [1983] 1984) or investigating storytelling as a political praxis (Stone-Mediatore 2003).

Foucault is generally left out of discussions of narrative in philosophy, and yet, as a philosopher, he is perhaps above all a master storyteller. Recounting the origins of whole "knowledges" (*connaissances*) or disciplines and the conditions that gave rise to them was the project of *The Order of Things* ([1966] 1973); *Madness and Civilization* ([1961] 1988) traces the origins of modern conceptions of mental illness—how a classical conception of "madness" is transformed into the "mental illness" of the nineteenth and twentieth centuries; *The Birth of the Clinic* ([1963] 1975) recounts the development of the modern concept of disease. If in his later work, in *Discipline and Punish* and the three volumes of *The History of Sexuality*, Foucault's emphasis turns more to the history of practices than of concepts, the telling of stories remains at the center of his project. It seems clear that the extraordinary range of Foucault's appeal across the humanities and social sciences is owing to the narrative presentation of his analyses, together with the possibilities his method offers to tell new stories—stories that centrally feature neither actors nor agents but, instead, the development of ideas and practices.

As Gary Gutting reports, Foucault's histories have been alternately valorized for their important transformation of the questions they pose and excoriated for their "mistakes," dismissed as "bad history" (Gutting 1994, 47–50). But Foucault's histories are not "histories" in the conventional sense—their aim is not finally to record, in the words of Leopold von Ranke, "*wie es eigentlich gewesen ist*" (how it really happened); they are not concerned with identifying what Foucault called the "origin" *(Ursprung)* of this or that condition, discipline, or practice. As Foucault explains in "Nietzsche, Genealogy, History," his genealogies are not intended to uncover the "timeless and essential secret . . . behind things" but are designed to expose the greater secret—"the secret that they have no essence or that their essence was fabricated in a piecemeal fashion" (Foucault [1971] 1977, 142). He is interested, as he put it in an interview the year before, in "the possibility of a discourse which would be both true and strategically effective, the possibility of a historical truth which could have a political effect" (Foucault [1976] 1980, 64).

Rather than an origin, then, genealogy takes as its objects *Herkunft* (descent) and *Entstehung* (emergence). In tracing a descent, the aim is not

the restoration of "an unbroken continuity that operates beyond the dispersion of forgotten things; its duty is not to demonstrate that the past actively
exists in the present, that it continues secretly to animate the present, having
imposed a predetermined form to all its vicissitudes" ([1971] 1977, 146).
Indeed, rather than erect foundations, "the search for descent...disturbs
what was previously considered immobile; it fragments what was thought
unified; it shows the heterogeneity of what was imagined consistent with itself"
(ibid., 147). Examinations of emergence—such as the study of punishment
Foucault undertakes in *Discipline and Punish*—similarly challenge a conception of history as looking for what he calls a "final term of an historical
development." That punishment, for example, has had a variety of uses besides
a concern with "setting an example," challenges conventional approaches that
"place present needs at the origin." The diverse purposes that punishment has
served "may appear as a culmination," Foucault writes, "but they are merely
episodes in a series of subjugations," responses to a variety of needs: "revenge,
excluding an aggressor, compensating a victim, creating fear" (ibid., 148).
Among the disturbing possibilities genealogical method offers, then, is the
opening of space for the telling of more than one story, a possibility that itself
calls into question the nature of knowledge, that is, of truth itself.

Foucault describes history as "the endlessly repeated play of dominations"
(ibid., 150). This play of dominations "gives rise," he writes, "to the universe
of rules," which are used to inflict violence and consolidate power. However,
the rules, according to Foucault, "are empty in themselves....They are
impersonal and can be bent to any purpose." For Foucault this means that

> the successes of history belong to those who are capable of seizing the rules, to
> replace those who had used them, to disguise themselves so as to pervert them,
> invert their meaning, and redirect them against those who had initially
> imposed them; controlling this complex mechanism, they will make it func-
> tion so as to overcome the rulers through their own rules. (ibid., 151)

Remarking on the resonance of this passage with the deeper project of
genealogy, Ladelle McWhorter changes the word "rule" to "story" to emphasize the transformative possibilities genealogical method offers:

> The success of history belong to those who are capable of seizing these
> stories, to replace those who had used them, to disguise themselves so as to
> pervert them, invert their meaning, and redirect them against those who
> initially told them; controlling this complex mechanism, they will make it
> function so as to overcome storytellers through their own stories.
> (McWhorter 1999, 60)

In making this change, McWhorter underscores both the critical function
stories perform in Foucault's own work and the possibilities his method offers
not only to cast wary eyes on "truths" that have been narratively cast as
immutable but also to transform these truths—to tell new stories.

Storytelling is relevant not only to Foucault's genealogical work. Indeed,
one way to understand what he means by an "archaeological analysis," as it
plays out in each study preceding *Discipline and Punish* is to consider it a

method for telling different kinds of stories. In *The Archaeology of Knowledge*, he describes what he calls the four interrelated "elements" that constitute a given "discursive formation," that is, the "conditions" of the appearance of different "knowledges." As I have already noted, archaeologies can focus on particular objects, enunciative modalities, concepts, or strategies. In any archaeological investigation, Foucault observes, one element of a discursive formation emerges as the most salient. In *Madness and Civilization*, the complex production of objects—the discipline of psychology itself, as well as psychology's own objects: the "madman," his "mental illness," and its "symptoms"—concerned him, while the theoretical choices, conceptual systems, and enunciative modalities he characterized as "easy to locate," "relatively uncomplex," and "fairly homogeneous and repetitive." The modification of enunciative modalities at the end of the eighteenth and early nineteenth centuries were most prominently featured in *The Birth of the Clinic*; in *The Order of Things*, the rules for the formation of concepts (in "General Grammar, Natural History, and the Analysis of Wealth") constituted the center of his investigation, while the role of strategic choices was indicated but undeveloped (Foucault [1969] 1972, 65).

Unlike the discussion of the three rules preceding it in *The Archaeology of Knowledge*, Foucault's definition of discursive strategies does not emerge from a retrospective summary of their operation in the archaeologies he has already undertaken. Rather, Foucault gives the formation of strategies a more schematic treatment, underscoring the importance of analyzing the formation of strategies in their interaction with each of the other three rules. In other words, he explains, discursive strategies may be discerned in the interstices—the spaces between the more fully developed plots and subplots to which the other rules give rise. It is in his discussion of strategies that Foucault most clearly signals the close relationship between an archaeological analysis and the analytic of power that animates so much of the work immediately following the publication of *The Archaeology of Knowledge*.

Focusing on each of the "directions" indicated by the elements of an archaeological analysis, then, provides us with new stories. Telling these stories, using Foucault's methods, is the project of this book. The chapters that follow consist of individual stories that make up a larger story about the construction of race and gender in the United States and demonstrate the centrality of the family in these constructions in the second half of the twentieth century. Each of the four chapters corresponds to one of the four elements that constitute a discursive formation. The close connection between archaeological analysis and the functioning of power are demonstrated in the chapters themselves, analyses that are at the same time stories highlighting different decades in the recent history of the family in the United States. Rather than a formal study of Foucault's own work, then, *Family Bonds* is an effort to produce new genealogies. This is the kind of project, according to Jana Sawicki, that Foucault himself hoped his work would prompt (Sawicki 1991, 15).

Chapter 2, "The Family in the Tower: The Triumph of Levittown and the Production of a New Whiteness," sets out to "objectify" the family as an institution unmistakably connected to other institutions that appear outside it. The chapter takes the example of the construction of Levittown, the definitive suburb conceived and built following the Second World War, to examine the junction of power evident in the making of new communities in the 1950s and 1960s, namely, the power of the state, together with the power most closely associated with Foucault's work, the disciplinary power revealed in Bentham's design of the Panopticon. The story of Levittown provides an opportunity to study how a more conspicuous form of power—resulting in the production of what I call "a new whiteness"—dovetails with the disciplinary enforcement of the proper roles of men and women. The case of Levittown thus encapsulates one of the central claims of the book regarding the privileged place of the family in the production of gender and racial difference.

The two chapters that follow explore in more detail the production of gender as a function of disciplinary power and of race as a function of regulatory power, respectively. They also concern subjects that interested Foucault himself: the regulation of sexuality and the biopolitical control of populations. Foucault speaks at some length about these two kinds of power and how they come together in the "society of normalization." Since the mid-eighteenth century, he recounts, normalization has marked the institution of standards of health particularly aimed at containment of the "abnormal." These standards arise together with the complex of mechanisms that make possible a state regulation, "the capillary ramifications of which," he says, "constantly reach into the grain of individuals themselves, their time, habitat, localization, and bodies" (Foucault [1999] 2003, 47). In this application of power, we encounter what he describes as "the juxtaposition of, the confrontation between, two mechanisms and two types of discourse that are absolutely heterogeneous: on the one hand, the organization of right around sovereignty, and on the other, the mechanics of the coercions exercised by disciplines" (Foucault [1997] 2003, 38). While we should appreciate the distinctive qualities of these two expressions of power, we must at the same time attend to the ways that each implicates the other.

Chapter 3, "Boys *Will* Be Boys: Disciplinary Power and the Production of Gender," concerns the disciplinary production of gender that appears to occur within the family. Examining the development of the diagnosis and treatment of Gender Identity Disorder in children, it continues the analysis begun in chapter 2 by detailing the function of the family as a panoptic institution, splayed out onto other institutions typically understood to be located outside the family. Gender Identity Disorder (GID) emerged as a new diagnosis in the 1970s and flourished in the 1980s after the removal of homosexuality from the *Diagnostic and Statistical Manual of Mental Disorders (DSM)*. In following accounts of the earliest cases through the later refinements of the nature of the "disorder," we see the nature of the power vested in psychology to define deviant gender expression and the bounds of normality. We also see in the case of GID how the power to police these bounds must be significantly located within the family, which involves a complex form of "self-discipline." Examining the development of

GID also provides an opportunity to consider the nature of the archaeological rule governing enunciative modalities, particularly the institutional sites from which statements are made, and the assignment of subjective positions, that is, the way that individuals' roles and the social positions into which they are cast are enforced. From the application of this notion to the case of GID, we see how "experts" come to play a role in the lives of individual families. At the same time, we see how the ways in which individuals come to understand themselves as gendered are enforced by means of discourses that are produced outside the family but that come to work inside it.

While chapter 3 is concerned primarily with the disciplinary power of gender, working, as it were, from the inside of the family out, the production of race I take up in chapter 4 could be inversely described as working from the outside in. "Of Monkeys and Men: Biopower and the Production of Race" takes up the analysis of race as a Foucaultian "concept." Here I consider the practices associated with government coordination of scientific investigations into violence to examine the way that race is deployed in the plan to implement preventive measures as interventions into violent behavior. The racism evident in the specific practices locating violent tendencies in targeted populations exemplifies what David Theo Goldberg, following Foucault, calls the "preconceptual ground" of racist discourse. The elements that structure this order, which comprises the axes of "classification and order, value and hierarchy; differentiation and identity, discrimination and identification; exclusion and domination, subjection and subjugation; entitlement and restriction, and in general way, violence and violation" (Goldberg 1990, 301), have been central, historically, to the scientific rationality from and in which the "profusion of the themes, beliefs, and representations" of this discourse emerge (Foucault [1969] 1972, 63). The attention directed at "the violent body" is aimed not at the internalization of an authoritative gaze by the individuals themselves but rather at the individualizing of a group against whom the population needs protection. This is an expression of what Foucault calls in *The History of Sexuality* "biopower" or later, in his 1975–76 lectures at the Collège de France, the power of "regularization." Rather than a diffused gaze that can be employed by anyone, in other words, the authority of the regulatory gaze is consolidated—for use by the state.

The concluding chapter, "Thinking Gender, Thinking Race: Strategies and Contradictions," reflects on the nature of the project as a whole, which is an effort not only to demonstrate a different way to think gender and race together but also to account for the very difficulty of doing so. Focusing on the fourth archaeological "rule," concerning discursive "strategies," this chapter highlights the strategies already at work in the preceding chapters and in so doing emphasizes the analytic of power that shapes our thinking of gender and race. It is not only, I contend, that gender and race function distinctively as materialities even as they work in concert but also that, as the preceding chapters illustrate, the discursive representation of each works to exclude the other. Much like the famous "reversible figure-ground" images from Gestalt psychology, where a vase becomes visible only when the faces in profile are forced to the background and vice versa, one category of difference becomes visible just at the moment that the other category recedes; only one category is visible at a time. However, while we may not be able to "see" both simultaneously, we can move our gaze from one to the other and in so doing make each visible—and more: We can become aware of the ways that each shapes the other and how the very evidence of this shaping itself recedes into the background.

The Family in the Tower

The Triumph of Levittown and the Production

of a New Whiteness

The object does not await in limbo the order that will free it and enable it to become embodied in a visible and prolix objectivity; it does not preexist itself, held back by some obstacle at the first edges of light. It exists under the positive conditions of a complex group of relations.
—*Michel Foucault*, The Archaeology of Knowledge

In 1958 sociologist Herbert Gans moved to Levittown to be a participant-observer in a new suburb. His hope was that his work would bridge the gap between an intelligentsia critical of the glut of suburban building that was destroying farmland and creating aesthetic wastelands and the lower-middle class so eager to move their families to these new towns. Gans cast his project as concerned with the dynamics of community development—how a group of strangers come to understand themselves as a community and the relationship of that sense of community to the intentions and aspirations of the builders.

One of the prominent attractions of Levittown was the planned homogeneity—of both the houses and their inhabitants. Not surprisingly, the subject of racial integration was from the start a contentious one that provoked anxiety in the new suburbanites. To them, integration signified the fragility of newly won middle-class status, the instability of their property values, and the intimacy their children might experience with the prospective "Negroes next door." Theirs were anxieties tied to a growing body of "knowledge" about the conditions of the community Levittowners were forming: about who Levittowners were, what their community meant, and what was necessary to promote and sustain the identities bound up with the fortunes of their new town.

Gans does not comment on the way in which this new knowledge was constituted. Yet, his own acceptance of this knowledge is revealed when, amid rumors that, after completing his research, he had sold his house to a black family, Gans capitulates to what he describes as "intense" pressure exerted by his neighbors to sell his house to whites. Although Gans, friend to pro-integration leaders in and outside Levittown, "thought about" selling his home to a black family, he decided not to for fear that his continuing fieldwork would be, as he put it, "endangered" (Gans 1967, 405fn).

To judge Gans is not my aim. I am interested, rather, in the way that he constructed his decision, the set of truths to which he subscribed and that he perpetuated. Gans acknowledges his acquiescence to a body of rules governing Levittown and its residents. These rules were enforced by means of a local distribution of "truth" as Gans experienced it. In this chapter I discuss the ways in which race imbues the kind of knowledge that we take to be common sense, the knowledge that circulates "on the ground," among the individuals who became Gans's neighbors and friends. At the same time, I note the conspicuous operation of state power active in the making of race during this time, which explicitly determined who counted as "white" and who "nonwhite." This power, I contend, played a significant role in the shaping of this "common sense." How we come to know what we think we know is in part a function of power that, in turn, reinforces the rules that determine the possibilities for action and understanding.

Why should social and political philosophers be interested in a historical example such as Levittown? Philosophers of race have traced the development of racial thinking to its first appearance in the mid-sixteenth century at the "Great Debate" at Valladolid, through the modern period and into the nineteenth and twentieth centuries (see, e.g., Goldberg 1993; Eze 1997). But we know much less about the ways that racial categories permeate daily life, that is, how they shape the narratives through which we make sense of the world. In the construction of Levittown, we find a critical site for the production of race in everyday life—one that implicates both the power of the state and the seemingly pedestrian practices of home financing and also explains the attitudes of people who sought above all to defend their dreams. Levittown provides a rich example of the way in which state or regulatory power is deployed to create a new community, what would become the prototypical suburb. Levittown allows us to be eyewitness to the creation of a body of truths about individuals and race.

The first part of this chapter recounts that creation by focusing particularly on the relationship between a new conception of "whiteness" that emerged at this time and the exercise of state power that supported that conception. The story of Levittown should be written as the tale of the production of gender in everyday life, too, one that also implicates the state in its efforts to restore familial order after World War II. The second part of this chapter accordingly focuses on women's "return" to the home (coinciding with the postwar building of Levittown) that followed their aggressive recruitment to the workforce during the hostilities. This other story of Levittown, I show, is not simply a postscript to the first story of the production of race but is rather an essential corollary to it, albeit one that, as I detail at the end of this chapter and in the chapters that follow, differs in important ways from the first. The deliberate construction of women's place in the homes of Levittown was a crucial component in residents' understanding of themselves and their places in the world; at the center of the conception, I argue, lies Levittowners' certainty about their status as white people.[1]

Finally, the story of Levittown is also a story about families. Defining a discursive object such as "family" is a complex business, all the more so because the very definition relies upon a certain amount of "taken-for-grantedness." However, in Jeremy Bentham's placement of the warden's family at the center of his famous design of the Panopticon prison, as I show in the concluding section of the chapter, we find an opportunity to disturb that taken-for-grantedness: Bentham's plan reveals the operation of a power in the institution of the family that also informs the design of Levittown. Michel Foucault takes up Bentham's machine as an exemplary model of what he calls "disciplinary" power. While a "state" power was clearly active in the organization of Levittown and similar projects of the time, attending to this distinctive power—the power that circulates within and through families—provides a means of understanding how conceptions of race and gender, together with the dominant conception of family that undergirds these conceptions, are produced and promulgated.

Legislating the American Dream

The 1944 founding of Levittown, New York—the first of what would become a succession of Levittowns and similar housing efforts in the years after the Second World War—inaugurated a historic shift in the conception of housing and the construction of living in the United States (Hayden 1984, 6–9; Jackson 1985, 234–38). Each identical house lining Levittown's gently curving streets was, as architectural historian Dolores Hayden writes, "designed to be a self-contained world" with a fully equipped kitchen, a Bendix washing machine installed in the laundry alcove, and an expansive living room that would eventually have a television set built into the wall (Hayden 1984, 6). Roads were constructed to allow the working husband convenient access to New York City via the newly built Long Island Expressway or the Long Island Railroad; homes were equipped to satisfy the needs of his wife and children.

The construction of Levittown marked the first time that a working class, composed almost entirely of returning GIs and their families, could afford to live in the suburbs. This constituted a notable change from the suburb's early nineteenth-century origins, when only those with the means to afford commuting via horseback or carriage enjoyed the genteel option of suburban living (Stilgoe 1988, 122; see also Palen 1995, 27–29). Starting in the late 1830s, the introduction of steamboat service around Manhattan, along the Hudson, and to and from Long Island and Brooklyn, together with the railroad, greatly expanded the residential possibilities for the middle class. Citizens seeking "the rewards of hard work" looked to the suburbs to provide them with the "right education, moral home life, aesthetic understanding, [and] stability" (Stilgoe 1988, 122) that suburbs were reported to afford their residents. Sociologist John Palen provides details of further incentives for white middle-class urbanites to leave the city when technological advances provided the means to do so. High on the list was the "high tide of southern and eastern European immigration to the United States," confirmed by the 1900 census, which reported that as much as three-quarters of urban centers

Figure 2.1. Levittown, New York, 1947. (Levittown History Collection, Levittown Public Library)

like New York, Boston, and Chicago were of "foreign stock." Palen writes that "the new suburbs allowed those who feared the menace of 'rum, Romanism, and rebellion' to escape to segregated neighborhoods.... By the time of World War I, the pattern of a segregated urban area had become the norm" (Palen 1995, 40).

Unsurprisingly, the vaunted rewards of suburban life would continue in subsequent decades to elude the city's working classes, composed mostly of immigrants (Coontz 1988, 289).[2] The suburbs also remained closed to black Americans due to their especially depressed economic status. In *The Social Origins of Private Life*, Stephanie Coontz recounts how, throughout the latter part of the nineteenth century, blacks were increasingly excluded from "skilled trades and even factory work" (ibid., 314), a result, in part, of the way in which "new immigrant labor, far from pushing native-born blacks up in the occupational scale, generally pushed blacks out of the industry or job category entirely" (ibid., 292). As blacks were systematically excluded from a growing part of the labor force, they were refused the possibility of realizing the middle-class dream that was extended to European immigrants at the end of the Second World War.

In the postwar period, the expansion of the Federal Housing Authority (FHA), together with the GI Bill (the Servicemen's Readjustment Act of 1944), provided financing for projects such as William Levitt's (Jackson 1985, 238) and allowed veterans to purchase homes with minimal down payments and guaranteed low-interest mortgages for up to thirty years

(Coontz 1992, 77). Not only was it possible for working-class families to leave the cramped quarters they often shared with in-laws and extended family in the city (Jackson 1985, 235), but it actually cost *less* to buy one of the new suburban houses than to rent a smaller apartment in the city. The proud new owners, some of whom waited days in line at the Hicksville, New York, sales office for the opportunity to buy one of Levitt's "boxes" (Hayden 1984, 6; Jackson 1985, 237) during this period formed a community made of growing families like themselves—so much like themselves in fact that the first issue of Levittown's newsletter included the observation that "our lives are held closely together because most of us are within the same age bracket, in similar income groups, live in almost identical houses and have common problems" (quoted in Jackson 1985, 235).

The homogeneity that characterized Levittown was not accidental. Critical was the significant role that the state, through federal financing of mortgages, played in the creation of this American dream. The first important government player was the Home Owners Loan Corporation (HOLC). Established at the urging of Franklin D. Roosevelt in 1933, HOLC protected families against foreclosure—an increasing problem since the depression—by introducing the long-term mortgage (ibid., 196). The process of assessing the government's new investment in housing produced in turn an important innovation in real estate appraisal:

> With care and extraordinary attention to detail, HOLC appraisers divided the cities into neighborhoods and developed elaborate questionnaires relating to the occupation, income, and ethnicity of the inhabitants and the age, type of construction, price range, sales demand, and general state of repair of the housing stock. The element of novelty did not lie in the appraisal requirement itself—that had long been standard real estate practice. Rather, it lay in the creation of a formal and uniform system of appraisal, reduced to writing, structured in defined procedures, and implemented by individuals only after intensive training. The ultimate aim was that one appraiser's judgment of value would have meaning to an investor located somewhere else. (ibid., 197)

The method of appraisal established by HOLC employed a rating system with letter and color codes that corresponded to the estimated desirability of a specific block in every major city; these codes were recorded on "secret 'Residential Security Maps' " circulated at HOLC and clandestinely made available to crediting banks (ibid., 199). An area categorized as being of the first or highest quality was designated grade A and denoted by the color green. The fourth and least desirable was grade D and designated red (hence "red-lining"). Newness of housing and homogeneity of a neighborhood's inhabitants (shorthand for "American business and professional men") were valued over older housing and ethnic or "mixed" residential composition (officially characterized, as HOLC put it, as Jewish "infiltration") (ibid., 197). The notation of a " 'rapidly increasing Negro population' and the resulting 'problem in the maintenance of real estate values' " would be ample cause for a downgraded designation, sometimes described as "hazardous" (ibid., 201).

The Federal Housing Authority took over where HOLC left off. Beginning with its founding in 1934 as part of FDR's New Deal, the FHA stimulated the building of suburban developments and innovated the standardization of housing that Levittown would epitomize ten years later. Adopting the HOLC appraisal system, the FHA trained its underwriters to evaluate a neighborhood's "appeal" and "protection from adverse influences," in addition to the assessment of adequate utilities and transportation (ibid., 203, 207). The valued homogeneity, along with the housing legislation's stated preference for single-family houses, prefigured the terms on which Levitt's federal support depended. Not only did the FHA establish a body of requirements and guidelines specifying the preferred dimensions of lots and housing (and, by implication, family size), but it also encouraged racialized zoning and endorsed restrictive covenants to prevent what it called "inharmonious racial or nationality groups" from lowering the value of the government's investment (ibid., 208).

The GI Bill also created a mortgage program to supplement the FHA's, officially sanctioning the expectation that veterans "should return to civilian life with a home of their own." Coupled with the severe housing shortage—a function of both the diversion of resources to the war effort and of surging marriage and birth rates—the GI Bill forced the government to ease restrictions on home builders while increasing its financial support (ibid., 232–33).

It is tempting to speculate about the possibilities for a different kind of suburban life that might have been, had home builders like Levitt used the leverage they enjoyed after the war to widen the road to suburbia and to throw their neighborhoods open to more. It was not out of the question. Drawing on the example of the integrated new town of Vanport City, Oregon ("Kaiserville"), historian Dolores Hayden has written of the real possibilities for housing reform that the 1940s opened and then foreclosed.[3] Levitt himself recognized the deliberate choice he was making. He said, "We can solve a housing problem, or we can try to solve a racial problem. But we cannot combine the two" (quoted in ibid., 241).

Foucault's conception of power as something that circulates but is not possessed (e.g., Foucault [1976] 1990, 94) indicates, however, how little sense it makes to blame Levitt the man for the policies pursued in his developments. More important, to follow Foucault, was the position Levitt had come to occupy as the most influential builder of homes in the postwar era (Hayden 1984, 12; Jackson 1985, 234). Despite Levitt's protestations to the contrary, his frank explanation to a reporter for the exclusion of blacks may be taken to indicate either his own preferences or the constraints imposed by the FHA's system of financing: "[It was] not a matter of prejudice, but one of business. As a Jew I have no room in my mind or heart for racial prejudice.[4] But, by various means, I have come to know that if we sell one house to a Negro family, then 90 to 95 percent of our white customers will not buy into the community" (quoted in Hayden 1984, 6–7). With the precision that marks his declaration—"90 to 95 percent"—Levitt reflects a certainty, a claim to truth grounded in empirical reality. Such a claim marks a key moment in the production of knowledge. Levitt's statement asserts itself as truth not simply by repeated insistence ("90 to 95 percent," he told his audience whenever a new Levittown was opened, as if his organization had made a survey on the point). More important, the statement itself promotes the subtextual intention of government policy, an intention advanced by the increasing establishment of alliances with individual homeowners' sense of "how things are." But even as Levitt's claim is fortified by government policies of segregation on the one hand and the sure "knowledge" of his buyers on the other, his claim also conceals other, competing truths. In particular, what Levitt's certainty obscures is the degree to which the society of which he spoke was already in flux: Ethnic distinctions that had so famously divided America's immigrant communities in the cities were being blurred in the suburbs.

Given that Levitt's was a guiding hand in shaping the policy that determined not only the composition of Levittown but also that of American suburbs for decades following, is it possible, if he and others, such as his West Coast counterpart, Henry J. Kaiser, had pressed the point, that the government would have supported integrated communities?[5] It should by now be clear that the description of power as something that circulates but is not possessed by no means implies that individuals cannot be influential actors in the production of effective truths. Indeed, as Foucault puts it in a 1976 lecture, "individuals... are in a position to both submit to and exercise this power. They are never the inert or consenting targets of power; they are always its relays" (Foucault [1999] 2003, 29).

While claims such as Levitt's concerning the overwhelming number of white buyers who would not purchase homes in an integrated community derive their potency from the impression that they are true in the obstinate way of fact, reflections of a reality unresponsive to the desires of the well-meaning, these truths are themselves produced and promulgated by means of individuals; while these individuals do not "possess" or "appropriate" power, "power is exercised through networks" that shape individuals— that make them among its "first effects" (ibid., 30). Even though the possibilities for integration in the mid-1940s might have seemed far fetched, in a testament to Foucault's analysis, changes that a mere two decades earlier had seemed unimaginable were then in process; significant transformation in the "racial" composition of the suburbs of New York was already under way.

Becoming White

The policies of the FHA encouraged young European American families— among them the Catholics and Jews who had themselves been excluded from the suburbs before the war—to forsake ethnic enclaves in the city for the American dream. It was at this point, as George Lipsitz writes, that

> ethnic differences became a less important dividing line in American culture, while race became more important. The suburbs helped turn European

Americans into "whites who could live near each other and intermarry with relatively little difficulty." But this "white" unity rested on residential segregation and on shared access to housing and life chances largely unavailable to communities of color. (Lipsitz 1995, 373–74)

Access to the suburbs, in other words, brought with it admission to the "whiteness" that had characterized suburban living since its origins. The production of a simple racial division between white and black was dramatically reflected in the increasing difference between the suburb and the city. Of the neighborhoods ethnic whites left behind, many were destroyed in the urban renewal following the war, while others became minority areas of another stripe, ever more densely occupied as a result of the housing shortage aggravated by urban renewal (ibid., 373; see also Jackson 1985, 206). Although white ethnic neighborhoods thrived before the war, Douglas Massey and Nancy Denton recount that, "unlike black ghettos, immigrant enclaves were never homogeneous and always contained a wide variety of nationalities, even if they were publicly associated with a particular national origin group" (Massey and Denton 1993, 32). Massey and Denton suggest that this heterogeneity contributed to a lower "degree of isolation" relative to blacks in ghettos, a contributing factor that made ethnically identified neighborhoods a "fleeting, transitory stage in the process of immigrant assimilation" (ibid., 33). Kenneth Jackson echoes this finding, writing that the period following World War II marked the beginning of "racial and economic polarization . . . so pronounced that downtown areas lost their commercial hold on the middle class." As the suburbs came to symbolize a "haven in a heartless world," cities "became identified with [a racialized] fear and danger rather than with glamour and pleasure" (Jackson 1985, 276).

The expansion of the category of whiteness that attended the opening of the suburbs to ethnic European Americans also entailed a "possessive investment in whiteness" (Lipsitz 1995, 371). Lipsitz argues that this "investment"—conceiving of whiteness as an exclusive "property" to be cultivated and, more important, protected (Harris 1993)—had been encouraged "from the start," that is, from the first European settlement of the suburbs (Lipsitz 1995, 371). However, the racism on which the investment is predicated did not remain the same: The rule of white supremacy that characterized the antebellum South, for example, is not the racism effected in "the putatively race-neutral liberal social democratic reforms of the past five decades" (ibid., 372), in which the FHA figures so prominently. Though the racist policy making Lipsitz and others understand as deliberate action on the part of governmental agencies (ibid., 371; Massey and Denton 1993, 19) is a key constituent of the postwar production of the possessive investment in whiteness, this investment is marked in the initiation of new suburban residents into the club of whiteness. A clause in the contract of new homeowners in Levittown, New York, suggests the codification of the residents' whiteness and the "proper" relationship to the racial other that it attends: "No dwelling shall be used or occupied by members of other than the Caucasian race, but the employment and maintenance of other than Caucasian domestic servants shall be permitted" (quoted in Popenoe 1977, 123).[6] Such an initiation calls for an examination of the way in which *the residents themselves* took on the enforcement of the racial boundaries they had been encouraged to cross.

The difficulty that characterized Levittown's desegregation testifies both to the effects of the assimilation of ethnic Europeans and to the success of the creation of the suburb that facilitated that assimilation. Levittowners' own resistance to desegregation marks a definitive moment in the process by which boundaries dividing geographies and bodies, suburbs and cities, white and black were deeply etched during this period. The means by which this resistance—an effect of the operation of whiteness—was achieved recalls Foucault's discussion of disciplinary practices in *Discipline and Punish* (1975). Just as the soldier at the end of the eighteenth century was conceived as "something that can be made" (ibid., 135), ethnic Europeans could be "made white" as a result of the entitlements afforded returning GIs. "Becoming white" on Levitt's terms entailed molding a kind of suburban lifestyle whereby habits that typified immigrant city life were "corrected" via rule-books distributed as homeowner's manuals.[7] That the first houses in Levittown were available for rent with the option to buy only after a year (Jackson 1985) signals the consequences of a failure to conform to the expectations specified in the manual, namely eviction.

The Levittowners, Herbert Gans's study of the third Levittown in New Jersey, which opened in 1958 (called Willingboro since the early 1960s, the township's original name), offers an important account of the way in which the claim to whiteness represented by suburban home ownership was assumed by Levittowners. While Levitt's own publicly repeated confirmations of the exclusion of blacks from successive developments could have once been credibly attributed to his dependence on federal funding, those same declarations made a decade later cannot adequately account for the persistence of racist exclusion in the absence of such constraints. Something else had to account for Levitt's public refusal to sell houses to black people in Levittown, New Jersey, after the state of New Jersey had passed legislation outlawing discrimination in connection with federally subsidized housing (Gans 1967, 372). The intervention of a New Jersey senator with the FHA, appeals to the governor, picketing of model homes by a local Quaker group: Nothing would change Levitt's mind, not even the suit brought by two black families who had been refused sale.[8]

Fighting the suit, Levitt was not only contesting New Jersey state law but also resisting considerable grassroots pressure exerted by Jewish and pro-integration groups nationwide (ibid., 372–73). But for what the Levitt organization characterized as compelling economic incentive, Levitt would have been forced to acknowledge the racist underpinnings of his policy. Instead, Levitt's representative justified the company's policies by reference to economic realities that government financing policies had created in the 1930s: "Our firm is liberal and progressive, but we don't want to be singled out or used as the firm which should start the other builders off. If there is no other builder who can keep Negroes out, we will not do so either; we will go with the group if the state makes us, but we don't want to lose millions by being the first. . . . We could not afford to take such losses" (quoted in ibid., 372). Levitt's fear of financial loss was not wholly unfounded and stood credibly at the time for a reasonable refusal to allow integration of his housing. After all, the presence of black residents had twenty years earlier caused the government to downgrade the classification of a neighborhood to "hazardous."

More immediately, the last of the houses in Levittown, Pennsylvania, were selling sluggishly in the wake of what was described as a "stone-throwing riot" occasioned by the arrival of a single black family, the Myerses, to whom a house had been discreetly sold (ibid., 375; Popenoe 1977, 123). The congregation of a "milling crowd of about five hundred angry people"—which the local police declined to disperse (Gans 1967, 375)—speaks to the degree to which, having assumed the mantle of whiteness, the new residents were determined to protect their investments, even to the point of taking it upon themselves to enforce the exclusion of the racial other now signified by "the Negro." The tale, Gans suggests, was inflated (two stones were thrown), demonstrating the ways in which this narrative of inevitability, of facts that are known, came to represent the hopelessness of the cause. Levitt's refusal to integrate in the context of the events in Pennsylvania—the development that would ever after be known as "the one that had the riot" (ibid.)—cannot then be explained simply in terms of Levitt's own individual preference or decision. His refusal speaks, rather, of a whole network of understanding, of the formation Foucault called "power/knowledge."

"Power/knowledge" (*pouvoir/savoir*) is a helpful term to identify the way in which "the truth" about racial composition and property values was regulated at this time. Readers of Foucault will be familiar with his examinations of the production of scientific truths through history and their implication with relations of power; his accounts of the making of new truths in the history of science, for example, demonstrate the ways in which what comes to count as "true" and "real" is a function of the power invested in scientific disciplines and how the status of "truth" then fortifies this "power." The example of Levittown offers us an opportunity to see that power/knowledge circulates not only at the level of science but is pervasive in daily life.

The formation of the improbable "mob" of Levittown, Pennsylvania, can thus be understood both as an effect and another instantiation of the power/knowledge circulating there. Theirs was an apparently spontaneous response to what they took to be a violation of the conditions of their home ownership, many of which were unspoken. At the same time, of course, we must not neglect the resonance of *pouvoir* with more ordinary conceptions of power, with *force* or *puissance*, the kind of power most commonly associated with institutions, exerted from above or from without, for this kind of power, issuing from a federal government, also established the conditions of the milling homeowners' "truth."

Racism on the part of his buyers, then, no less than his own, strongly motivated Levitt to stave off integration for as long as possible, if only to instill confidence in the buyers Levitt still needed to attract, confidence that theirs would be an all-white neighborhood. The assurance that one's investment was safe from the intrusion of people of color was increasingly important in the wake of the building of highways and urban redevelopment that displaced thousands of black families and contributed to the worsening conditions of the inner city. Gans reports that discussion of integration elicited the most hostility from

> working class people who had left the city because their neighborhood was becoming predominantly Negro. Unable to afford another move, they were fearful that the same mass invasion of lower class Negroes would occur in Levittown, confronting them with a sudden and visible decline in property values and status. Having just achieved suburban home ownership, and being at the top of the working class socially and occupationally, they sensed that such an invasion could only pull down their prestige. (Gans 1967, 373)

Gans's treatment of "The Racial Desegregation of Levittown" elides the role of federal policies in changing the face of ethnic neighborhoods from which Levittowners hailed (Jackson 1985, 243). His account nevertheless illustrates how, at least by the late 1950s and early 1960s, the possessive investment in whiteness that a move to Levittown entailed was not simply a function of federal policy or even the greed of builders like Levitt. Had that been the case, Gans would probably not have found among the Levittowners with whom he lived that "most whites who got along well with their neighbors were reluctant to sell to Negroes if the neighbors opposed it" (Gans 1967, 379).[9]

Suburban Order: Roles and Regulations

As I noted in the introduction to this chapter, Gans acknowledges his own capitulation to a body of rules governing Levittown and its residents. These rules were enforced locally, via rumor, as Gans recounts, but the force of rumor to ensure order is itself grounded in a disciplinary mechanism that Foucault calls "the distribution of individuals in space." Here I focus on the multiple levels on which the distribution of individuals can be seen to be operating in Levittown.

The "enclosure" that discipline may involve (Foucault [1975] 1979, 141) is manifested in the relative isolation of the suburb from the city, for example, in the parkway designs of Robert Moses in and around New York City, preventing buses and other transport likely to carry "undesirable" people onto selected parts of the island (Caro 1974, 318, 951–52; Winner 1980, 123–24). Refined by Levitt in the diversion of through traffic to the development's periphery (Jackson 1985, 236), the suburb was physically set apart from the city and its inhabitants. Within Levittown, a vaunted privacy was secured by the construction of houses to suit only nuclear families no longer connected to their neighbors as in the city but joined instead by newly acquired similarities of status.

This feature evokes the second principle of discipline, namely, "partitioning." More "flexible and detailed" than the simple "enclosure" of a factory, monastery, or town (Foucault [1975] 1979, 142), partitioning requires that "each individual has his own place; and each place its individual" (ibid., 143). In Levittown, not only did each individual family have its own domicile separate from and yet identical to every other house on the block, but within the house, each family member also occupied a distinct place, as well. Women belonged in the modern kitchen installed in every house, while the children belonged in the front yard, where their mothers "could watch [them play] from the kitchen windows and do their washing and cooking with a minimum of movement" (Jackson 1985, 235). When not at work, men would be occupied by the "do-it-yourself" basement finishing, porch building, and eventually "additions" that the design of small houses on large lots accommodated (Hayden 1984, 8).

Perhaps Levitt's remark that "No man who owns his own house and lot can be a communist. He has too much to do" (quoted in ibid.) best captures the image that guided Levittown's design. It also suggests the sort of "machinery," in Foucault's terms, that Levittown would be required to establish and maintain. The regular division of houses and subdivisions that served to "individualize" families allowed Levitt and his organization to supervise the maintenance of the town, ensuring the value of this and future Levittowns. The attention devoted to the smallest details of upkeep is indicated by the prohibition of outdoor clotheslines (drying clothes in the sun required the use of "specially designed, collapsible racks") and the supervision of lawn cutting, to which home owners were subject in their first years. According to Jackson, the firm would take over the task if the family neglected it, "sending the laggard families the bill" (Jackson 1985, 236).

The vigilance of the Levitt organization bears comparison with the disciplinary supervision of which Foucault speaks, which came to characterize institutions as diverse as factories and schools (Foucault [1975] 1979, 145–49): "In organizing 'cells,' 'places' and 'ranks,' the disciplines create complex spaces that are at once architectural, functional and hierarchical. It is spaces that provide fixed positions and permit circulation; they carve out individual segments and establish operational links; they mark places and indicate values; they guarantee the obedience of individuals" (ibid., 148). Levitt's design was not simply concerned with how to organize space to best serve the needs of those understood to form members of a household; the ordering of neighborhood and familial spaces that characterized Levittown actually prescribed those roles, enforcing them by means of the uniform placement of houses and individuals. For Levittown, like other "great operations of discipline," "it was a question of organizing the multiple, of providing…an instrument to cover it and to master it; it was a question of imposing upon it an 'order'" (ibid.). Levitt's preoccupation with fussy details such as clotheslines or tidy lawns may appear excessive; taken as constitutive of a disciplinary regime, however, his concerns demonstrate the prescience of one who understands that "the slightest incompetence, if left unnoticed and therefore repeated each day, may prove fatal to the enterprise" (ibid., 175).

Constructing Women's Place

In a discussion of the effects of the GI Bill, cultural historian George Sánchez suggests that the rationale that guided federal housing policy in the 1940s was animated by a vision of the social order prevailing before the war. The segregation that marked fighting units from which soldiers returned was reproduced by the entitlements that "consistently, if covertly, heightened the racial divide" (Sánchez 1995, 389). Though the interracial congregation of workers necessary to maintain and expand industries essential to the war effort at home (e.g., Hayden 1984, 4) did not reflect the organization of soldiers fighting abroad, rather than extending the social changes the war had occasioned, postwar federal policies instead reproduced the segregation that had been enforced among military units. Since white soldiers did not fight with soldiers of color, they would not be forced to work or compete with racial minorities in business or education upon their return home.[10]

Nor were they forced to compete with women. Just as racial divisions were temporarily upset by the pressing needs of war, so, too, were the rules of gender bent during wartime to allow women to replace conscripted workers. While women were not in combat with men overseas, images of Rosie the Riveter at home beckoned them to work as welders, carpenters, and a variety of employment previously closed to them. Furthermore, industry giants such as Henry Kaiser—themselves supported by considerable government subsidies—went to great lengths to accommodate women workers and their families. In less than a year, Kaiser built Vanport City, Oregon, and equipped it with multiple nursery schools, kindergartens, grade schools, and supervised playgrounds designed for the nine thousand children who would live there. The director of childcare at Vanport City remarked that "In the past, good nursery schools have been a luxury for the wealthy. The Kaiser Child Service Centers are among the first places where working people, people of average means, have been able to afford good nursery education for their children" (quoted in Hayden 1984, 161). In the absence of wartime profits it could not be hoped that the "unprecedented . . . range of services" (ibid.), which included "infirmaries for sick children, child-sized bathtubs so that mothers don't need to bathe children at home, [and] cooked food services so that mother can pick up hot casseroles along with their children" (ibid., 4; see also Michel 1999, 142–44), could possibly be maintained. Nevertheless, the immediate halting of child-care services by employers and states, together with the sweeping layoffs of women workers after the war (Hayden 1984, 161), suggests that the considerations motivating these closings were not merely economic but also part of a more encompassing concern over the complexion of American family life.[11]

The wartime opening of jobs to women who had previously been barred from them occurred concurrently with the racial integration of areas of employment that had been the exclusive domain of white men; however, disparate mechanisms enabled white men, upon their return home, to resume and furthermore consolidate their place in the workforce at the expense of white women and people of color. I have discussed the way in which racial segregation was enforced through housing policies that forbade entrance into the new suburbs by nonwhites, exacerbating the density of inner cities through urban renewal. By contrast, the "restoration" of white women to their occupations as homemakers was enforced by means of the promotion of a middle-class ideal symbolized by the preinstalled Bendix washing machines that promoted familial "privacy and autonomy" by permitting women, as historian Ruth Cowan writes, to "wash their dirty linen at home" (Cowan 1983, 149–50).[12] Put simply, racial segregation was secured by keeping blacks (and other nonwhites) *out* of the suburbs, while the subordination of middle-class white women as wives was enforced by keeping them *in*.

The particular manifestation of gender regulation in postwar suburbia has received broad feminist treatment since Friedan's *Feminine Mystique* (e.g., Mainardi 1970; Oakley 1974a, 1974b; Hartmann 1981; Barrett and McIntosh [1982] 1990; Cowan 1983; Wajcman 1991).[13] Outfitting of single-family houses with the commodified spoils of the "miniaturization of technology" that made relatively inexpensive, mass-produced refrigeration and vacuum systems available and thereby necessary to the "dream house" (Hayden 1981, 25) was among the means by which the isolation of women was ensured. The higher expectations of cleanliness and order that increased household technologization brought occupied women full-time with household chores, the work that was "never done" (ibid., 26; Wajcman 1991, 84); at the same time, the lack of child care made young children a mother's sole responsibility. Finally, the absence of public transportation made her also the chief "transporter of goods" (Cowan 1983, 83–84), as well as the family "chauffeur" (Langdon 1994, 46).

The production of wives at this period was thus accomplished in no small measure by the architectural innovations that Levittown assembled. Even as they were intended to spare her effort or save her time, appliances and the strategic placement of rooms dictated women's movements.[14] Unlike the mechanisms of power that barred people of color from entering suburban life (save as domestic servants) through the complex of federal policies and zoning restrictions that formed a protective wall around the suburb, the operation guiding the suburban woman's movements in her house exemplified a more refined method of regulation, one that strikingly resembles what was for Foucault the premier "architectural figure … [embodying] a whole set of techniques and institutions for measuring, supervising and correcting the abnormal": Jeremy Bentham's Panopticon (Foucault [1975] 1979, 199–200).

The Panoptic Family

In Bentham's vision of the ideal "inspection house," individuals—whether prisoners, madmen, or schoolchildren—are consigned to isolated cells arranged in rings stacked around a central tower occupied by a supervisor. The supervisor, who, Bentham notes, could be "anyone" (ibid., 202), enjoys

Figure 2.2. Levittown, Pennsylvania, 1959. (Temple University Libraries, Urban Archives, Philadelphia, PA)

unimpeded powers of surveillance even as he is invisible to his charges. Windows on the central tower give onto corresponding windows in each cell, backlit by a window on the other end. The design provides visual access to each cell while the "lateral arrangement" of the cells precludes the inmates' interaction with one another. The supervisor's continuous presence is rendered unnecessary by the effects of the panoptic arrangement, for its design produces a relation whereby one, "subjected to a field of visibility... assumes responsibility for the constraints of power; he makes them play spontaneously upon himself; he inscribes in himself the power relation in which he simultaneously plays both roles; he becomes the principle of his own subjection" (ibid., 202–3).

The image of "several million American women cook[ing] supper each night in several million separate homes over several million stoves" (Cowan 1979, 59, cited in Wajcman 1991, 87) is a striking one to consider in the context of Bentham's plan: a woman in each house located along Levittown's orderly streets, preparing dinner for her family in the space recognized as that to which she "belongs," the kitchen window giving on to the front yard so that she can watch her children play on the unfenced lawn, a window into which those outside may also look *in*. The orderly arrangement of kitchen "cells" offers itself as an exemplar of disciplinary surveillance, ensuring that each individual woman assumes her proper task in the home. If it seems unreasonable to compare Levittown with the "total institution" (Goffman 1961; cf. Foucault [1975] 1979, 205) of the Panopticon, further examination of panopticism suggests that the "encompassing tendencies" (Goffman 1961, 4) of both are borne out in Bentham's own treatment of panopticism in the letters that constitute the text, *Panopticon, or, The Inspection-House, &c.* (1787).

In his discussion of panopticism in *Discipline and Punish*, Foucault argues that the Panopticon "must be understood as...a way of defining power relations in terms of the everyday life of men" ([1975] 1979, 205). It is therefore surprising that Foucault's discussion obscures the extent to which Bentham's formulation of the panoptic operation depends on a prior disciplinary institution that complexly delineates "the everyday life of men," namely, the family.[15] A first instance of this dependence may be found in Bentham's fifth letter, titled "Essential Points of the Plan," in which he notes that a "very material point is, that room be allotted to the lodge, sufficient to adapt it to the purpose of a complete and constant habitation for the principle inspector or head keeper, and his family. The more numerous also the family, the better; since, by this means, there will be as many inspectors, as the family consists in persons, though only one be paid for it" (Bentham [1787] 1962, 44–45).[16] Doubt concerning the necessity of motivating family members to assume the inspector's position is groundless, Bentham continues, since their seclusion "will naturally and in a manner unavoidably, give their eyes a direction conformable to that purpose, in every momentary interval of their ordinary occupation." Just like their counterparts "in towns," the members of the warden family will look out their windows to supply their entertainment. "The scene," Bentham remarks, "though confined, would be a very various, and therefore, perhaps, not altogether unamusing one" (ibid., 45).

Bentham's descriptions suggest that the support of the family in promoting the illusion of constant supervision in the panoptic operation should not be understated; the positioning of the family in the warden's tower is essential for its operation. The inclusion of the members of the warden's family in the apparatus bespeaks the efficiency of the machine, for the power that it puts into play upon the prisoners is already at work in the family itself. While Foucault speculates that the "Panopticon may even provide an apparatus for supervising its own mechanisms" (Foucault [1975] 1979, 204), Bentham's text suggests that such a provision is rather more consequential: "Another very important advantage," Bentham writes in another letter, "is that the *under* keepers or inspectors, the servants and subordinates of every kind, will be under the same irresistible controul with respect to the *head* keeper or inspector, as the prisoners or other persons to be governed are with respect to *them*" (Bentham [1787] 1962, 45; emphasis in the original). In other words, the family's maintenance of the "apparent omnipresence" of the "head keeper" is itself founded upon the very same effects of power that the family of inspectors maintains vis-à-vis the prisoners: the panoptic operation of the family itself. Though the position of the family in the tower goes unmentioned by Foucault in *Discipline and Punish*, Bentham himself treats the family as a locus (indeed a focus) of the panoptic operation.

There is a sense, however, in which families, understood in more ordinary terms, resist the characterization that would liken them to Bentham's constabulary clan. Conceived in ideal terms, the family is a domain of nurturance and development, not a "means of correct training"; it is a field of support, not of surveillance. But perhaps the persistence of that normative ideal, positioned in opposition to the panoptic representation of the family, is precisely what enables families to exercise considerable power both among their members and as an ideal to which other families ascribe. The idealization of the family as a field of support can mask the power circulating within it. Images of nurturance can render that power tolerable and thus sustainable.

We may say the same of the valued notion of privacy sought by the buyers of Levitt's single-family houses, which might appear to set ordinary understandings of "family" apart from Bentham's carceral design. Privacy after all signifies a space of not being observed, which panopticism explicitly disallows. The position of the warden, constructed as a supreme observer within the prison, vividly illustrates the prohibition of private space, for even the inspector himself is immersed in the mutually enforcing levels of the Panopticon. The threat of an unexpected arrival of some outside inspector activates disciplinary effects within and upon the head inspector himself, which ensures, in turn, that the head inspector's "fate [is] entirely bound up with [the functioning of the disciplinary mechanism]" (Foucault [1975] 1979, 204, 207). The anonymous surveillance that produces individuals out of juridical subjects in the prison thus also serves to individualize the inspector, who is himself observed by those outside the prison, be they state inspectors or amusement-seeking passersby (Bentham [1787] 1962, 46).

Even as a space of "not being observed" is disallowed by the institution, however, such a space seems nevertheless to be conceptually required by its complement, "observing." Indeed, the strata of surveillance at work in the Panopticon are constructed within not only a hierarchical scheme but also one in which the synchronous occupation of rigidly maintained binary positions (i.e., observer/observed) is essential. Even as we might understand that there is and can be no private space in the Panopticon, the notion of privacy is nevertheless essential to its operation. It is constitutive, in other words, of the binary formation in which the panoptic operation is grounded, much the way that the idea of freedom is essential to the regime of power that precludes it, as Foucault argues in the first volume of *The History of Sexuality* (Foucault [1976] 1990, 86).

"But What Will the Neighbors Think?"

What buyers of Levitt's houses were seeking was in part the privacy that city living made scarce, but Bentham's placement of the family in the tower should, I have argued, call that notion into question. Though marked wholly as "private," domestic space is itself divided architecturally between "public" (e.g., dens, dining areas) and "private" (e.g., bedrooms , bathrooms). However, like the inhabitants of the Panopticon, who take on the roles of both watcher and watched, members of households similarly assume both roles. Failures of observation, both of others and of oneself, will prompt the correction necessary for restoring the discipline that animates the observation. Already we have seen how rules—concerning visible displays of laundry or neat lawns, for example— functioned to enforce among families the proper stylization of middle-class life.

There were of course other rules in force—within the private space of the family—that were not written in rulebooks. These are perhaps especially visible in the management of female sexuality, which came, at this moment, to function as an important "transfer point," as Foucault puts it (ibid., 103), for the enforcement of the idealized image of middle-class family life.

Wake Up Little Susie, Rickie Solinger's history of the treatment of single pregnancy before *Roe v. Wade*—the years marking the founding and settlement of Levittown—provides an extended study of the operation of the disciplinary gaze, in this case, the gaze trained on sexually active women. The specter of promiscuity and of being labeled a "whore" reflected popular attitudes toward women's sexual expression but functioned, too, to maintain what would actually come to be called "sexual discipline" in the early 1960s (Solinger 1992, 214), whereby women were exhorted to assume their own regulation.

Solinger observes that the phrase " 'he ruined her,' archaic by mid-century, had been meaningfully replaced by 'she got herself in trouble' " (ibid., 35). This shift, retaining the social stigma attached to the woman, implies that a woman's sexuality was understood as a matter of *self-control*, relaxed at her peril. Unwed pregnancy constituted the visible sign that the internalized discipline had faltered and that she had relinquished "responsibility for the effects of power." The opprobrium that followed, associated not only with her but also with her parents, effectively reveals what could be construed as the failure of the parents as "head keepers" of domestic space, charged with maintaining disciplinary order at home. The presumption of parental responsibility can also clarify why preservation of familial privacy is at such a premium.

Solinger's composite of the 1957 case history of "Sally Brown," pregnant at sixteen, a young, white, middle-class woman from a "medium sized city in Western Pennsylvania," provides a useful illustration of the disciplinary gaze at work. The following is Solinger's construction of the response of Sally's parents to the news of her pregnancy:

> Mr. Brown, a businessman for twenty years with deep roots in his community, was bitterly obsessed with what the neighbors, the community and their friends at church would say if they knew about Sally. He proposed a sensible solution: to send Sally away and tell the townspeople that she was dead. . . . Mrs. Brown put her own plan into action. She contacted the high school and informed the principal that Sally would not be returning for the second half of her junior year because she'd been offered the wonderful opportunity to spend the Spring semester with relatives in San Diego. She then called up the Florence Crittendon Home in Philadelphia and arranged for Sally to move in. (Solinger 1992, 1)

The question "What will the neighbors think?" marks the extension of the panoptic operation into the space beyond the bounds of the private sphere, into the neighborhood occupied by other families. The surveillance characterizing private familial space and that characterizing the public space of the neighborhood are analogues: The "neighborhood," whether taken to be the families occupying nearby houses or more loosely as a community comprising extended family, or those who share a common religious affiliation or are members of the PTA, enjoins individual families to incorporate the community's expectations, just as a family compels individual members to adopt its values. However, as Solinger's composite illustrates, the two do not operate independently of one another: The actions of the Browns are motivated in no small measure by the disgrace that will not only be associated with Sally but will also be visited upon the family as a whole. Perhaps the lesson is this: If the operation of disciplinary power within families is predicated upon its regulation *among* families—that is, by the community—discipline among families can be understood to be maintained at the same time *within* families.

The Browns' sensitivity to the neighbors' opinions illustrates an observation Foucault made in and then clarified after *Discipline and Punish*, namely, "that the fundamental point of anchorage of the [disciplinary] relationships, even if they are embodied and crystallized in an institution, is to be found *outside* the institution" (Foucault [1982] 1983, 222; emphasis added). In the same way that the relationships that Bentham describes as most essential to the panoptic operation may be mapped onto the family, the configuration of the power beyond its bounds cannot be overlooked. This includes not only neighbors but also the media (Solinger 1992, 222), a psychiatric establishment that ascribed various pathologies to young women who engaged in premarital sex (ibid., 16, 86–102) or wanted to raise the babies themselves rather than allow them to be adopted (ibid., 6), and a judicial system charged with rendering decisions regarding pregnant girls and unmarried mothers (ibid., 34–35).

The impulse to send Sally away reveals the complex apparatus required to support the image of the middle-class white family. Solinger's comparison of the treatment of young single black women with that of single white ones exemplifies, too, the distinctive kinds of power at work with respect to racialized conceptions of "the family"; the stark differences between "white" and "black" that were produced and reinforced during this period were mirrored in the vastly different treatment of unmarried mothers of different races. As black families were largely kept out of suburbia, so too were black mothers excluded from the homes for unwed mothers, be they the Salvation Army, serving a less-educated, lower-middle-class white clientele, or private agencies and physicians serving middle- and upper-class women. Young black women relied for the most part on public welfare agencies, which frequently ill-treated them (ibid., 7, 12). Physicians and psychiatrists regarded the pregnant young white woman as sick, suffering from any of a number of mental disturbances, including "confused sexual identity" (ibid., 87, 90–91); given the proper care, there was every hope that she would recover, relinquishing her child and preparing for marriage and legitimate maternity (ibid., 16, 96). Young black women, by contrast, were seen as behaving "naturally," following their native "hypersexuality and immorality...[as] the Negro woman who gave birth, as it were, to black America, with all its defects" (ibid., 27). The threat that all single mothers posed to what Solinger calls the "white family imperative"—the requirement that white women willingly marry and raise children with their husbands (ibid., 20)[17]—was managed, then, both by promoting the illusion that white women conformed to the norm (hence the importance of putting unmarried white mothers-to-be out of sight) and by exposing young black women in need of assistance. As the suburbs kept black families out and white women in, so too were unmarried pregnant women either sequestered or exposed, according to race.

As Bentham himself understood, panopticism functions not only to circulate power, as it clearly does in the Panopticon, but also to produce knowledge. In Solinger's history of single pregnancy we find an excellent illustrative case of the way that an apparatus of power functions simultaneously to promulgate the "truth" about white girls and, by extension, what is true about white families. Foucault's formulation of the term "power/knowledge" is developed from Bentham's own expectation that the Panopticon would serve as a "laboratory…[that] could be used as a machine to carry out experiments, to alter behavior, to train and correct individuals" (Foucault [1975] 1979, 203). It is a "privileged place for experiments on men, and for analyzing with complete certainty the transformations that may be obtained from them" (ibid., 204). As I proposed at the outset, Herbert Gans's study presents not only a discrete case but, more accurately, a nested series of cases of disciplinary power in action as well. Levittown was a great experiment in living, creating a multitude of small laboratories and subjects for study and manipulation—from Levittowners' daily routines to their expectations for themselves and their families. Insofar as Gans himself becomes an object of scrutiny when it comes time to sell his house, it is testimony to the flexibility of the machine and its insistence that all of the participants play both roles, observer and observed. More than he may himself have understood, Gans was a true participant-observer, his study marking another moment of surveillance that served to reinforce the vision of Levittown that has animated planned communities in the decades since. The suburb has come to emblematize middle-class living and, with it, the division between men and women, white and black that it shaped. "Thanks to its mechanisms of observation," Foucault reflects, the Panopticon "gains in efficiency and in the ability to penetrate into men's behavior; knowledge follows the advances of power, discovering new objects of knowledge over all the surfaces on which power is exercised" (Foucault [1975] 1979, 204).

The construction of Levittown, together with the systematic exclusion of the racialized other and the regulation of gender it entailed, provide telling examples of the function of family in the production and enforcement of difference. The chapters that follow focus more finely on the differences between the production of gender and the production of race. Even as they differ in important ways, their respective operations are, as the story—or stories—of Levittown show, imbricated with one another: The formation of Levittown as a new white town depended on its exclusion of the racial other. The history provided by Rickie Solinger offers, too, a more detailed analysis of the central role the figure of the family plays. The proper image of white motherhood, the fulcrum of white family, is maintained within the family, whereas the excoriation of black women that would soon become the shorthand for the "problem" of the black family may be understood to come from outside it.

3

Boys *Will* Be Boys

Disciplinary Power and the Production of Gender

> *The statement, as it emerges in its materiality, appears with a status, enters various networks and various fields of use, is subjected to transferences or modifications, is integrated into operations and strategies in which its identity is maintained or effaced. Thus the statement circulates, is used, disappears, allows or prevents the realization of a desire, serves or resists various interests, participates in challenge and struggle, and becomes a theme of appropriation or rivalry.*
> —*Michel Foucault*, The Archaeology of Knowledge

In 1977 George A. Rekers, a self-styled pioneer in the treatment of gender dysphoric behavior in children, together with his colleague James W. Varni, presented a case study of one of their subjects:[1]

Nathan was referred at the age of four years, and lived in an intact family with two sisters, aged five years and eleven years. Of etiological significance, Nathan had a chronic blood disorder which required that he remain indoors under very protective circumstances to avoid even mild physical injury. As a consequence, his peer play had been almost exclusively with his two sisters. There was limited interaction between Nathan and his father or any other male figure. He frequently verbalized his wish to be a girl, and identified himself predominantly with female roles, occasionally displaying pronounced feminine voice inflections. Even though both boys' and girls' dress-up were available at pre-school Nathan dressed exclusively in girls' clothing. His stereotypic feminine gender-role behaviors elicited comments from other children, such as "You can't be a little girl." This concerned Nathan's teacher and parents, and ultimately led to referral for treatment. (Rekers and Varni 1977b, 428)[2]

Subsequent to his evaluation by independent clinical psychologists, an evaluation that included the mother's completion of "parent-report inventories on child gender behaviors," Nathan was determined to be "extremely effeminate," and he was formally diagnosed with "confused gender identity and moderate cross-gender disturbance."

Treatment began in the clinic playroom, where Nathan was presented with two tables, one displaying "affect toys" and the other "dress-up" toys. Affect toys consisted of like numbers of "toys associated with 'maternal nurturing' (e.g., baby dolls with accessories)" and "toys associated with 'masculine assertion' (e.g., a set of cowboy and Indian figures)."[3] During several sessions in which Nathan was instructed to play alone for five-minute intervals, observers located behind a one-way mirror logged masculine and feminine behaviors "on independent multiple push-button response panels wired to an Esterline-Angus multiple pen recorder" (ibid.). A videotape recorder was added to the live observers once Nathan's mother and father were each separately included in Nathan's sessions, having been told to refrain from joining in his play.

In the next phase of treatment, Nathan's mother was "trained to reinforce the boy's masculine play" (ibid., 429). Equipped with a "Farrell instruments bug-in-the-ear receiving device," she was prompted by an unseen experimenter to encourage Nathan's play with boys' toys by smiling and complimenting him and to discourage his play with girls' toys by "ignoring it and picking up a magazine to read" (Rekers and Varni 1977a, 179). No further mention of the participation of Nathan's father is made.

A period of what the authors refer to as "self-regulation" followed. Nathan was provided with a wrist counter and instructed to press the counter when playing with boys' toys. Prompted by an experimenter hidden from view through his own bug-in-the-ear device, Nathan was told, "O.K. if you played with just boys' toys for the last (1, 2, 4, 6 . . .) minutes(s), you can press the wrist counter" (ibid.). Over the course of several sessions, Nathan was gradually weaned from this prompting and told to press the counter "when he thought about it."

Having established significant improvement in the ratio of masculine-to-feminine play, the authors moved to replicate their success in the preschool setting. During free-play period, Nathan was observed, unbeknownst to him, by experimenters introduced to the class as "student teachers." After initial or baseline behaviors were recorded, self-regulation was once again instituted with Nathan's wearing of the wrist counter during free play. Nathan "was told and occasionally reminded, 'You may play with any of the toys you wish. You may give yourself points on the wrist counter only when you are *not* wearing the girls' dress-up clothes' " (Rekers and Varni 1977b, 430; emphasis in the original). After several sessions of self-monitoring—interrupted by a "reversal probe session" that measured his behavior without the wrist counter—Nathan was again given the wrist counter for a protracted period of self-reinforcement, in which he rewarded himself with candy after accumulating points on his wrist counter.

Twelve months after the completion of the treatment, Nathan was evaluated once more, both in the clinic and at home. "Based upon the test data," the study concluded, "the independent post-treatment follow-up diagnosis was 'male gender identity' and no emotional disturbance" (ibid., 430–31).

Nathan's is among the first case studies that tracked the development of a new diagnosis that emerged just at the moment that homosexuality was removed from the *Diagnostic and Statistical Manual of Mental Disorders (DSM)*.[4] This coincidence, first noted by Eve Kosofsky Sedgwick (1991), has generated a great deal of interest by critics who have suggested that Gender Identity Disorder (GID) continues to pathologize homosexuality.[5] My interest in the development of the diagnosis of GID, however, more immediately concerns the way its treatment reveals the distinctively disciplinary enforcement of gender difference in everyday life, as well as the ways that the family is implicated in that enforcement. Beginning in the mid-1970s and extending to today, discussions of GID in the professional literature suggest that its treatment is designed to reactivate mechanisms of gender enforcement that are supposed already to be in place. Examination of this work makes those mechanisms visible, casts them in relief, and so affords a new perspective on how gender difference is produced as if naturally.[6]

The first part of this chapter elaborates on the nature of the panoptic organization of power that, I argue, is responsible for the production of gender within the family. In contrast to a grosser, more familiar conception of power that issues from clearly visible institutional sites, the disciplinary power that Foucault identifies with the panoptic apparatus is characterized by its *invisibility*. As Bentham understood, it is the dynamic of "being seen" coupled with invisibility that is fundamental to the operation of disciplinary power. The prisoners cannot see the warden, and the warden (and his family) cannot see the inspectors outside the tower. In mapping the ladder of surveillance—from outside inspectors to prisoners in their cells—onto the participants in the diagnosis and treatment of GID—from schoolteachers and doctors to parents and children—I aim to call attention to the way that invisibility, coupled with an acute recognition of being seen, works to inculcate the internalization of the gaze that is the hallmark of panopticism.

As the constituents in the tower must occupy their place, so, too, must they *know* their place. Just as the prisoners in their cells cannot dictate the terms of their imprisonment, the warden in the tower cannot dictate the terms of surveillance. These are defined not by individuals but by the structure of the institution itself. In the development of the diagnosis and treatment of Gender Identity Disorder, we encounter a uniquely revealing moment in which psychiatry forgets its place and then, to all appearances, corrects itself. The second part of the chapter is accordingly devoted to an examination of the mechanisms of that correction that may be found in the latter-day justification of the diagnosis. This justification is periodically revised in order to meet challenges to the diagnosis, including the need to avoid emergent political pitfalls or diagnostic conflicts such as those implied by the explicit pathologization of homosexuality in early descriptions of GID.

In arguing that a disciplinary expression of power best describes the operation of gender, however, I do not claim that sexual difference, (i.e., the division of the human world into men and women, boys and girls) and the constellation of norms with which that difference is associated can so neatly be described as a function of this species of power. The legal changes affecting the different rates of the institutionalization of gay youth, for example, as I suggest in the last part of the chapter, together with the changes in mainstream psychiatric understandings of homosexuality, speak to what Foucault sees as a "confrontation" between disciplinary mechanisms and those bound up with a juridical exercise of power. It is in medicine, however, which has come to play such a prominent role in our lives, or what Foucault describes as "the general medicalization of behavior, modes of conduct, discourses, desires, and so on" (Foucault [1997] 2003, 39), that this confrontation is most evident. In the final section of the chapter I discuss two cases that highlight both the limits of disciplinary power and the points where the production of gender importantly intersects with the production of sexual difference more broadly understood. The apparatus with which these "limit cases" is associated, I conclude, points to a distinctive operation of power—one that is more closely associated with the production of sexual difference tout court.[7]

The first case is that of the treatment experienced by some gay teens during the same period that GID emerged as a diagnostic category. As the accounts of these teens attest, the removal of homosexuality from the *DSM* did not result in the depathologization of homosexuality entirely. The story of Paul Komiotis, a teenager committed to a treatment center for homosexual behavior, indicates not only the continued pathologization of sexual deviance but the operation of a more conspicuous form of power in the regulation of sexual difference as well. Naomi Scheman has argued that "heteronormativity" (the regulation of desire) "is bound up with the unambiguous division of the world into men and women" (Scheman 1999, 62). The story of Paul Komiotis and other teens like him demonstrates that the means of that division have been more recently expressed in far cruder ways than the kind of "ordinary" enforcement of gender to which the diagnosis of GID points.

The second case involves what might appear to be an extraordinary instance of the enforcement of sexual difference in the story of a mother, "Mary," whose child's sex does not conform to restrictively binary categories. The very existence of children with intersex conditions, or what are now called "Disorders of Sex Development"[8]—and particularly those resulting in ambiguous genitalia— defies the categorizations of sex and constitutes a challenge to the prevailing sexual order.[9] The correction that Mary's daughter underwent was surgical rather than behavioral; like the story of Paul Komiotis and others like him, it demonstrates the arduous character of the concealment that must be effected in the maintenance of dominant conceptions of sexual difference. Together, these two cases reveal an enforcement of sexual difference that functions in tandem with the disciplinary enforcement of gender. The juxtaposition of these cases allows us to specify both the different operations of power that work to produce gender and sexual difference, and the effects of this division.

To begin, let us return to the case of Nathan and the chain of events set in motion by his first attendance at school, for here we see the characteristic effects of a distinctively disciplinary expression of power.

The Schoolyard: Nature's Tribunal

What is perhaps most striking about the conditions of Nathan's referral to Rekers is the evident influence of the other children's judgment of Nathan's desire to play "like a girl." As the case study reports, what alarms Nathan's teacher and his parents is not his behavior itself but rather *the other children's response* to Nathan. Teasing and name-calling of boys who "reject their male role," Rekers and his colleagues explain, is not only "virtually certain to occur" but also constitutes "one of the manifest symptoms of child gender disturbance" (Rekers et al. 1977, 3). The status of peer response as a definitive sign of pathology suggests that it is imbued with a particular kind of power. While it may strike us as a truism that children's response to one another is meaningful in terms of their social and emotional development, we must wonder about the fact that the authority that sanctions Nathan's subjection to evaluation by Rekers and his team is vested in Nathan's four-year-old classmates.

Throughout the professional literature concerned with Gender Identity Disorder, children's seemingly natural assumption of conventional gender roles (granting some degree of variability, to be sure) is taken as axiomatic. Where feminism's critique of normative gender roles is explicitly raised, its arguments are dismissed, most often with the assertion that even "sex-role liberated parents report that in these times of societal change their own children remain quite traditional in sex-role behavior" (ibid.). Commentary such as this implies a certain abiding quality (that is not to say essential nature) of "traditional sex-role behavior" that makes it resistant to even the best-motivated social change. Presumably this resistance is continuous with the apparent inevitability of the teasing and name-calling that have been identified as the telling signs of the disorder.

One could speculate that the impunity with which children goad nonconforming peers derives from their collective positioning as a kind of natural tribunal whose judgment is unencumbered by the liberal notions of equality and fairness that bind adults through the social contract. Such a view would share a certain logic with the assertions of Rekers and others that traditional gender roles are persistently assumed by children despite attempts to encourage them to behave otherwise. Their intolerance of deviant gender expression, one could suggest, issues as intuitively as does their performance of traditional gender roles. While characterizing children as natural arbiters of gender norms might account for the way in which their judgment of Nathan results in his evaluation and subsequent treatment, such a characterization calls for a more adequate account of how such power is conferred upon a group of individuals who are not generally conceived as powerful.

In *Discipline and Punish*, Foucault contrasts disciplinary power with the ordinary understanding of power as something that can be "possessed as a thing" and wielded against another (Foucault [1975] 1979, 177; see also Foucault [1976] 1990, 94). Disciplinary power, according to Foucault, is instead an expression of power that is associated with what he calls, in *The Archaeology of Knowledge*, "the assignment" of subjective positions (Foucault [1969] 1972, 95), whereby individuals are allotted roles in the social world, positions that provide different possibilities for the exercise of power. In the first volume of *The History of Sexuality*, Foucault clarifies that "power is not an institution, and not a structure; neither is it a certain strength we are endowed with; it is the name that one attributes to a complex strategical situation in a particular society"

(Foucault [1976] 1990, 93). In the previous chapter we saw how the state exercised a specific kind of power to enforce a particular conception of the position a white woman was to assume in suburbia. In this chapter we see how power relations are distributed more widely among individuals and form the "dense web that passes through apparatuses and institutions, without being localized in them" (ibid., 96). Power is for Foucault inaccurately described as issuing "from above" or "outside;" instead, it is more instructive to understand first the way it "comes from below" (ibid., 94).

Recall that in Bentham's design of the Panopticon, the members of the family—or any occupants, really—who have places in the central tower take up positions of surveillance vis-à-vis each of the inmates (and one another). Nathan's classmates are similarly enjoined, enlisted in a panoptic apparatus that operates to ensure the production of properly gendered subjects. If the exercise of the classmates' gaze is evidenced by their teasing, it should be counted among the "essential techniques" of disciplinary power. Foucault describes such techniques as "always meticulous, often minute techniques, but they defined a certain mode of detailed political investment of the body, a 'new micro-physics' of power [that] had constantly reached out to ever broader domains, as if . . . intended to cover the entire social body" (Foucault [1975] 1979, 139). Loosed from its discursive field, the children's forthright announcement to Nathan that "You can't be a little girl" resists characterization as a subtle expression of power. Conceived within the terms of its field, however, their blunt repudiation is precisely the sort of "capillary intervention" (Foucault [1976] 1990, 84) that epitomizes a microphysics of power. It is consequential not for its sheer force but for the disciplinary effects it can provoke, that is, for its ability to "reach out to ever broader domains." The children's intervention in the case of Nathan activates a complex machinery of interlocking institutional interests—embodied by his teacher, his parents, and an entire team of psychologists, assistants, and technicians—functioning to subject Nathan to a "field of visibility" whereby he will learn, as his peers have already learned, to assume "responsibility for the constraints of power. . . [to] become the principle of his own subjection" (Foucault [1975] 1979, 202–3). Located at the extremities of this "productive network of power which runs through the whole social body" (Foucault [1977] 1980b, 119), not only is the children's exposure of Nathan's violation instrumental in rousing the apparatus that will therapeutically draft Nathan into his prescribed role, but their intervention effectively results, too, in the treatment of Nathan's mother.

The (Re)Production of Mothering:
The Case of Nathan's Mother

Nathan's mother receives no diagnosis. Baseline measures of her behavior are not taken, nor is her performance rated at treatment's end. Nowhere does the case study describe the examination and training that she undergoes as "treatment." Nevertheless, the arresting similarity between the instruction or "correction" Nathan's mother receives in offering gender-appropriate responses to Nathan's play and the prompting Nathan himself receives suggests that she, too, is undergoing treatment.[10] The surveillance to which she is submitted—behind the two-way mirror in the laboratory play room, in her home, and through scrutiny of the results of her enforcement of Nathan's behavior while he is outside her home—operates here as a continuous test of her performance.

Although it is unmarked in Nathan's case, work on GID in the decades following has gone to some length to investigate and detail the pathological tendencies of the mother of the gender dysphoric child.[11] In a representative statement concerning the psychosocial or nonbiological factors marked with etiological significance in GID are

> Parental attitudes and behaviors regarding psychosexual socialization. A consistent empirical and clinical observation is that parents are prone either to tolerate or to encourage the emerging cross-gender behavior, which ultimately appears to contribute to the consolidation of a cross-gender identity in a child. The reasons for such tolerance or encouragement seem to vary. In some instances, it appears related to an intense desire of the parent's [sic] particularly the mother's, to have a child of the opposite sex. (Zucker et al. 1993, 58)

This is the tentative conclusion offered in the study of two-year-old "Jackie," who liked to play with dolls and whose mother had undergone pregnancy with the expectation and hope of bearing a little girl whose name was to have been "Jacqueline."[12]

In a frequently cited and often reprinted study of "twenty-five extremely feminine boys" diagnosed with GID, psychologist Susan Coates and her colleague Ethel Spector Person suggest that such boys "appear to exceed normal children in behavioral disturbance and separation anxiety" (Coates and Person [1985] 1987, 209). "Extreme Boyhood Femininity: Isolated Behavior or Pervasive Disorder?" suggests a correlation between the prevalence of separation anxiety in boys diagnosed with GID and an intensely close but disturbed relationship with their mothers (ibid., 210) who themselves suffer from depression and personality psychopathology (Bradley and Zucker 1990, 210; Zucker and Bradley 1999a, 377; see also Marantz 1984).[13] In 1990 Coates identified the disorder of mothers of boys with GID as a "maternal psychopathology" attributable to their "fear, anger, and devaluation of men" (Coates 1990, 423), associated with the mothers' own "gender role difficulties" (ibid., 429). The array of behavioral problems manifest in boys with GID —problems that, it is pointedly argued, cannot be explained exclusively in terms of the ostracism they face upon entrance into school (Coates and Person [1985] 1987, 211)[14]—is owing rather to "deeper" disturbances that may find their source in their mothers' pathological condition.[15]

In contrast to the absence of the overt psychological evaluation of Nathan's mother, the mothers involved in the study of the twenty-five boys were "assessed using the Rorschach, Beck Depression Inventory, and the Gunderson

Diagnostic Interview for Borderlines. In addition, they received a structured interview that focused on their relationships with their own parents, on their relationship to their child during the first 3 years of life and on their own psychological status during the child's first 3 years of life" (Coates and Person [1985] 1987, 203–4). The characterization of the mothers of gender dysphoric children as themselves cases warranting clinical intervention reveals that the prolific mechanisms of surveillance by which persons are individualized within the psychiatric domain cannot readily be disentangled from the disciplinary mechanisms to which their sons are subject on the playground: It is by way of these same mechanisms that the mother's own orientation, that is, her position *as a mother,* is subject to surveillance. If, as Rekers et al. remark, "the serious social development problems...of gender disturbed boys are usually detected by the time the child enters school or is observed by other social agencies outside the home for the first time [when they are]...forced to interact with peers, both male and female, and to stand under the observing eye of teachers, other parents, and the general community" (Rekers et al. 1977, 5), so, too are the mothers of such boys "detected" and observed by these same agencies.

The aim of panopticism, as Bentham understands it, is exposure and correction of deviance from the established norm. The ingenious character of the machine means that no element truly stands outside it. The example of Nathan's mother makes clear that while parents may be understood in one sense to function as "head keepers" of domestic space, "subjects" of the gaze as their children are positioned as its "objects," it turns out that, like the children in the schoolyard or the warden in the tower, mothers, too, occupy both roles. The same would appear to hold true for those professionals who might otherwise appear to occupy positions "outside" the machine.

Justifying the Diagnosis: Securing the Professionals' Place

Case studies of GID clearly illustrate that disciplinary surveillance individualizes those judged to be deviant. Nathan is singled out by his classmates and taunted, and this taunting serves both to provoke intervention with respect to Nathan's behavior and to deter other children from engaging in similar behavior. Discipline, however, does not function solely by means of punishment or the threat of punishment but also by means of the "play of awards," which makes it possible "to attain higher ranks and places" (Foucault [1975] 1979, 181), that is, to occupy favorable subject positions. Thus, Nathan is praised when playing with the rubber knife or the "cowboy and Indian pieces" and is later told to help himself to candy when he accumulates points on his wrist counter by choosing pirate costumes in favor of playing "mommy" in a game of house.

But what of Nathan's schoolmates? On the school playground, that disciplinary field recognized as such by sissy boys and too-butch tomboys,

Nathan's fellow preschoolers are entirely supported in their judgment and encouraged not only in their own performance of "normal" behavior but also in their enthusiastic enforcement of everybody else's. Where the other children's behavior is affirmed as normal, Nathan's is condemned as pathological. Where the other children's behavior is conceived as a kind of free expression of their nature (both in terms of their gender expression and their teasing of Nathan), Nathan's behavior is understood to have been perverted, perhaps by his mother.

The efficacy of the disciplinary apparatus is evidenced by the fact that, in the face of what might otherwise be called harassment, seldom is the possibility entertained that children's intolerance of gender nonconformity is itself a problem that should be addressed. The remarkable success of Nathan's treatment or that of Becky, the seven-year-old girl who habitually spoke in "lowered, masculine tones" (Rekers and Mead 1979), is not regarded as indicative of the possibility of progressive change in children's attitudes with respect to gender roles.[16] Rather, the implications of the meaning of successful treatment are contained, discursively managed to pertain only to the necessity of treating the individual rather than intervening in the teasing that might itself be recognized as harmful.[17]

In the history of the diagnosis, teasing plays a crucial role in the justification of treatment of children whose behavior does not conform to their assigned gender. This "necessity" of treating the individual child afflicted with GID is figured as moral imperative in the articulation of the rationale defending the treatment of children in the 1970s. Rekers and his colleagues wrote that "the negative stereotypical labels applied to [boys like Nathan], such as 'sissy' or 'fag,' markedly restrict their freedom to choose, in an open fashion, a course of behavior by which they might avoid sex-role stereotyping" (Rekers et al. 1977, 5). Appropriated to identify Nathan's behavior as "stereotypically feminine" and *therefore* restrictive, the very concept of "stereotype," intended to shed a critical light on conventional expectations with respect to categories like gender, is neutralized and redeployed in the service of promoting treatment for gender-variant boys. This same deployment, in turn, fortifies the authority of the other children's position as enforcers and thus reinforces an apparatus that maintains everyone's proper "place."

The diagnosis and treatment of GID is concerned with deviance from the norm, but the norm—gender difference—is a highly contested one. Given that specialists in the field are self-consciously aware of the debates surrounding gender difference,[18] one might reasonably anticipate a certain sophistication to inform the arguments supporting the diagnosis and treatment of GID. However, when, in 1977, Rekers and his colleagues wrote in "Child Gender Disturbances" that "evidence indicates that gender identity problems in childhood are strongly predictive of sexual orientation disturbance in adulthood"[19] (ibid., 7), that outcome was taken as sufficient reason to warrant intervention.[20]

Despite the fact that four years earlier "homosexuality" was removed from the *Diagnostic and Statistical Manual of Mental Disorders* (*DSM*) as an official diagnostic category, Rekers and his collaborators unapologetically maintain that intervention in the interest of preventing homosexuality is a legitimate therapeutic good and vehemently oppose using psychotherapy as a means of helping an individual to "adjust to his homosexual orientation and behavior" (ibid., 9).[21] The provision of psychotherapeutic support to those identifying as gay, Rekers maintains, is "irresponsible," and the failure to intervene "seriously reduces the possibility of choice for the individual and actually unjustly narrows a person's options" (ibid.). And what of the propriety of preventing behavior that is no longer considered pathological? This is a question Rekers simply refuses to consider.[22]

Reading the early work on GID recalls an observation Foucault made during an interview regarding criminological texts. In responding to the suggestion that he is "very hard on criminology," Foucault responds:

> Have you ever read any criminological texts? They are staggering. And I say this out of astonishment, not aggressiveness, because I fail to comprehend how the discourse of criminology has been able to go on at this level. One has the impression that it is of such utility, is needed so urgently and rendered so vital for the working of the system, that it does not need to seek a theoretical justification for itself, or even simply a coherent frame-work. (Foucault [1975] 1980, 47)

Like such texts—and their representation of crime, which renders the police state a welcome and necessary intrusion into the lives of ordinary citizens (ibid.)—so, too, does the discourse of GID render as necessary and good this institutional intervention, this policing of gender, to which we are all subject.[23]

However, if this policing does not necessitate a "coherent framework" to buttress its operation, it must nevertheless approximate, or at least appear to operate within, such a framework. Rekers is a case in point: It is likely Rekers's failed attempts to justify more adequately treatment of GID as an effective prophylaxis against (a no longer pathological) homosexuality to which his much-diminished position in the field may be attributed. Discourse with scientific pretensions such as that concerning GID requires more credible agents than the man who has authored books like *Shaping Your Child's Sexual Identity* (Rekers 1982b) would seem.[24]

More credible agents have since taken up the mantle of GID, most prominently Susan Bradley and Kenneth Zucker. Colleagues for many years at Toronto's prestigious Clarke Institute Child and Adolescent Gender Identity Clinic and Child Family Studies Center, both have served as members of various subcommittees responsible for the introduction of and subsequent revisions to the *DSM* entry on Gender Identity Disorder. In a professional overview of the literature in 1990 Bradley and Zucker describe, in terms not so very different from those of Rekers a decade before, the two short-term goals of treatment for GID: "The reduction or elimination of social ostracism and conflict, and the alleviation of underlying or associated psychopathology. Longer term goals have focused on the prevention of transsexualism and/or homosexuality" (Bradley and Zucker 1990, 482). What distinguishes this later characterization from that of Rekers is the "underlying or associated psychopathology" ascribed to GID and given tremendous weight by the work of professionals like Susan Coates.[25] The correlation of GID with later homosexuality, as well as with the "underlying pathology" with which it is purportedly associated, locates GID incontestably within the purview of psychiatry as the diagnosis and treatment of mental illness. It works, furthermore, to steer psychiatry clear of the bounds of moral legislation toward which earlier figures like Rekers were clearly headed.[26]

The development of the diagnosis over nearly three decades is reflected in changes to the diagnostic criteria. In 1980 GID first appeared in the third edition of the *DSM*. As Eve Sedgwick notes, GID in its earliest version was nominally gender neutral but was

> actually highly differential between boys and girls; a girl gets this pathologizing label only in the rare case of asserting that she actually is anatomically male (e.g., that she has or will grow, a penis); while a boy can be treated...if he merely asserts "that it would be better not to have a penis"—or alternatively, if he displays a "preoccupation with female stereotypical activities as manifested by a preference for cross-dressing or simulating female attire, or by a compelling desire to participate in the games and pastimes of girls." (Sedgwick 1991, 20)

Later definitions of GID (American Psychiatric Association [*DSM-III-R*] 1987, [*DSM-IV*] 1994) mitigate this disparity by specifying "features" of GID in girls—including persistent marked aversion to feminine clothing, insistence on wearing stereotypically masculine clothing, or "repudiation of female anatomic characteristics." A girl's avid interest in sports and rough-and-tumble play also begin to figure in discussions of the disorder at this time, even though it is not counted among the diagnostic criteria with respect to girls. Indeed, there is a conspicuous proliferation of detail about GID symptoms in later definitions, allowing an increasing range of behaviors to count as indicia of GID.

For instance, while GID in boys was initially described in general terms as a preference for cross-dressing and playing with dolls (*DSM-III*), the description in *DSM-IV* mentions the simulation of long hair using towels, aprons, and scarves; playing house; drawing pictures of beautiful girls; and watching television shows or videos of favorite female characters.[27] Similarly, the description of GID in girls becomes increasingly detailed. In addition to a preference for boys' clothing, it comes to include a preference for short hair, having powerful male figures such as Superman as fantasy heroes, asking to be called by a boy's name, or being misidentified as boys by strangers. Most important, perhaps, by 1994, the diagnostic criteria for GID no longer required that cross-gender behavior be accompanied by a "stated desire to be, or insistence that he or she is, the other sex" (*DSM-IV*). This revision reflects a notable shift in emphasis toward any nonstereotypical behavior and represents an effective transformation of the standard articulated in previous formulations. In addition, the removal of the express gender preference requirement opened the possibility that greater numbers of children could be located within the spectrum of disorder. While Rekers initially concluded in 1977 that GID is extremely rare and "might appear only once in every 100,000 children" (Rekers et al. 1977, 4–5), by 1990 practitioners were concluding that "GIDC [Gender Identity Disorder in Children] or its subclinical variants may occur in two percent to five percent of children in the general population" (Bradley and Zucker 1990, 478)—an estimated prevalence at least two thousand times greater than the original.

In their 1999 text Zucker and Bradley substantially revised these findings, including a chapter on the difficulty of establishing rates of prevalence, arguing that GID is "an uncommon child psychiatric condition (like, say, autistic disorder)" (Zucker and Bradley 1999a, 24). In each case, estimates of prevalence appear calculated to justify the diagnosis and the treatment of the disorder. Its rarity—that is, its unusual deviation from the norm—was initially important in establishing the diagnosis of GID, while claims of higher prevalence served through the 80s and 90s to justify greater resources, including the swelling of the professional ranks enlisted in the cause of treatment. When, beginning most forcefully in the late 1990s, more critical perspectives were brought to bear, a high prevalence, many argued, represented not a true disorder but a mere "variance" that could, like any instance of nonconformity, pose problems for a child (see, e.g., Lock, Carrion, and Kleis 1997; Corbett 1998; Bartlett et al. 2000; Rosenberg 2001). At this point the rarity of GID was once again asserted, justifying its treatment as a genuine disorder (see, e.g., Zucker and Spitzer 2005, 37: "It is well-recognized that GID has a very low prevalence in the general population").

Because a disorder concerned with properly gendered behavior must blur the line between "legitimate pathology" and "social deviance," justification must occupy, implicitly or explicitly, an important place in the literature. In the abstract of one paper Rekers et al. raise the question of "the nature of informed consent in children for [the] intervention" required by the treatment of GID (Rekers et al. 1977, 2). This question is nowhere addressed in the body of the paper, which perhaps implies that the consequences of an untreated condition, namely eventual homosexuality, would so limit a person's choices as to indubitably constitute an overriding ethical duty to act on behalf of the child with GID. Moreover, the authors write, "Once parents and professionals have concluded that a boy has a gender disturbance, a therapist cannot ethically *refuse* to treat a child. The therapist *cannot impose his values* against those of the child's parent" (ibid., 9; emphasis added). Richard Green, writing in *The "Sissy Boy" Syndrome" and the Development of Homosexuality*, more frankly admits the priority of parental authority and casts the "rights of parents to oversee the development of their children [as] a long established principle. Who is to dictate that parents may not try to raise their children in a manner that maximizes the possibility of a heterosexual outcome? If that prerogative is denied, should parents also be denied the right to raise their children as atheists?" (Green 1987, 260). Kenneth Zucker later criticizes this line of reasoning by remarking that "a treatment rationale based on 'the rights of parents to oversee the development of children' would equally well justify a couple's efforts to obtain the assistance of a professional therapist in raising one or more of their children as homosexual" (Zucker 1990, 29).

Zucker's criticism of Green (and implicitly of Rekers) reflects more than a difference of opinion with respect to matters of professional ethics. His remarks contain an admonition of his colleagues with regard to what might appear to be an overstepping of the bounds that define their roles and secure their professional authority. There should be no question that professional psychological assistance of the sort that specialists of GID provide should be regarded as necessary for correcting an illness for the child's own good; such treatment is not commonly understood to be undertaken to satisfy parents' wishes. Zucker's intervention is not simply a critique of the rationale that informs both Green's and Rekers's defense of treatment of GID; it also reflects a clear recognition of the place that both parents and psychiatric professionals occupy within a greater disciplinary field. If it is not for Rekers to determine through the lens of undisguised homophobia whom to treat and why, it is also not within parents' power to baldly "shape their child's sexual identity." In other words, even as the view that parents are a formative influence is widely accepted, a parent's role is defined as fostering children's "healthy, natural" impulses. A conception of parents' positions as head keepers who inculcate a self-discipline is—with respect to gender roles at any rate—best rendered invisible: the better to reinforce an understanding of gender as the division of behaviors that our conceptions of men and women, boys and girls *normally* entail. While doctors' intervention could risk calling attention to the enforcement that takes place, their positions as helping professionals can be deployed precisely to reinforce the apparatus that naturalizes conventional expectations of gender. Much as the design of Bentham's machine makes visible a generalized apparatus of discipline operating in society, the diagnosis and treatment of GID makes visible the specific mechanisms functioning in the disciplinary enforcement of gender.

If, in the early years of the development of the diagnosis, GID was frequently and explicitly linked to homosexuality, it may be owing to the fact that homosexuality once functioned primarily in a disciplinary mode; that is to say, the specter of homosexuality was clearly linked to norms of gender, and, to some greater or lesser extent, gayness was equated with gender deviance. While at the outset homosexuality was marked within the discourse of GID as a failure to treat a disorder of gender, ultimately the introduction of the diagnosis of GID and the removal of homosexuality reflected a greater sociocultural change that functioned—at least to some extent—to disentangle "gender" from "sexuality." The result was a greater openness for gay people but also, paradoxically, a far harsher form of treatment of the deviance that it continues to represent even today.

Locating Disciplinary Limits: The Case of Gay Youth

Foucault remarks that "the individual to be corrected appears to require correction because all the usual techniques, procedures, and attempts at training within the family have failed to correct him" (Foucault [1999] 2003, 58). If we understand the treatment of GID as a kind of harnessing of the "usual" means of correction, one of the failures of this correction would appear to result in a child's homosexuality. Attending to the effects of this alleged failure, we may better appreciate the distinctively disciplinary character of gender enforcement, as well as its limits; we may, in other words, specify where a disciplinary apparatus ends and where the expression of a different kind of power begins.

From the early 1970s at least through the mid-1990s a continuous effort was made to yoke the officially recognized diagnosis of GID to homosexuality.[28] In the earliest work by Rekers, homosexuality was noted as a "risk" of untreated GID. By the late 1990s Zucker and Bradley routinely note, without judgment, the results of Green's study that demonstrate that most boys who were identified with GID would come to identify as gay (though conversely, most gay men would not have been diagnosed with GID). Homosexuality is no longer directly pathologized, but it is nevertheless taken up in discussions associated with GID, Zucker and Bradley explain, because "clinicians are frequently consulted about, or by, lesbian and gay youth" (Zucker and Bradley 1999a, 339).

Zucker and Bradley's continued work in this area speaks to a kind of indirect intervention with respect to the sexual orientation of gay youth, but there was, during this same period, an apparent increase in a more direct sort of "treatment" of these young people. Stories reporting the disturbing abuse of lesbian and gay youth in mental hospitals and residential treatment centers began to appear in the mid-1990s in a variety of media.[29] "Setting Them Straight," Bruce Mirken's exposé of the therapeutic treatment of gay teenagers, recounts the story of Paul Komiotis, who was sent to Rivendell in Utah, part of a national chain of psychiatric hospitals. Much of Komiotis's treatment "involved a device called a plethysmograph that uses electronic sensors attached to the genitals to measure the subject's sexual arousal. But in Komiotis's case, the procedure went a step further. 'They'd put electrodes on our private parts,' he explains, 'and show us pictures of men and women. When you got attracted to people of the same sex you got a little electric shock to your penis, strong enough to sting' " (Mirken 1994, 55). Mirken reports that Komiotis was also subjected to regular sessions with Mormon church representatives who would "tell us that homosexuality was wrong and could be changed through God." The experiences of Komiotis and others suggest that what Sedgwick calls the "war on effeminate boys" has since been waged on the defiant bodies of gay teenagers (Sedgwick 1991).[30]

While the treatment of GID in children is relatively noncorporal and noncarceral, gay and lesbian teenagers are clearly seen to require a harsher kind of intervention. From a "therapeutic group home" in the Midwest, sixteen-year-old Phil wrote to Mirken: "I'm sorry I didn't write sooner. I tried to write you a letter by hand, but it was too frustrating. It's the drugs. I get Melleril shots, PRN, Haldol, Clozapine, and a pink hormone pill. I try to move and it is really hard because it makes me all stiff and that's why I couldn't write. They know I am gay, but they don't say that is the reason that I am here. They say it is depression, but I didn't feel depressed until I got locked up here" (Mirken 1994, 57).

Shock treatment, drugs, isolation, and "covert desensitization"—the process by which a patient is conditioned to associate "undesirable" behaviors (in this case homosexuality) with negative or repulsive images and "desirable" behaviors (heterosexuality) with positive or pleasant images—are all among the "therapies" to which gay and lesbian teenagers have been subjected (see also, e.g., Burke 1996; Mournian 1998). Lyn Duff, a young lesbian who escaped from Rivendell (since renamed Copper Hills Center) and whose court battle prevented her mother from returning her, reports having been sedated, hypnotized, placed in physical restraint, and administered "hold therapy"—in which she was held down while staff members screamed at her to admit she was hurting her family by being lesbian (Mirken 1994, 56).

Either by behaving in ways that belie normative gender expectations or by "acting out," lesbian, gay, and transgender youth have been entered into treatment as a result of an incongruous array of "problem behaviors" that are indicative (or thought to be indicative) of a developing homosexual orientation. As a result of participating in a political demonstration, attempting suicide, being sexually active, withdrawing socially, coming out to a teacher, or hanging out with "those kinds of kids"—even seeking assistance for peer harassment[31]—teenagers have found themselves delivered to treatment centers, sometimes for years at a time.[32]

In lectures delivered soon after *Discipline and Punish* was published, Foucault elaborates on his analysis of disciplinary power by distinguishing it from what he describes as a "statist" form of power he calls "regulatory" (Foucault [1997] 2003, 250). In this chapter I have argued that the treatment of GID—or, more accurately, the everyday enforcement of gender roles that the diagnosis and treatment reveals—exemplifies a disciplinary expression of power; this includes anonymous and invisible surveillance of the individual and a system of rewards and punishments aimed at the reinforcement and internalization of "correct" standards of behavior. In the treatment of gay youth, we find an expression of power that appears to be distinct from and yet significantly connected to this power.

In both the Collège lectures of 1975–76 and in the first volume of *The History of Sexuality*, which appeared at the same time, Foucault takes up the special case of the regulation of sexuality, which he understands to involve the imbrication of these distinctive expressions of power at work in the treatments of children with GID and gay youth, respectively:

> On the one hand, sexuality, being an eminently corporeal mode of behavior, is a matter for individualizing disciplinary controls that take the form of permanent surveillance . . . But because it also has procreative effects, sexuality is also inscribed, takes effect, in broad biological processes that concern not the bodies of individuals but the element, the multiple unity of the population. Sexuality exists at the point where body and population meet.

And so it is a matter for discipline, but also for regularization. (Foucault
[1997] 2003, 251–52)

Unlike younger children, whose performance of gender roles can be subject to
disciplinary correction, gay teenagers' open or "discovered" expression of a
desire that is incongruent, as Rekers understands it, with "normal sexual
identification" (Rekers 1982a, 1982b) reveals a failure of disciplinary power,
that is, a failure of the power directed at the level of individual bodily comport-
ment. However, in addition to the failure of disciplinary power it signals,
"perverted sexuality," as Foucault notes, "has effects at the level of the population." These effects, he says, are a function of "the theory of degeneracy," which
casts perversion as a dangerous genetic condition entering the population: As
Foucault puts it, "anyone who is debauched is assumed to have a heredity.
Their descendants also will be affected for generations, unto the seventh
generation and unto the seventh of the seventh and so on" (Foucault [1997]
2003, 252). Perhaps the danger that is still projected onto homosexuality today
can be understood as the historical legacy of the stigma embedded in this
theory. Concealment of the treatment of gay youth such as Paul Komiotis
serves to contain what would otherwise be the rippling effects of his gayness,
the stigma of which would attach to his family and mark them, too, as deviant.

The Junction of Discipline and Regulation:
The Case of Children with Intersex Conditions

Juxtaposing the treatment of children diagnosed with GID with the treatment
of gay teens highlights the different mechanisms that both maintain what
Kathryn Pauly Morgan calls the "gender border" (Morgan 2005, 298) and
contain transgressions of that border. This juxtaposition illustrates, too, the
important role that medicine—as knowledge, practice, and institution—plays
at the crossroads where gender and sexuality, disciplinary and regulatory
power, meet. Foucault describes medicine as a "scientific knowledge of both
biological and organic processes (or in other words, the population and the
body)," but, starting in the nineteenth century, medicine also "becomes
a political intervention-technique with specific power-effects" (Foucault
[1997] 2003, 252); that is to say, medical knowledge can be put to work in
the disciplinary subjection of bodies and the regularization of populations. If
medicine here occupies a privileged place at the border, perhaps it is owing to
the special function it has in determining what counts as the norm with
respect to sexual difference. While the development of the diagnosis of
GID and the institutionalization of gay youth suggest medicine's role in the
"normalizing society," it may be in the cosmetic surgical correction of ambiguous genitalia—a routine approach to what has been known as "intersex
management"—that that role is made most evident.

About one in two thousand children is born each year with ambiguous
genitalia.[33] Accepted protocols for treating children born with genitals that

are neither clearly male nor clearly female include corrective genital surgery and gender reassignment.[34] Starting in the 1950s and common by the late 1960s, when the work of sexologist John Money and colleagues became widely accepted, boys born with a condition called "micropenis," that is, having a penis shorter than 2.5 centimeters at birth, or girls with "clitoromegaly," defined as having a clitoris larger than one centimeter at birth, were referred for surgical correction. For boys this would mean clinical castration and reassignment as girls; for girls it has meant clitorectomy. "Mary's story," an account of a mother whose daughter was discovered to have a form of intersex, vividly illustrates the convergence of these different kinds of power and their effects.[35]

Mary was a young mother in the mid-1980s when she saw her daughter, "Jessica," come out of the shower after a ballet lesson one afternoon. Out of the corner of her eye, Mary noticed what she described as a "growth" emerging from her daughter's labia. Mary immediately called the doctor, who agreed that Mary should bring her daughter in the following morning. Her daughter did not ask why they would be going to the doctor. "Jessica was the type of child who never questioned me. She never spoke back. Never. Because she wanted to make me—us, her parents—happy, and not displease us."

After a brief examination, Jessica's pediatrician sent her that same day to a pediatric endocrinologist. A sonogram revealed that Jessica did not have a uterus but undescended testes.[36] Mary recounts:

> The pediatric endocrinologist asked to speak with me alone. Jessica was in a different room. The doctor and I then sat and she explained to me that Jessica had XY chromosomes and Jessica would not be able to bear children. She also explained to me that this was something I should never, ever bring up with Jessica. I should never talk about it with Jessica. We should just take care of it as quickly as possible so that Jessica could live a normal life. I agreed to this because it was what she asked me to do. I was very young at the time. I was just in my late twenties.
>
> Naturally I was shocked; I was stunned, I was saddened. I went home and told my husband, who had just come back from work. I told him all about it, what the pediatric endocrinologist said. I had never seen him cry before but he just broke down and sobbed in my arms. That's when it impacted me the most.... There were a lot of tears, a lot of feeling bad for Jessica, knowing that she couldn't have children naturally.

Mary was instructed to tell her daughter that "her ovaries hadn't developed properly and they would have to come out." Jessica was not told that her testes would be removed because doctors feared they would become cancerous. Nor was she informed of the clitorectomy that would be performed at the same time.[37]

Only a month later Jessica was in the recovery room of the children's hospital. Mary remembers finding her daughter moaning in bed as she recovered from the anesthesia. Mary thought it was only from the pain, but years later Jessica told her that, having reached down, she realized that "a piece of her was gone." In the week that Jessica spent in the hospital, nothing was said about the clitorectomy. Doctors did inform her, however, that she would soon have to return to the hospital to evaluate the effects of what they called "the plastic surgery."

Mary remembers that before surgery, immediately after, and in the follow-up evaluation, "scores of male residents would come in to examine" her daughter. Mary had consented to the examinations because she knew that her daughter was being treated in a teaching hospital. Years later, Jessica obtained her medical records and confronted her parents with what she had learned. It was then that Mary would hear from her daughter's mouth about the terrible effects not only of the surgery and the deception that accompanied it but also of the repeated examinations she had endured.

In retrospect, it seems obvious to Mary that her daughter, who regarded her enlarged clitoris as perfectly normal, would have experienced the surgery and the examinations as painful violations, but if at the time she entertained such thoughts, she put them out of her mind. She remembers asking whether she should seek counseling for Jessica and in response was told the story of another girl with Jessica's condition who, as a teenager, had stolen a look at her records when her doctor was called out of the room. That girl, the doctors informed Mary, had had to be placed in a psychiatric institution as a result of learning "the truth." The surgery had taken care of the problem, Mary was told, and further discussion would only raise potentially damaging questions for Jessica. What was important was that Jessica look normal. If she looked normal, she would be able "to live her life as a normal girl."

The repeated invocation of "the norm" in the treatment of Mary's daughter signals the operation of what Foucault calls in *Discipline and Punish* a "disciplinary régime" (Foucault [1975] 1979, 193). In the "management" of intersex, the norm is explicitly constituted by the standardized measurement of genital size. A baby girl's clitoris should not measure more than one centimeter, and an adolescent girl's clitoris should not extend beyond her labia. A failure to conform to "the norm" brings upon the individual with ambiguous genitalia a whole technology of power that is at the same time visited upon the entire family. The application of power evident in the account of Jessica's mother is strikingly similar in many ways to that revealed by the treatment of Gender Identity Disorder.

Certainly, the treatment of children such as Nathan can appear (and certainly, judging by retrospective accounts of some children who have undergone it, is experienced) as arduous in nature.[38] However, as I have argued, embedded in Bentham's own account of the working of the panoptic "machine" is the case that the everyday application of disciplinary power can and frequently does manifest itself in ways that would not generally be understood as "power" in the ordinary sense of "domination"; such applications are instead expressed in ways that we may take to be the routine acts of loving and attentive parents. We take for granted the importance of inculcating in children any number of skills and behaviors by their parents. From feeding oneself with the aid of cutlery to looking both ways before crossing a street, from toilet training to offering one's hand in greeting to another—these are among the behaviors children must learn, the regular, controlled performance of which is promoted by disciplinary means.

As the case of Nathan makes clear, the performance of gender norms is most often like any behavior that parents are expected to cultivate in their children. A girl may be told not to sit a certain way because it is not "ladylike"; boys are typically instructed not to cross their legs at the knees "like girls," for example; more subtly, children may be clothed or provided toys that encourage certain kinds of play. In these ways Mary's memory of her daughter's childhood suggests an ordinary and successful activation of these mechanisms. Mary relates that Jessica was a very good girl; she was obedient, interested in appropriately feminine activities like ballet dancing, and expected to fulfill her role as a woman by marrying and having children of her own one day. When the pediatric endocrinologist recommended prompt surgery, Mary was given to understand that this treatment would keep Jessica's development as a woman on track. Furthermore, any revelation of the truth about the aim of the surgery, namely, to make her more closely resemble the "female" that she in fact was not, would derail those efforts and could furthermore result in Jessica's mental illness.[39]

What distinguishes Jessica's experience and that of other children with ambiguous genitalia from what we might call the "ordinary" gender training of children is the conspicuous mark of power left on her body. One might argue that all of us wear the mark of gender on our bodies; indeed, it would be plausible to see the range of these marks on a continuum, with the various appurtenances of gender—be they specific articles of clothing or grooming standards—at one end and "corrective" surgery for individuals with ambiguous genitalia at the other. While such a characterization would rightly call attention to the ways that gender is "produced," as Foucault would say, it could serve to trivialize the significant differences between the traces of the usual mechanisms of power that enforce gendered behavior and the literal scars borne by children submitted to cosmetic genital surgery.

The Confluence of Disciplinary Power and Sovereign Right

The distinction Foucault makes between disciplinary power and a grosser expression of the power of regularization (so aptly called in the case of intersex management) suggests an important qualitative difference between what could be described as the enforcement of gender difference on the one hand and the enforcement of the division of the sexes on the other. At the same time, the imbrication of the two kinds of power, the way each is articulated upon the other, as Mary's story makes clear, allows us to appreciate how a continuity can exist in the expression of power's disparate forms. In emphasizing the difference between the two expressions, my aim is not to deny this continuity but to permit a finer analysis and understanding of the mechanisms that make us take for granted the division of the world into men and women, boys and girls. Understanding these mechanisms can help us, too, in specifying the nature of the harms suffered by children and teens like Paul Komiotis and Jessica.

More than in the case of Nathan, it is tempting to make recourse to a language of rights and their violation in seeking to understand the practices of normalization to which both Jessica and Paul Komiotis were subjected. While we may certainly marshal arguments against the training that Nathan underwent, its remarkable similarity to the uncontroversial varieties of parental training renders more difficult a clear drawing of lines distinguishing one kind of correction from another. Indeed, we may understand this difficulty to emblematize a disciplinary regime, but the practices involved in institutionalizing gay youth and in performing cosmetic genital surgery on children with intersex conditions differ in important ways from Nathan's treatment. While, as I have maintained, disciplinary power is active in both cases, the story of Paul Komiotis particularly exemplifies the way in which "in our day," Foucault argues in a 1976 lecture, "power is exercised through both right and disciplines.... The techniques of discipline and discourses born of discipline are invading right, and the normalizing procedures are increasingly colonizing the procedures of law" (Foucault [1997] 2003, 38). If we understand Komiotis's institutionalization to have been motivated by disciplinary forces (e.g., an effort to conceal and, hopefully to eradicate, the deviance that his parents experienced as a source of their own shame), that motivation is, at this historical moment, propelled by and exercised through a newly consolidated force of right with respect to teenagers in the United States.

In "Mental Hospitalization of Troublesome Youth: An Analysis of Skyrocketing Admission Rates" (1988), psychologist and legal scholar Lois Weithorn explains the recent history that has paved the way for the specific expression of this right. She recounts how, in the 1980s, a dramatic increase in the rates of adolescent institutionalization followed on the heels of legal reforms enacted in the 1970s that checked the authority of courts and mental health professionals to commit adults against their will, establishing "procedural protections and substantive standards.... [that] did not extend to juvenile hospitalization procedures" (Weithorn 1988, 779–80). These reforms left a gap in the mental health regulatory scheme that the industry fully exploited in the wake of the decriminalization of status offenses (e.g., truancy or running away from home) that had previously placed juvenile offenders under the authority of the justice system (see, e.g., Schwartz, Jackson-Beeck, and Anderson 1984).

At the same time, laws affording great latitude to parents to oversee their children, such as the 1979 Supreme Court decision in *Parham v. J. R.*, endorsed "unbridled discretion for parents ... and admitting staffs in decisions concerning juvenile admissions to [psychiatric] facilities" (Weithorn 1988, 809). In his dissent in *Parham*, Justice Brennan expressed his concern that "the decision by parents 'to surrender custody of their child to a state mental institution' signaled an existing 'break in family autonomy' " (ibid., 811n). Weithorn elaborates: "When a confused parent reaches out for help, he may gratefully acquiesce to whatever treatment option seems most readily available. Because of the vulnerable position in which he finds himself, the parent may be unduly swayed by advertising or by the availability of insurance coverage and may not be aware of, or have immediate access to, other more appropriate and less restrictive options" (ibid., 812).[40]

Without having access to the details of the situation of Komiotis's parents, we cannot assess the degree of their vulnerability. If we suppose, however, that they sought medical care for their son out of a genuine concern that he was ill, his experience would attest to the way that medicine functions as a site of "a perpetual exchange or confrontation between the mechanics of discipline and the principle of right" (Foucault [1997] 2003, 39); a case such as Komiotis's demonstrates also the way that a regulatory power can be redeployed to protect a prevailing disciplinary regime.

While the case law Weithorn addresses did not explicitly involve parental consent for the surgeries to which Jessica was subject, Mary's story similarly illustrates this confrontation of discipline and right. It has in common with Komiotis's the fact that in both cases the parents were empowered to make decisions on behalf of their underage children. However, unlike the case of Komiotis, in which his parents were presumably acting on their own beliefs concerning homosexuality as a pathological condition or perhaps even as a social or moral wrong, Jessica's parents were in a position more closely resembling Jessica's own; that is to say, they were not acting on their own beliefs that an intersex condition required surgical correction but were themselves subject to "doctors' orders." What is perhaps even more vexing about the surgical treatment of intersex is its clear violation of accepted principles of bioethics, cardinal among them the informed consent, which is routinely withheld in these cases.[41]

Because Jessica's mother is charged with making her daughter's decisions, her story, perhaps even more than Jessica's own, demonstrates the importance of attending to the disciplinary expression of power embedded in the social fabric. In thinking about a situation such as theirs, we would be remiss if we did not ask, "What can be done?" Foucault's analysis emphasizes the ways that the very formulation of the questions we might pose concerning the possibilities for resistance are themselves grounded in networks of power and that appreciating the mechanics of that power can provide us insight into the openings that that network must, as Foucault understands it, afford.

It may appear that the answer to the gross violations such as those endured by a Paul Komiotis or a Jessica is what Foucault describes as a "recourse or a return to . . . right" (ibid.), such as the right to make a choice based on full information. Because we may so readily describe the experiences of Komiotis, as well as that of Jessica and her parents, as violations of rights, both legal and moral, it would seem that a proper response to such violations would rest in the assertion of a "sovereign right" to one's own body. Foucault cautions against such a conclusion, however, and indeed, both stories suggest that assertions of right can take us only so far. In a lecture at the Collège de France, Foucault told his audience that the invocation of right "against discipline will not enable us to limit the effects of disciplinary power" (ibid.). Foucault's claim is amply—and tragically—illustrated in the stories of Komiotis and Jessica, for, as I have claimed, the violations of right experienced by both teenagers (institutionalization and clitorectomy, respectively) are grounded in a distinctively disciplinary enforcement of gender norms natively resistant to the sorts of intervention that can be marshaled in the name of right. To the extent that they cloak the individual in some theoretical protection against official actions by the state, rights are intelligible only in the context of a regulatory expression of power.[42]

The limits of making recourse to rights within a disciplinary regime is perhaps more visible, however, in the case of Jessica and her family. Neither Mary nor her husband—not to mention Jessica herself—was given a choice regarding the surgery that Jessica would undergo. In fact, as Jessica's mother recalled the unfolding of events that led to the surgery, it becomes clear that choice was not at issue at any point. What the story suggests is that the invocation of some right is precluded by the presentation of "facts" about the problem to be corrected—facts that are rendered true by a construction of gender that is not decreed from on high but from a dispersed apparatus that makes of gender difference something that goes without saying and, with it, makes it imperative to correct any presentation of genital ambiguity— a "social emergency," in the words of the American Academy of Pediatrics (2000, 138). Jessica's story illustrates how desperately correction of intersex is needed by a system that will find a way—in spite of regulations it itself institutes—to ensure that correction. In making this observation, I emphasize that I am not suggesting that it is inappropriate to invoke right where questions of cosmetic genital surgery are concerned;[43] instead, I am trying to understand how, in cases such as these, disciplinary power functions to block such an invocation in advance.

A pair of studies conducted by psychologist Suzanne Kessler illuminates the perhaps surprising disjuncture between right and discipline to which Foucault points. In one study, college students were asked to imagine that they had been born with clitoromegaly. In response to the question of whether they would have wanted their parents to sanction clitoral surgery if the condition were not life threatening, an overwhelming 93 percent of the students reported that they would not have wanted their parents to agree to surgery. Kessler reports that "women predicted that having a large clitoris would not have had much of an impact on their peer relations and almost no impact on their relations with their parents. . . . They were more likely to want surgery to reduce a large nose, large ears, or large breasts than surgery to reduce a large clitoris" (Kessler 1998, 101).[44] These findings, Kessler reflects, are not surprising given that the respondents characterized genital sensation and the capacity for orgasm as "very important to the average woman, and the size of the clitoris as being not even 'somewhat important' " (ibid., 101–2). Men in the study were faced with a different dilemma, the one facing parents of boys with micropenis. Their question was whether to stay as a male with a small penis or to be reassigned as a female. More than half rejected the prospect of gender reassignment. However, according to Kessler, that "percentage increases to almost all men if the surgery was described as reducing pleasurable sensitivity or orgasmic capability. Contrary to beliefs about male sexuality, the college men in this study did not think that having a micropenis would have had a major impact on their sexual relations, peer or parental relations, or self-esteem" (ibid., 103).

In the second study, Kessler and her team asked students to imagine that *their child* was born with ambiguous genitalia. The students in this study indicated they would make what Kessler describes as "more traditional choices" to consent to corrective surgery. Their rationales mirrored those of parents that can now be found on Internet bulletin boards devoted to the parenting of intersexed children: Students reported that they did not want their child to feel "different" and believed that early surgery would be less traumatizing than later surgery (ibid.). Like parents over the last fifty years who have faced these difficult decisions, the students did not reflect on the somatic experience of the child and, with it, the possibility of lost sensation that so concerned the students in the first study.

Kessler's paired studies confirm a kind of common sense that individuals, as individuals, are disinclined to compromise their erotic response for the sake of cosmetic enhancement. Thinking about our own bodies, their sensations and capacities, invokes a sense of our rights to self-determination: the rights, for example that propelled feminist praxis of the Second Wave. But parents, as parents—even prospective parents such as the students—want "what is best for their child," and the promise of a "normal life" figures prominently in that conception. The juxtaposition of the two studies raises an obvious, if nonetheless vexing, question: "Why would parents consent to procedures on behalf of their children that they would refuse for themselves?" Foucault's discussion of the incompatibility of individual right with disciplinary power helps to illuminate what we might characterize as the ambivalence to which the results of Kessler's studies point. Assuming the position of the parent, the second study suggests, prevents the students in the second study even from asking themselves the question that students were asked in the first. This failure of the parents to pose the question concerning what they themselves would have wanted is a testament to the pivotal role that the family plays in the disciplinary apparatus and the way it enjoins its members in the enforcement of the norm.

Finally, I want to identify a salient question that has throughout my analysis of Gender Identity Disorder also gone unasked, namely, the place of race in the disciplinary enforcement of gender. Kessler's studies indicate the ways that a question can be rendered unaskable within a discursive formation. Indeed, only a small portion of the studies on Gender Identity Disorder even break down their subjects by race and/or ethnicity,[45] implying that race and ethnicity are not relevant factors in deriving conclusions about children diagnosed with GID. If this silence suggests that whiteness is functioning in this discourse as the unmarked standard for measuring masculinity and femininity, the active withholding of data concerning race and ethnicity (see, e.g., Green 1987) exemplifies how questions can be preempted by the presentation of research and how data can be used to tell some stories but not others. In the next chapter we will see how another body of scientific research suppresses active discussion of race. However, rather than promote a conception of the white norm, this suppression is designed to promote a conception of racialized deviance.

4

Of Monkeys and Men

Biopower and the Production of Race

The hold of ideology over scientific discourse and the ideological function-ing of the sciences are not articulated at the level of their ideal structure (even if they can be expressed in it in a more or less visible way), nor at the level of their technical use in a society (though that society may obtain results from it), nor at the level of the consciousness of the subjects that built it up; they are articulated where science is articulated upon knowledge.
    —Michel Foucault, The Archaeology of Knowledge

That poverty, unemployment, slum housing, and inadequate education underlie the nation's urban riots is well known, but the obviousness of these causes may have blinded us to the more subtle role of other possible factors, including brain dysfunction in the . . . small number of the millions of slum dwellers . . . who engaged in arson, sniping, and physical assault. The real lesson of the urban rioting is that, besides the need to study the social fabric that creates the riot atmosphere, we need intensive research and clinical studies of the individuals *committing the violence. The goal of such studies would be to pinpoint, diagnose, and treat those people with low violence thresholds before they contribute to further tragedies.*
    —Drs. Vernon Mark, William Sweet, and Frank Ervin, letter to
    the Journal of the American Medical Association, 1967[1]

The long-awaited publication of Michel Foucault's 1974–75 and 1975–76 lectures at the Collège de France provides us with an opportunity to reconsid-er the potential contribution of Foucault's "analytics" of power for under-standing the contemporary operation of race. Unlike the deployment of gender, which, I argued in the previous chapter, is best understood as a function of disciplinary power, the deployment of race is primarily a function of "biopower," an expression of power that is bound up with the state apparatus. Appreciating the distinctive kinds of power associated with the production of gender on the one hand and race on the other affords us a chance to deepen our understanding of the ways that differences are produced and articulated in and through one another.

In this chapter I first discuss the lectures themselves to show how they take up the genealogy of race and the specific expressions of power with which it has been associated. I then take a contemporary example—from the 1990s—in the announcement of the "Violence Initiative," a program of the U.S. government that proposed to coordinate federally funded research into biological and genetic links to violence, as a case in point that demonstrates the workings of biopower, or what Foucault also calls the power of "regularization," in the production of race. My aim is to uncover the way in which the clumsy announcement of the Violence Initiative bespeaks the operation of the distinctive kind of power that characterized racist expression at the turn of the twenty-first century. The announcement is a particularly interesting example that marks a kind of discursive "break," revealing what is meant to be unspoken about race and the management of difference during this period. An unstated and "forbidden" vector of social control, race is nevertheless active in the statements that accumulate in the unfolding of the details of the initiative.

Foucault's understanding of the chiasmic operation of knowledge and power is an important theme throughout his work, and the treatment of the power of regularization is no exception. As Foucault's studies demonstrate, power/knowledge is exercised in ways that divert attention from one term or the other; for example, the scientific production of knowledge that makes use of disciplinary means appears most frequently to accumulate knowledge in a field that is putatively devoid of power relations; the scientific aim of objectivity seems even to demand that science claim freedom from the constraints of power or politics as constitutive of its own justification. Such a claim, as we saw in the last chapter, was, and continues to be, salient in the discourse of Gender Identity Disorder.

One might suppose that scientific work openly supported by the state would abandon a pretension to "purity"; even in this work, however, which is intended to promote public health, medical and scientific knowledge is presented in a way that disarticulates its pursuit from the more obvious aims of power. Attending to what Foucault calls a "preconceptual" ground, which, I argue, underpins the Violence Initiative, is essential to understanding the way in which state power can be exercised in ways that would otherwise appear repugnant to and even forbidden by the very institution that perpetuates its operation. Fundamental to the operation of this power in the example of the Violence Initiative is the explicit focus on the individual. However, as I argue in the final section, evidence suggests the significant presence of a shadowy figure in this discourse, someone "behind" the violent individual, namely, his mother. Attending to the representation of the violent individual's mother will provide us an opportunity to examine the complex effects appearing at the juncture where the disciplinary production of gender meets the production of race by biopower.

Biopower and the Racist State

In his 1975–76 lectures, Foucault takes up explicitly, for the first time in his work, the function of racism in the state and the specific techniques of power associated with it. In his summary lecture he addresses the development of the two different sorts of power he had undertaken to study in the course. The first of these is the power of the sovereign: In the early modern period, the power embodied by the sovereign was a "right of life and death" over his subjects (the right "to take life or let live"). In the nineteenth century this power underwent a transformation into what Foucault describes as a "right to make live and to let die" (Foucault [1997] 2003, 240–41; cf. Foucault [1976] 1990, 138). However, this characterization does not yet fully describe the power of the racist state or, rather, the extent to which the functioning of this power in the racist state depends on what Foucault calls "the level of the micro-relations of power" (Foucault [1977] 1980a, 199). In Foucault's work, this level of power is most closely associated with the "disciplinary" power he examines in *Discipline and Punish*. According to Foucault, a kind of power emerged in the mid-eighteenth century that significantly differed from, but nonetheless dovetailed with, disciplinary power. While disciplinary power was applied to individual bodies to train and make use of them, this new kind of power existed "at a different level, [functioned] on a different scale...and [made] use of very different instruments" (Foucault [1997] 2003, 242). This power, which he calls "biopower" both here and in the first volume of *The History of Sexuality*, was "applied not to man-as-body [as disciplinary power is] but to the living man, to man-as-living-being; ultimately...to man-as-species" (ibid.). It is biopower, Foucault argues, that "inscribes [racism] in the mechanisms of the state" (ibid., 254).

Biopower creates the distinctions—the "biological" distinctions—within the population that form the hierarchy whereby "certain races are described as good and...others, by contrast, are described as inferior" (ibid., 255). This standard is the one on which a new conception of "normalization," or what Foucault calls "regularization," is established. In this way, biopower—like the disciplinary power from which it developed—is founded upon a gathering of knowledge; it is a power that is grounded upon and made possible by this knowledge; at the same time, this accumulated knowledge is made to count as knowledge by virtue of the power it activates and supports. Among the generalized mechanisms of which the biopolitical state makes use is the measurement of biological processes of the populace—rates of birth, death, and fertility. These are, Foucault says, biopolitics' "first objects of knowledge and the targets it seeks to control" through natalist policy, for example, but also through efforts to contain disease (ibid., 243).

Where the Middle Ages were centrally concerned with epidemics, diseases that wiped out whole portions of the population and required "disqualification, exile, rejection, deprivation, refusal, and incomprehension; that is to say, an entire arsenal of negative concepts or mechanisms of exclusion" (Foucault [1999] 2003, 44), the morbidity problem starting in the mid-eighteenth century is more precisely described in terms of the endemic, which may be managed by attending to "the form, nature, extension, duration and intensity of the illnesses prevalent in a population" (Foucault [1997] 2003, 243). Foucault here extends his discussion of plague from the Collège course of the previous year ("Abnormal") and the "positive technologies of power" that accompanied it. Early in the course Foucault mentions the existence of a whole literature devoted to the "kind of orgiastic dream" of lawlessness permitted by the outbreak of plague. "But," Foucault writes, there was another dream of the plague; a political dream in which plague is rather the marvelous moment when political power is exercised to the full. Plague is the moment when the spatial partitioning and subdivision (*quadrillage*) of a population is taken to its extreme point, where dangerous communications, disorderly communities, and forbidden contacts can no longer appear. (Foucault [1999] 2003, 47)

Plague, in other words, creates the conditions that intensify and justify state regulation of the lives of its residents, "the capillary ramifications of which constantly reach into the grain of individuals themselves, their time, habitat, localization, and bodies" (ibid.). This is what Foucault terms the power of "normalization," a concept he draws from Georges Canguilhem ([1943] 1989). Normalization refers to a variety of techniques that draw on the concept of "the norm" for their founding and legitimization (Foucault [1999] 2003, 50). Emerging in the eighteenth century, normalization took as its privileged object the "dangerous" or "delinquent individual" (ibid., 25). Foucault's aim in these lectures is to trace the genealogy of this power and the change that occurred in the "medico-juridical body" such that its charge was no longer the "control of crime or illness" but rather the "control of the abnormal, of the abnormal individual" (ibid., 42). This shift corresponds to a change that occurred as the medieval understanding of criminality as a "disease of the collectivity, of the social body" gave way to an individualizing conception of "the criminal who as such is someone who may be ill" (ibid., 91), which appeared in the late eighteenth century.

This category of the "biocriminal," Foucault goes on to explain in his lectures the following year, "was conceptualized in racist terms" and made possible the state's exclusion of certain sorts of people by way of criminal execution or banishment (Foucault [1997] 2003, 258). But this racism, he claims, differed from the racism of the past. Unlike what he calls an "ordinary racism" consisting of "mutual contempt or hatred" or an "ideological operation" that allowed a state to "displace the hostility that is directed toward [it]," the distinctive expression of power that emerged at the end of the nineteenth century and was refined in the twentieth century was "bound up with the workings of a State that is obliged to use race, the elimination of races and the purification of the race, to exercise its sovereign power" (ibid.).[2] Racism was not invented in the nineteenth century or first used by the state at that time, but Foucault believes that it was at this moment that biopower inscribed racism as the basic mechanism of power exercised in modern states. It has emerged, Foucault argues, as a new individualizing pathologization that is "grafted," as he puts it, onto an older, ethnic racism that aims to defend society against the dangerous individual "carriers" who appear and who will, unchecked, transmit their condition to their heirs (Foucault [1999] 2003, 316).

In the United States at the end of the twentieth century, violence was understood in precisely the terms Foucault outlines. It was an individual pathology that would be passed on from generation to generation and necessitated the identification and elimination of "degeneracy," which would be regarded as an endemic: Violence was not be understood as a temporary danger but was instead a permanent factor that acted upon the population from multiple directions. It affected morbidity, certainly, but it also took an economic toll: Resources that would be devoted to educational development were diverted to the bolstering of law enforcement or the industry of prison construction that began in the 1980s and flourished throughout the 1990s; individual victims of violence might not have been able to work and would thus have put pressure on social welfare programs, as well as those individuals' families; finally, violence was a moral problem that corrupted the youth by means of the cultural media—music, television, cinema, video games—by promoting delinquency in those who were susceptible to violent behavior (see, e.g., Glassner 1999, 41–45).

The first identification of endemics, Foucault recounts, provoked the formation of programs of "public health" around the end of the eighteenth century. The progenitors of the Centers for Disease Control and the National Institutes of Health (NIH) would "coordinate medical care, centralize power, and normalize knowledge" of the nation's health. Public hygiene campaigns would be launched for the first time, and the population would be "medicalized"—made patients of the state (Foucault [1997] 2003, 244). In the late twentieth century, proponents of a "violence initiative" promised to do for the problem of violent crime what the proponents of public health in the nineteenth century strived to do for the problems associated with poor hygiene. Increasing knowledge of the biochemical processes associated with violence, those who sponsored the initiative argued, would permit the identification of violence-prone youngsters, who would, in turn, provide increasing understanding of these processes. As in the programs of public hygiene, the "enemy" of the people is not a "foreign body" that threatens the population from without but is located within the population itself "in the biological threats," as Foucault puts it, "posed by the other race" (ibid., 61).

The Problem of Race in the 1990s: The Case of the Violence Initiative

On February 11, 1992, within a week of the highly publicized opening arguments in the prosecution of the white police officers who beat African American Rodney King, Dr. Frederick Goodwin, then director of the nation's Alcohol, Drug Abuse, and Mental Health Administration (ADAMHA), unveiled a new federal plan to combat violence in America's ravaged inner cities, the Violence Initiative. In an address to the National Mental Health Advisory Council, Goodwin called violence an issue of "public health" that required the combined efforts of governmental agencies and the research apparatus they support to combat it. In the course of his presentation to the council, Goodwin made the following impromptu remarks:

> If you look, for example, at male monkeys, especially in the wild, roughly half of them survive to adulthood. The other half die by violence. That is the

natural way of it for males, to knock each other off and, in fact, there are some interesting evolutionary implications of that because the same hyper-aggressive monkeys who kill each other are also hypersexual, so they copulate more and therefore they reproduce more to offset the fact that half of them are dying.

Now, one could say that if some of the loss of social structure in this society, and particularly within the high impact inner-city areas, has removed some of the civilizing evolutionary things that we have built up and that maybe it isn't just the careless use of the word when people call certain areas of certain cities jungles, that we may have gone back to what might be more natural, without all the social controls that we have imposed upon ourselves as a civilization over thousands of years in our evolution.

This just reminds us that although we look at individual factors and we look at biological differences and we look at genetic differences, the loss of structure in society is probably why we are dealing with this issue.[3]

Designed to provide funds and promote the coordination of existing and projected scientific research into the causes and prevention of human violence, the Violence Initiative could have been expected to be welcomed in the face of widely publicized predictions that rising crime rates would worsen severely in coming years. But in the wake of Goodwin's unplanned oration and the wide press coverage it provoked, the Violence Initiative soon commanded national attention.[4] Goodwin himself did not expect that his connection of violent, hypersexual monkeys and poor urban youth would be received as a racist invocation of images that have, within "the sciences of man," as Donna Haraway has written, constructed blacks as "the beast" or " 'primitives' more closely connected to the apes than the white 'race' " (Haraway 1989, 153).[5] Nevertheless, Goodwin apologized ten days later, described his comments as "insensitive and careless," and insisted that "I have always said that in these studies it is crucial to focus on individual vulnerability and not on race" (Hilts 1992).[6]

Why is the association between marginalized racialized groups and violent behavior discouraged or even prohibited? After all, there are certain cases when it seems appropriate to consider the correlation between racial or ethnic origins and biological or genetic conditions (e.g., heritable diseases such as Tay-Sachs or the subset of breast cancers associated with Ashkenazic Jews, or sickle-cell disease, associated in this country with African Americans). This correlation is not only permitted but also encouraged, not for the protection of racialized groups but for the protection of individuals at risk.[7] The association of individual vulnerability with group membership can be a permissible vector of inquiry, but only under specific conditions: If an individual's risk is found to be associated with group membership, group membership should certainly figure in the calculation of risk for those individuals or their progeny. However, such diseases put only the individuals carrying the genetic "coding" at risk. While that coding and the diseases they mark may be passed on to another generation, these "bad" genes are not contagious—and this is a crucial distinction. There is no risk that "bad" genes will enter the population at large and render that population vulnerable to disease. Genetic maladies, in short, do not pose the danger to public health that communicable diseases—influenza, West Nile Virus, HIV—do; nor does genetic disease or a biological condition such as low levels of the neurotransmitter serotonin (associated, if imperfectly, with depression, anxiety, and aggression [Hamer and Copeland 1998])—function in the way that other problems of public health do. What is typically understood as a public health menace, on the other hand, is not associated with individuals. Toxic waste linked with various cancers or indoor air pollution linked with asthma, for example, are problems that affect individuals but do not find their sources in individual bodies; they are located, rather, in nonembodied agents. So the particular danger that Goodwin describes may be cast as follows: Violence as a threat to public health is a problem not for the individuals who may be found, in this research, to carry a genetic or biological marker associated with violence but is, instead, a problem for the rest of us.

If it seems clear that a government-funded initiative that targets a population of racially marked others who would be most prone to violent behaviors in an effort to protect those who would be, in turn, vulnerable to these individuals would provoke public controversy, it is because the specific expression of racism in the twentieth century (and evidently of the twenty-first, as well) differs from the old racism of the nineteenth century. In his 1974–75 lectures, Foucault characterizes this twentieth-century racism as one "whose function is not so much the prejudice or defense of one group against another as the detection of all those within a group who may be the carriers of a danger to it. It is an internal racism that permits the screening of every individual within a given society" (Foucault [1999] 2003, 317). Further details of the initiative that Goodwin provided just days after his apology would fill out the picture of what the Violence Initiative would entail and illustrate precisely Foucault's understanding of the way that the new racism is meant to function. Insofar as these details were made in the context of Goodwin's ham-fisted invocation of an older racism in the promulgation of the new, we can see how these comments, which might otherwise have gone unnoticed, only added fuel to the firestorm of controversy he had earlier ignited.

Goodwin described the plans for the initiative as including the establishment, as he put it, of "biological markers for the early identification of conduct-disordered youngsters. It aims to predict by the age of five—and at that point to intervene with—those children most likely to become disruptive and violent in adolescence" (cited in Breggin and Breggin 1994, 6). Protests lodged by Senator Edward Kennedy and Representative John Dingell (chairmen of ADAMHA's oversight committees) criticizing Goodwin's "extremist and appalling view" of urban problems (Holden 1992; Rensberger 1992), as well as those submitted by members of the congressional black caucus (Holden 1992; Sipchen 1992), prompted Goodwin's resignation as head of the ADAMHA. Reportedly at the urging of Senator Orrin Hatch, Goodwin was, however, immediately appointed head of the National Institute of Mental Health (NIMH) (Holden 1992), the agency that would be charged with overseeing the implementation of the Violence Initiative.[8]

That May, in his new capacity as NIMH director, Goodwin gave a talk at the American Psychiatric Association, titled "Conduct Disorder as a Precursor to Adult Violence and Substance Abuse: Can the Progression Be Halted?" In this address he elaborated on the specific methods the initiative might promote. Goodwin suggested that a method of "triage" could be implemented to identify children—beginning as young as two or three years of age—who manifested what he described as "early irritability and uncooperativeness" for possible treatment (Goodwin 1992b, cited in Sellers-Diamond 1994, 437). Inner-city elementary school teachers would be assigned the task of identifying up to 15 percent of their students as manifesting the specified behaviors. Goodwin speculated that telephone interviews could then be conducted with the children's parents in order to determine the type and intensity of intervention warranted in each case. For some, treatment would include the training of parents in ameliorative techniques.[9] Such practices, Goodwin told his audience, would include instructing parents "to assess and to monitor and to teach them how to use immediate and contingent and effective discipline for the antisocial behavior and consistent rewards for prosocial behavior" (ibid., 438). Older children might be sent to day camps; others who displayed more "overt psychiatric or neurological problems," including those whose aberrant behavior was determined to result from a learning disability such as Attention Deficit Disorder (ADD), could be subject to drug therapy, by which "a serotogenic imbalance may be corrected" (ibid., 438–40).[10] Taken together, these approaches were intended to fulfill the newly instantiated commitment of the NIMH "to design and evaluate psychosocial, psychological and medical interventions for at-risk children before they become labeled as delinquent or criminal" (Goodwin 1992b, cited in Breggin and Breggin 1994, 9–10).

The regrettable announcement of the Violence Initiative marked a period in which the specter of the "dangerous individual" came to occupy a prominent place in public discussion. Investigation of the violent tendencies of individuals necessitated increasingly detailed attention to the body and its operations. However, while this attention can resemble the detailed scrutiny Foucault associates with the disciplinary apparatus, this particular investigation of the body differs in important ways from that associated with the "disciplinary gaze": The attention directed at the violent body is aimed not at the internalization of an authoritative gaze by the individuals themselves but instead at the individualizing of a group against whom the population needs protection. Rather than a diffused gaze that can be employed by "anyone," the authority of the regulatory gaze is consolidated—for the use of the state.

The case—made in different ways over the last two or three centuries—that a propensity to criminal behavior (or poverty or deficits in intelligence, for that matter) could have a genetic or biological source in racial difference emerges time and again. In the early modern period, these efforts can be dated back to Europe's first encounter with the indigenous groups of South America and the ensuing debates concerning the "humanity" of native peoples; they continued in the United States into the eighteenth century in claims regarding the special vulnerabilities of slaves to various disorders, including "draeptomania" (the mental illness that provoked a slave to flee his enslavement) (see, e.g., Stampp 1956), and well into the twentieth century in studies that have claimed to confirm variable levels of intelligence between racial groups (see, e.g., Herrnstein and Murray 1994).[11]

As often as these arguments are advanced, however, robust refutations appear,[12] and the case that Frederick Goodwin made for a propensity to violent behavior among inner-city youth figures as yet another case in point: Public and professional support for these claims is resisted from a variety of discursive directions, not least of which is the claim that violent behavior has its source not in the genetic or biological makeup of an individual or family but in material conditions of poverty that disproportionately affect groups marginalized by racial difference. Perhaps more saliently, however, the associations that the proposed research plan has with eugenic science taint this kind of work both ethically and scientifically. For both of these reasons, it would appear, Goodwin was compelled to express his regret for his unfortunate choice of words and to affirm that the studies he would oversee would conform to acceptable guidelines—"to focus on individual vulnerability and not on race." To focus on race, in other words, broke the rules governing "enlightened" scientific inquiry.

No Offense Intended: The Preconceptual Ground of Racist Discourse

If scientific inquiry is to be conceived as uncorrupted by political bias, "race blindness" would certainly be an essential goal. But how are we to reconcile the standard explicitly maintained by scientists with what appears simultaneously to be its violation? Foucault's earlier, archaeological work is extremely helpful for its detailed treatment of the operation of discourse. To understand how power works in the production of race, we must think about power not only with subtlety but also with the understanding that power is discursively constituted. We must appreciate, in other words, how discourses—scientific and medical discourses especially—function to impose meaning through the construction of norms that are then taken up in other fields. The case of the Violence Initiative also provides us an opportunity to focus on the important connection between the archaeological method and the "genealogical" work that follows it. Recall that Foucault attends explicitly, if too briefly, to this connection in his inaugural lecture at the Collège de France, when he affirms that these approaches should "complete" each other (Foucault [1971] 1972, 234). I want now to focus specifically on the critical role that the discourse of race and, in particular, the insistence upon race blindness plays in the expression of biopower during this period.

The Violence Initiative generated tremendous and widely publicized controversy in the months following its announcement. An independently organized conference intended to investigate the assumptions and implications of behavioral genetic research into violence and crime was funded that same year by the

Ethical, Legal, and Social Implications (ELSI) Program of the National Center for Human Genome Research at the National Institutes of Health. Following the furor over Goodwin's presentation of the initiative, funding for the conference was first suspended and then rescinded before it was finally restored three years later, in 1995.[13] Goodwin's own related research into the use of psychotropic drugs to contain violence[14] also provoked a vociferous outcry from critics about the potential use of Ritalin and Prozac to "manage" inner city youth.[15] Most upsetting of all was the charge of racism and the widely cited characterization of the Violence Initiative by a small black newspaper in Washington, D.C., as a "Plot to Sedate Black Youth" (Williams 1994; Wright 1995, 69).

In response to the clamorous protest, a federal Blue Ribbon Panel was convened to determine whether racial motive was present in the Violence Initiative. The panel, chaired by Howard University's president at the time, Franklyn Jenifer, found, as Alfreda Sellers-Diamond recounts in "Disposable Children in Black Faces," that

> there was no evidence to support the allegations and suspicions levied against the DHHS [Department of Health and Human Services]. ... [It] concluded that a focus on violence as a public health problem was appropriate, and determined that none of the studies sought to establish a genetic link between race and violent behavior, thus effectively exonerating the Violence Initiative, if not the words of Dr. Goodwin. (Sellers-Diamond 1994, 430)[16]

That the Blue Ribbon Panel found no racial motivation in the initiative is perhaps not unexpected in view of the fact that *racist discrimination* against African Americans as a group is expressly prohibited. Invoking race as a causal factor to explain an individual's violent behavior is not allowed: The discursive proscription of overt, conscious, or intentional racism is juridically inscribed, for example, in the Equal Protection Clause of the Fourteenth Amendment (see Sellers-Diamond 1994, 431–32).[17] It is enforced, too, in the representation of racism as "irrational" or its reductive casting as a matter of "individual prejudice," as David Goldberg details in *Racist Culture* (Goldberg 1993, 7).[18]

It should come as no surprise, then, that it was to this eminent panel unthinkable that, in the hyperbolic terms of a book title critical of the initiative, the "Psychiatric Establishment" had declared a "War against Children" (Breggin and Breggin 1994) or that America's children could be regarded as "disposable," whatever their color. What is remarkable, however, is that, despite what seemed to be their rejection of Goodwin's ideas, the panel made clear that the only objectionable part of the initiative was the *language* Goodwin had used to describe the project. The panel's judgment reflected Goodwin's own conviction that all this fuss was really an unfortunate matter of a poor choice of simile: "If I had said that in the Wild West, where there was no structure, there was a hell of a lot of violence, no one would have noticed" (quoted in Wright 1995, 73).[19]

Goldberg's groundbreaking application of Foucault's archaeological method to racist discourse provides a means of understanding how and why the panel's conclusion misses the mark. Working from what Foucault would characterize as a model of the old racism, the panel's assignment was to identify racist intent in the language of agents or research designs. However, to uncover an instance of contemporary racism, it is necessary to examine what Foucault calls in *The Archaeology of Knowledge* the "preconceptual level." Examination of this level of discourse in the case of the Violence Initiative can also help to fill out the complex relationship between discourse and power in contemporary expressions of racism.

Preconceptions are those ideas, notions, or convictions of which one is not quite conscious and which it would be difficult to say one intends to advance. At the same time, preconceptions form the very framework of one's articulated ideas, notions, or convictions. The contemporary operation of what might be termed "racist discourse" functions by way of what Foucault calls "conceptual primitives"[20] or "manifestations of power relations vested in and between historically located subjects" (Goldberg 1993, 48). In "The Social Formation of Racist Discourse," Goldberg clarifies that these "are not *a priori* essences; they do not constitute an ideal foundation of the racist discursive formation. On the other hand, the set of primitives are not to be confused with the actual concepts and terms by which racist discourse is usually expressed" (Goldberg 1990, 301).[21] A "usual expression" of racist discourse in the sense that Goldberg means it may be located in the dominant discursive practices of a given period, which are characterized by those "preconceptual elements that have structured racist dispositions." Such elements, constituted by the axes of "classification and order, value and hierarchy; differentiation and identity, discrimination and identification; exclusion and domination, subjection and subjugation; entitlement and restriction, and in general way, violence and violation" (ibid.), have historically been central to the scientific rationality from and in which the "profusion of the themes, beliefs, and representations" of its discourse emerge (Foucault [1969] 1972, 63).

The axes Goldberg enumerates form the basis of hierarchized differences with respect to race and bear a moral implication as well. The "principle of gradation," derived from the system of racial classification, yields the conviction that "higher beings are ... of greater worth than lower ones" (Goldberg 1990, 302). By way of example, Goldberg recalls one historical manifestation of the principle that resulted in the treatment of " 'lower racial orders' as animals, subjecting their members to forms of labor and living conditions otherwise reserved for animals" (ibid., 303). What would now be regarded as a repulsive expression of racial superiority seems to have little in common with the contemporary gradations whose putatively race-neutral principle is implicit in the investigation of the correlation between violence and serotonin levels. After all, as one science reporter recounted in defense of the research, "many things [like gender and age] can apparently influence serotonin production, [but] race isn't one of them" (Williams 1994).

Science writer Robert Wright substantiates the operation of the principle of gradation when, in an article for the *New Yorker* published in 1995, he revisits the damning comparison between monkeys and humans: "The lesson [of the correspondence between levels of serotonin and monkey 'success'] would seem to be this: some individuals are born to be society's leaders, some are born to be its hoodlums; the chairman of I.B.M. was born with high serotonin, the urban gang member was born with low serotonin" (Wright 1995, 74).[22] Wright's speculation was borne out during the nineties by the pervasive repetition of appalling statistics regarding the incidence of crime and rates of incarceration that invariably detailed the differences between whites and blacks: "One in every 27 black men, compared with one in 205 white men, died violently [in 1992]. ...Black Americans, who constitute about 12 percent of the population, were arrested for 45 percent of the nation's violent crimes" (Williams 1994); "Nearly 7% of Adult Black Males Were Inmates in '94, Study Says," announced a *New York Times* headline in 1995 (Reuters 1995); and in 1996 another story reported that "almost 40 percent of black men in their 20's are imprisoned or on probation or parole on any given day" (Butterfield 1996). And so it goes, throughout the nineties and beyond.[23]

In considering these statistics, it is worth keeping in mind, as sociologist Troy Duster has pointed out, that rates of incarceration "are a function of incarceration decisions, a fact that social science research has long shown to be a function of social, economic, and political factors" (Duster 1994, 146; see also Reiman [1979] 2004). To take one example, the heated debate that has raged for the last decade over the significant disparity in the federal sentencing guidelines that apply following conviction for possession or distribution of crack cocaine as compared with powdered cocaine is a good illustration of this convergence of social, economic, and political factors.[24] To objections such as Democratic Congressman Melvin Watt's, that "poor young kids who can afford crack go to jail" and that "rich young kids [who get arrested for powder cocaine possession] go home and sleep in their own beds" (U.S. Congress 1995, H 10259), Republican Congressman Bill McCollum, *pace* Anatole France, responded, "If we are applying the law equally, then the law itself is not racist" (ibid., H 10275).[25] Made in full understanding that a disproportionate number of those arrested for possession of crack cocaine were black and from poor urban neighborhoods, McCollum's comments can be understood to reflect a late twentieth-century principle of gradation, whereby wealthy (white, suburban) youth were ushered into rehab, whereas poor teenagers of color were increasingly consigned to the fast-growing number of prisons, a disparity that also reflects a prevailing moral order.[26]

If McCollum's argument signals what Foucault calls a "regularity" in the series of discussions concerning race and crime, it may be understood to issue from the same preconceptual field as the proposals for the Violence Initiative. His conclusion that racism would be present only if there were an express race-based difference in the application of the law reveals the way in which focusing on the individual displaces race as the object of discourse and repositions it at the level of the preconceptual field from which the statement issues. The objects of the dominant discourse on violence, as a result, are not given in terms of race or poverty, for example, but rather are concentrated in the "dangerous individual" who is, as if incidentally, the young black male inner-city dweller, whose violent behavior may be coded in his biochemistry or perhaps etched in his genetic heritage. In this way race operates "conceptually" in Foucault's sense, whereby race appears to belong to or concern "quite different domains of objects... but [is] active among the statements... because [it] serve[s] as a general principle and as premises accepted by a reasoning... or because [it] function[s] at a higher authority" (Foucault [1969] 1972, 58). In Senator McCollum's statement, both of these criteria may obtain. McCollum's argument relies on a set of implied premises concerning the status of the individual before the purportedly race-neutral law. Furthermore, embedded in his efforts to maintain the existing sentencing guidelines is the claim that crack cocaine (almost wholly identified with poor urban neighborhoods) poses a more serious threat to this country, and so warrants such harsh measures. Congress's overwhelming 332 to 83 vote to uphold the guidelines in 1995 (U.S. Congress 1995, H 10283) suggests that these premises were not only acceptable but also compelling to the country's legislative body.

The discussion of the guidelines rather obviously points to the way in which the emphasis on the dangerous individual renders permissible (by making deniable) a focus on blackness. But the debate over the guidelines also suggests the state's interest in promulgating images that objectify the racial other. The story of the Violence Initiative likewise illustrates the ways in which a focus on the individual masks a biopolitical targeting of the racial other. There is, however, more to the story, for that focus on the individual also masks the implication of the family as its object.

The Dangerous Individual's Mother

At the same time that the headlines of the late 1980s and 1990s featured prominent stories about increasing crime rates and the decreasing age of criminal offenders (see, e.g., Davis [1990] 1992, 287; Butterfield 1995), another sort of "dangerous individual" was featured right alongside. Poor, single mothers—notoriously inscribed in the figure of the "welfare queen"—became "omnipresent in discussions about 'America's' present or future even when unnamed" (Lubiano 1992, 332). Although no explicit mention of such mothers was made in the public discussions of the Violence Initiative, their presence was nevertheless unmistakable. As Wahneema Lubiano writes, the dangerous (black) individual is "the creation of his pathological 'nurturer[,]'... she who reproduces the culture" (ibid., 339). Frederick Goodwin's comments about violent monkeys and jungles may have been written off as so much bluster, but his remarks made plain reference to an important body of ongoing NIH research into the role of mothers in the making of violent individuals.

The research to which Goodwin referred is most closely associated with primatologist Stephen Suomi, best known for having identified a "dramatic biochemical difference" in the small percentage of male, adolescent monkeys who are violent for no apparent reason who become what one science writer for the *Washington Post* described as "outcasts—repeat offenders for whom there is no place in rhesus society" (Rensberger 1992). Suomi was particularly concerned with the role of "maternal nurturance" in the making of the violent individual. "What interests many of us," Suomi said at the time, "is that serotonin levels of monkeys—and their personality differences—can be traced back to an animal's early beginnings. ... It makes a big difference what kind of mothers they had and what their genetic heritage was" (quoted in ibid.).

According to a 1994 report in the *Journal of NIH Research*, Suomi demonstrated that infant monkeys who were removed from their mothers and raised by what were characterized as foster mothers in groups with their peers displayed a marked propensity to violence as juveniles, a finding that Suomi understood as a result of "poor early attachment" (quoted in Touchette 1994), with which a low level of serotonin is associated (see, e.g., Higley and Suomi 1996; Suomi 2003). In addition, he found that animals with "low concentrations of [serotonin], like their human counterparts, tend to drink more alcohol" (Suomi 2002, 275), a significant finding in the context of violence research, given that statistics show that "more than half of all violent crimes involve the use of alcohol" (Touchette 1994).

The conclusions drawn from such research concerning the importance of a primary nurturing relationship for a child could have spoken to the need for state-sponsored programs to help facilitate the development of this crucial mother-infant bond. That the research did not lend itself to such recommendations may be owing to a second set of conclusions Suomi drew, namely, that an important genetic component also contributed to a child's propensity to violent behavior: According to Suomi, having been separated from their mothers, offspring of violent parents have a "tendency to get involved in fights ... [and to] fight longer and harder than others even raised apart from their biological parent" (quoted in Mestel 1994, 32). And yet, as Suomi elaborates in a follow-up study, "allelic variation in the serotonin transporter gene ... is associated with deficits ... for peer-related, but not mother-reared, [male] rhesus monkey adolescents and infants" (2002, 275; see also Suomi 2003, 137). This finding suggests that genetic factors may play a role, but only if environmental conditions (such as the absence of a mother) activate them— which one might imagine could speak, once again, to social policies supporting stable families.

And what of female monkeys? If "early rearing by peers" results in anti-social offspring prone to excessive consumption of alcohol, females with absent mothers "are significantly more likely to exhibit neglectful and/or abusive treatment of their firstborn offspring than are their mother-reared counterparts." The reproduction of bad mothering is evidenced, in other words, by the "strong continuities between the type of attachment relationship a female infant develops with her mother and the type of attachment relationship she develops with her own infant(s) when she becomes a mother herself" (Suomi 2002, 275)—the attachments that are understood to be critical in predicting the violence of a young male. Findings by Suomi and his colleagues regarding deficiencies in child rearing and genetic flaws together not only suggest a kind of inevitability of the problem of violence in certain populations but also cast the mother of the violent individual as irremediably transgressive, a "monster," in Foucault's terms.

In his 1974–75 lectures, *Abnormal*, Foucault's discussion of the monster details the historic identification of monstrosity with "possible criminality" through the early modern period. Beginning in the Middle Ages, monstrosity was understood as a transgression of the law—civil, religious, and natural (Foucault [1999] 2003, 63). The monster was a criminal, but criminality was not yet understood as monstrous. "Then," he says, "starting in the nineteenth century... monstrosity is systematically suspected of being behind all criminality" (ibid., 81). Despite this change, monstrosity as such remained somehow beyond the reach of the law. Foucault explains that the monster occupied an unusual position as "the limit, both the point at which law is overturned and the exception that is found only in extreme cases." As a result, the monster's presence provoked an ambiguity with respect to the law. Even as it constituted its violation, the monster remained out of the law's immediate reach. While the subjection of criminals to the law is magnified in their violation of it, the monster, by contrast, "triggers the response of something quite different from the law itself. It provokes either violence, the will for pure and simple suppression, or medical care or pity" (ibid., 56). If, for Foucault, the notion of monstrosity comes to be understood as standing behind criminality, one twentieth-century instance of monstrosity seems to be embodied by the criminal's mother, the "moral aberration" responsible for the crack dealer, addict, or violent predator. She, like the monster, is a despised figure who provokes anxiety (ibid.), but (or precisely because) she herself escapes unmediated juridical intervention.

Throughout the 1980s and well into the period of welfare reform in the 1990s, the vilification of the welfare queen was a staple of popular discourse that increasingly attached the idea of welfare to race and specifically to blackness (Lubiano 1992, 340; Williams 1995, 5; Davis 1997, 275). Though the welfare queen was juxtaposed with the violent youth, the two were rarely explicitly linked in popular discourse.[27] Scientific discussions of violence overtly individualized the afflicted boys and men even as they had a much broader reach; by contrast, discussions of welfare queens far more openly connected their objects with deeper social problems. As Lubiano puts it, the "welfare-dependent single mother" came to function at this time as

> the synecdoche, the shortest possible shorthand, for the pathology of poor, urban, black culture. Responsible for creating and maintaining a family that can only be perceived as pathological compared to the normative (and thus allegedly "healthy") family structure in the larger society, the welfare mother is the root of greater social pathology. (Lubiano 1992, 335)

Lubiano's analysis of the welfare queen details the state's interest in the promulgation of narratives that set white against black, where the one is associated with "normality" and "health," and the other with "abnormality" and "degeneracy"—the very terms by which, according to Foucault, monstrosity, or the source of the pathological state responsible for the "delinquent," is cast. Foucault describes this imagined source of pathology—the ultimate target of biopower—as the "background-body": It is the "fantastic body of physical or functional or behavioral abnormalities that is the origin of the appearance of the [dangerous] 'condition' " (Foucault [1999] 2003, 314). And "what," asks Foucault, "is this background-body, this body behind the abnormal body? It is the parents' body, the ancestor's body, the body of the family, the body of heredity" (ibid., 313).

One of the prototypical monsters Foucault singles out in his lectures is the "hermaphrodite," one who violates the laws of nature by occupying the "impossible" position of being two sexes (ibid., 71). Despite the opportunity presented in his analysis, Foucault characteristically overlooks the salient role that sexual difference, broadly conceived, may play in the transgression that monstrosity marks. The figure of the welfare queen offers us an opportunity to explore the vexing position gender undeniably occupies in late twentieth-century constructions of monstrosity. One of the most important ways that the welfare queen is transgressive is the ambivalence with which she, together with the "flip side of the pathology coin," the "overachieving black lady" (Lubiano 1992, 340), occupies the position of "woman." Indeed, in the discursive interweaving of blackness with gender, the welfare queen and the black lady do not figure as women; their narrative construction opposes them to "real" women.

As Hortense Spillers puts it in "Mama's Baby, Papa's Maybe," African American women, by virtue of their historic situation, are excluded from "the traditional symbolics of female gender" (Spillers 1987, 80). While Spillers's claim may appear dangerously reactionary—that black women do not really count as women—her point, following Foucault, concerns the discursive operation of these categories of gender and race, that is, the ways these terms both convey and are limited by sedimented meaning. Lubiano's elaboration on this point forcefully shows how the deployment of the figures of the welfare queen and the professionally ambitious (and likewise unmarried) "black lady," propelled by programs of affirmative action, reinforces the prevailing racial order precisely in their denying to black women the status of "woman." Examining the distinctive operations of power Foucault describes provides a means of understanding how these categories can work simultaneously to effect mutual exclusion, even as the one can be harnessed to reinscribe the other.

Lubiano's analysis of the role of gender in the narrative production of the welfare queen, however, differs substantially from the gender that is enforced by disciplinary means. As we saw in the previous chapter, disciplinary power at work in the maintenance of the strict division of the sexes and its proper embodiment by boys and girls functions on the principle of *internalization* of the standards, rules, and norms associated with it. While the violation of gender norms in the child diagnosed with Gender Identity Disorder, discussed in the previous chapter, clearly results in intervention from agencies beyond the family, that intervention is nevertheless concentrated in a kind of reactivation of the family's "normal" enforcement of its members. In one of his Collège de France lectures in 1975, Foucault describes the mechanism of this power as associated with the "individual to be corrected" and as a function of "the family exercising its internal power or managing its economy, or even more...its relations with the institutions adjoining or supporting it" (Foucault [1999] 2003, 57). Disciplinary power, then, is prototypically a species of power that comes "from below"; with respect to the institution of the family, it can be understood as the power that circulates primarily *within* the institution rather than a power that is imposed *upon* it.

However, if the production of gender can generally be identified with and understood as a function of disciplinary power, it would be a mistake to understand the power associated with the production of the welfare queen as similarly directed toward a correction of the individual. With regard to the figure of the welfare queen—or the black lady, for that matter—"correction" cannot be understood to be an issue at all; their deviant status results precisely from their resistance to correction. Lubiano identifies the welfare queen as a function of a more encompassing kind of power associated with a state apparatus (Lubiano 1992, 327),[28] which Foucault's lectures suggest is concerned not with the disciplinary correction of the individual but is focused instead on the identification of "the incorrigible" monster whose management calls for "politico-judicial powers" (Foucault [1999] 2003, 61) that are regulatory in nature.

The violent individual and the welfare queen are discursively joined to one another in and through a third figure that has lurked in the background all along, namely, that of the family. The monstrous mother vilified in the 1980s and 1990s recapitulates, as both Spillers and Lubiano point out, the "matriarch" of the Moynihan Report, issued more than two decades earlier. In *The Negro Family: The Case for National Action*, the report's official title, Moynihan decries the shameful history of slavery in the United States and linked this history to poverty and what he took to be the "unstable" family structure of black families (Moynihan [1965] 1967, 29), which were implicated, in turn, in "a disastrous delinquency and crime rate" (ibid., 38). However, Moynihan also maintains that, while "three centuries of injustice have brought about deep-seated structural distortions in the life of the Negro American...the present tangle of pathology is capable of perpetuating itself without assistance from the white world" (ibid., 47).[29] That is to say, while the construction of black poverty finds its roots in white oppression, white people can no longer be held responsible for the present state of things; "something else" must account for its perpetuation. While for Moynihan this something else was constituted by the family and family structure that effectively "reversed" the gender roles of men and women, making black women matriarchs and leaving black men with "unusually low power" (ibid., 30), the Violence Initiative altered the focus to biology and genetics—a familial legacy of another sort.

Thinking Gender, Thinking Race

Strategies and Contradictions

A discursive formation does not occupy... all the possible volume opened up to it of right by the systems of formation of its objects, its enunciations, and its concepts; it is essentially incomplete, owing to the system of formation of its strategic choices. Hence the fact that, taken up again, placed, and interpreted in a new constellation, a given discursive formation may reveal new possibilities.

—Michel Foucault, The Archaeology of Knowledge

At the outset of this project I asked whether the difficulties of thinking gender and race together reflected the distinctive expressions of power associated with the production of each. My exploration of these differences—drawing primarily on Foucault's genealogical work—has been interwoven with an examination of the specifically discursive elements, that is, the "rules" governing discursive formation that stand out in the selected illustrations. At the same time that I have made a case for appreciating a kind of analytic separability of gender and race, however, I have also pointed to ways that the material production of differences cannot be so neatly disentangled one from another; indeed, it is evident that, at every moment, both gender and race are thoroughly and simultaneously at work in each other's production. Even so, as my own series of studies indicates, the telling of the stories that reveal the production of difference seems always to feature one kind of difference against another.

This is not surprising, for, as Foucault points out in *The Archaeology of Knowledge*, one element of a discursive formation tends to emerge as the most salient in a given investigation; similarly, one species of difference appears to manifest itself more prominently. The preceding chapters have provided several examples of what may be considered a problem of representation, whereby the chiasmic production of racial and sexual difference is concealed by discursive attention to the operation of a single category of difference that appears narratively to exclude, or at least push aside, the other. We see this phenomenon at work beginning with the story—or rather, the juxtaposed stories—of the founding of Levittown. One story relates the state-sponsored racial exclusion that made possible the establishment of a homogeneous community of "whites," many of whom had suffered discrimination as ethnic minorities. The other tells the tale of the disciplinary restoration of women to their place in the home, which also shaped the prescribed roles for husbands and children. Even as each story clearly implicates the other at every point, however, they resist a certain narrative union; each appears to constitute its own story. In the introduction I argued that this distance between the stories of race and gender was a function of the differences in power with which each production of difference is associated. The power deployed to enforce racial exclusion, in other words, which issues primarily from the state, works differently from the disciplinary power located within the family.

Foucault's treatment of the rules governing discursive formations in *The Archaeology of Knowledge* suggests that this separability, this distinguishing of what he calls discursive "themes," has a correlative function within a discursive formation, the "formation of strategies." Foucault provides just a preliminary sketch of this, the fourth rule, but stresses that discursive strategies nevertheless have an essential function in discursive formation. His choice of the term "strategy," the ordinary usage of which so clearly evokes what he calls "non-discursive practices" in *The Archaeology of Knowledge*, suggests the unique character of this rule. In writing that a particular discourse "gives rise to certain organizations of concepts, certain regroupings of objects, certain types of enunciation, which form, according to their degree of coherence, rigour, and stability, themes or theories" (Foucault [1969] 1972, 64), Foucault indicates that strategies should be examined in their implication with other rules, a recommendation he does not make with regard to "objects," "enunciative modalities," or "concepts," though these are clearly interrelated (ibid., 72). The production of the "dangerous individual" as an object of criminological discourse, for example, is unthinkable in the absence of the formation of enunciative modalities, in particular the assignment of subjective positions—with respect not only to the position of the dangerous individual but also to the production of "experts" who are authorized to name him, treat him, and talk about him in prime time. Yet it remains possible to distinguish the different elements in the analysis, to talk about the formation of objects and of enunciative modalities, and to discuss the relation between them. In elaborating the different directions from which one will study the formation of strategies, by contrast, Foucault explicitly characterizes that particular investigation in terms of the relation of strategies to the other rules of archaeological analysis.

Foucault's discussion of the analysis of discursive strategies suggests, then, that their examination is implicit in the studies featured in this project. Thus, my aim in this concluding chapter is to highlight some of the ways that these strategies have already been in evidence and to detail the nature of their operation. By appreciating the implications of the work of strategies in the discursive production of race and gender, we may begin the process of unraveling the interpretive knots they help to form. In the first part of this chapter I return to the story of the desegregation of Levittown to examine what will turn out to be the kinds of strategic erasures that are effected in that story and that call attention to the limits on the ways that race and gender can be thought together. The second part of this chapter examines in more detail the elements of strategies that Foucault enumerates in *The Archaeology of Knowledge*. In the development of the diagnosis of Gender Identity Disorder and the introduction of the federal Violence Initiative, the cases featured in chapters 3 and 4, may be found several examples of the kinds of "contradictions" that, as Foucault explains, function to make certain statements possible by excluding other statements. These contradictions operate, as I have already suggested, to mask the complementary way that these categories of difference are in fact produced, a point upon which I elaborate in the section that follows, concerning the discursive element Foucault terms "authority."

Gender and Race: Now You See It, Now You Don't

In his discussion of the racial desegregation of Levittown, New Jersey, Herbert Gans refers to what he suggests is an overblown tale of the "stone-throwing riot" that occurred in the Pennsylvania Levittown following the quiet purchase of a home by the Myerses, an African American family. Gans's account casts the tale as one of race, economics, and fear concerning status and home values that translated into "bad business" for Levitt and similar builders. There was, according to Gans, "no violence and only two stones were thrown" (Gans 1967, 375), but there may be more to what one Levittown resident and print journalist called the "Ordeal in Levittown." As David Bittan tells it in a 1958 *Look* magazine article, the hot August day that the Myers family arrived was unremarkable. Neighbors took the Negro man touching up the woodwork and the Negro woman with mop in hand to be a painter and a maid. But "at 11:00 A.M.," two days after the new family took up residence in the Dogwood section of the development, "housewives began to gather outside the Myers house. Questioning of their mailman had confirmed that Negroes had moved in."[1] Bittan continues:

> By seven, cars were bumper to bumper on Deepgreen Lane. By 10, hundreds of persons spilled over the sidewalk, screaming curses and insults. At midnight, two stones shattered the picture windows of the Myers house. . . . For eight straight nights, the mob ruled Dogwood Hollow. It defied township police and state troopers sent by [the] governor. . . . Then a stone felled a policeman. State troopers charged with flailing riot sticks. (Bittan 1958, 84–86)

In contrast to Gans's understated characterization of the situation in Levittown, which suggests that the dispersal of the several hundred people gathered outside the Myers home marked the end of the strange, sad episode, Bittan summarizes for *Look* readers the increasingly disturbing reports he made as a local newspaperman as, in the days and weeks following the initial incident, burning crosses appeared on the lawns of a Jewish family next door, known to be friends of the Myerses, and on the property of some sympathetic Quakers nearby. According to Bittan, threats were uttered on the telephone and by passersby on foot. The house opposite the Myerses' blared "Old Man

Figure 5.1. The "Levittown Betterment Committee" meets outside the VFW hall three days after the arrival of the Myers family, August 16, 1957. (Temple University Libraries, Urban Archives, Philadelphia, PA)

River," "Dixie," and "Old Black Joe" (see also Myers 2005, 69) and raised a Confederate flag from its roof.[2] The company providing fire insurance to the Myerses cancelled their policy since they had by then been labeled a "bad risk," and white friends took on the task of protecting Daisy Myers and the three young children while Bill Myers went to work.

It is not clear whether Gans's surprising depiction of this same incident as one in which "no violence" occurred is a matter of fading collective memory—a mark, perhaps, of how quickly change was taking place during this turbulent period (the following June, the *Look* reporter tells us, another black family moved in "without incident"; the community had "learned it [could] live with Negroes"[3])—or whether, as I suggested in the previous chapter, the discursive construction of whiteness disallowed its association with violence.

There is, however, a moment in this story that remains wholly undeveloped and perhaps, in the context of this discussion, undevelopable. It might not be quite right to view as instigators of a riot the housewives who, questioning their own narrative explaining the presence of black people in their neighborhood, gathered outside the Myerses' new home that August day. Perhaps there might be another dimension to this story, one relating to the specific nature of white women's roles in the enforcement of whiteness at this time and in this place.[4] But because the story of the Myerses' arrival in Levittown is told as a story exclusively about race, it entails particular kinds of erasures with respect to gender, and the questions that would need to be raised to break this silence go unasked.

Figure 5.2

We may find an image that captures the confounding inability to regard simultaneously the operation of race and gender in what are sometimes called "reversible figure-ground" drawings, popularized by Gestalt psychologists. In one of the best-known of these drawings (see figure 5.2), a vase is visible against a contrasting background. When we look at the vase, the background recedes, but focusing on this background reveals the distinctive outline of two faces in profile. Despite the fact that the contours of the vase define the faces and vice versa, each image becomes visible only when the other image is forced to the ground; only one is visible at a time. The juxtaposed stories of Levittown, I suggest, similarly demonstrate the difficulty in "seeing" both race and gender simultaneously, even as the production or operation of one kind of difference actively informs another. However, the reversible figure-ground drawing also indicates a way to recognize and reconcile this complicated symbiosis by understanding the function of discursive strategies, the ways that the displacement of the visibility of one kind of production in favor of another finally permits an operation of power "beyond our view."

Elements of Strategies

The first "direction" Foucault addresses in the study of the formation of strategies concerns "points of diffraction," that is, "points of incompatibility" within a discursive formation that may be identified when "two objects, or two types of enunciation, or two concepts . . . appear . . . without being able to enter—under pain of manifest contradiction or inconsequence—the same series of statements" (Foucault [1969] 1972, 65). In the work associated with the diagnosis of Gender Identity Disorder, these points of incompatibility emerge in the general postulation of heterosexuality as at once "natural" (thus rendering homosexuality a "perversion") and "constructed" (a function, that is to say, of a "proper" upbringing and susceptible to therapeutic reconstruction). Similarly, an axis of diffraction marking the research into the cause of violent behavior may be discerned in the question of whether a tendency to commit impulsive or disruptive acts is innately determined or environmentally impelled. As we have seen in each case, the two perspectives may coexist and, as

Foucault writes, may be conceived as "points of equivalence." Each issues "in the same way and on the basis of the same rules; the conditions of their appearance are identical . . . and instead of constituting a mere defect of coherence, they form an alternative . . . [appearing] in the form of 'either. . . or' " (ibid.): *Either* GID is a matter of individual pathology located in the child, *or* it is a function of parental encouragement. *Either* violent behavior is a result of flawed genetic inheritance in the individual perpetrator, *or* it is a social phenomenon, a reaction by an oppressed minority to poverty and racist exclusion.

The later characterization of the etiology of GID as a result of maternal psychopathology—a combination, of sorts, of flawed genes and flawed parenting—demonstrates how the "points of equivalence" that make up the diffraction may also become what Foucault calls "link points of systematization," constituting, "on the basis of each of these equivalent, yet incompatible elements, a coherent series of objects, forms of statement, and concepts" (ibid., 66). In the same way, the proposition that "violence might be the result of a loss of 'civilizing' social factors comparable to those in monkey society that usually keep the adolescent male's naturally violent behavior in check" (Rensberger 1992), exemplifies the juncture of two presumably incompatible "points"—"nature" and "environment"—that ground the discursive circulation of primatological research on violence. The study of the "natural" artifact of primate society preserves and resolves the diffraction within a discursive field characterized by the convoluted play of identity and difference: Humans are and are not like monkeys; violence is and is not a function of heredity or of upbringing. "Intersections of irreconcilable influences" (Foucault [1969] 1972, 150), accordingly, are not of the order of "appearance or accident of discourse . . . [but] constitute the very law of its existence." Moreover, Foucault writes, "it is on the basis of such a contradiction that discourse emerges, and it is in order both to translate it and to overcome it that discourse begins to speak; it is in order to escape that contradiction, whereas contradiction is ceaselessly reborn through discourse, that discourse endlessly pursues itself and begins again" (ibid., 151). In the face of the depathologization of homosexuality and feminist challenges to traditional gender roles, the American Psychiatric Association began again with GID; in the face of the civil rights movement, a new rationale was formulated to maintain what David Theo Goldberg calls "technologies of racial classification" (Goldberg 1990, 295).

An important effect of this diffractive proliferation of discourse is the formation of what Foucault calls "discursive sub-groups," which function, he writes, as the "raw material" for a given "theme" (Foucault [1969] 1972, 66) under consideration. In this sense, the decades of institutionalized pathologization of homosexuality come to mind as constituting a subgroup of GID; the discourse concerning welfare in the United States and the vilification of its recipients during the 1980s and 1990s (Lubiano 1992; Fraser and Gordon 1994; Williams 1995, 2–14) would seem to serve as suitable fodder for the discursive production of the violent young black man.

However, a subgroup, as Foucault understands it, is not merely raw material but also, at the same time, another constituent of the discursive field to which the theme also belongs (Foucault [1969] 1972, 66). The work of Mike Davis provides a vivid illustration of the specific operation of subgroups in the discursive production of blackness by examining vexed portrayals of black mothers as victims and victimizers during the late 1980s. In his prophetic *City of Quartz*, Davis recalls the media frenzy over the discovery of a "Mama Crip" in the wake of the enactment of Los Angeles's Street Terrorism Enforcement and Prevention (STEP) Act of 1988. Affirmed with enthusiastic bipartisan support, STEP made gang membership—the definition of which included active participation in, or assistance to a gang—a felony (Davis [1990] 1992, 282).[5] Parents of gang members could also be prosecuted under STEP for failure to "exercise 'reasonable care' to prevent their children's criminal activities." According to Davis, the "bad parent provision" was tested the following year with the arrest of the thirty-seven-year-old mother of a fifteen-year-old son who was arraigned for participation in a gang rape. "In an elaborately contrived exposé for the press," Davis recounts, "detectives and city attorneys feigned horror at discovering the Oedipal command post of the gang conspiracy" (ibid., 283). According to an article in the *Los Angeles Times*,

> Authorities said they were stunned at the pervasive atmosphere of gang activity within the household. "It looks like the headquarters for the local gang," said Robert Ferber of the city attorney's gang unit. "There was graffiti all over the walls." "I was amazed. I couldn't believe my eyes," said Southwest LAPD Detective Roy Gonzaque. "In all my 20 years on the police force I have never seen anything like this. It was obvious that the mother was just as much a part of the problem because she condoned this activity." (ibid.)

"Rehabilitation" of this woman was, according to the city attorney's office, an issue unworthy of consideration; the LAPD promised to pursue arrests of other parents like her (ibid.).

The portrayal of the Mama Crip takes its place among those images promoted by conservative figures like George Gilder, who traces what he called, in the *Wall Street Journal*, "The Roots of Black Poverty" to state sponsorship of "affirmative action programs [that] have artificially elevated black women into economic power over black men," thereby leaving them without a place "in the family" (Gilder 1995).[6] The alternate portrayal of black women as (federally assisted) trespassers in "such male bastions as the cockpits of fighter planes, police squad cars, fire stations, construction sites and university athletic teams," not to mention law, medicine, or academia, and as " 'matriarchs' cowering in their triple-bolted apartments in fear of [gangs of young men]" (ibid.)—or as Mama Crips—speaks to the deployment of diffraction, the discursive mechanism that "enables various mutually exclusive architectures to appear side by side or in turn" (Foucault [1969] 1972, 66).

But what are we to make, then, of the narrative "options" opened by the multiplicity of discursive architectures that tell different stories? What is the status, for example, of the revelation that Mama Crip turned out to be a hard-working single mother of three and that the STEP charges against her were dropped when reporters discovered the police investigation to have been "hasty and error ridden" (Davis [1990] 1992, 283)? Or Justice Clarence Thomas's tale of his "welfare dependent" sister, Emma Mae Martin, who, it turned out, had received public assistance for a brief period when she cared for the sick aunt who served as her children's caretaker while Martin herself worked two minimum-wage jobs?[7] (Painter 1992, 201–2). Why do the possibilities opened up by these stories—ones that might challenge a prevailing organization of power from as many directions as make up that organization—go largely unrealized?

We must look, Foucault suggests, to the "economy of discursive constellation" to understand the mechanisms—or "authorities"—that convey particular choices within a discursive formation (Foucault [1969] 1972, 66). These may be discerned, he says, in the relationship between a given discourse and those contemporary with it. Thus, the subgroups of the discourse on violence, for example, constituted by the conservative platform on welfare and affirmative action that has effected so much political (re)action since the early 1980s are manifestly implicated in the measures—proposed and undertaken—concerning the treatment of violent youth. Foucault's observation that the "discourse under study may also be in a relation of analogy, opposition, or complementarity with certain other discourses" (ibid.) suggests, too, that the discursive formation of the Violence Initiative may be operating more closely with that of GID than is immediately apparent.

Complementary Deployments

Diagnosing GID: Enforcing Whiteness

Until this point, the histories of GID and the Violence Initiative have been presented largely in parallel; each has served heuristically to illustrate different rules regulating a particular discursive formation. The distribution of institutional sites and the different subject positions that define them have been central concerns in my analysis of the diagnosis and treatment of GID; the function of the preconceptual level within a discourse has been my focus in the examination of the rationale for the measures proposed to address youth violence. As each story exemplified the work of different elements within a discursive formation, each also revealed the distinctive expressions of power salient in their own operation: Where disciplinary power characterizes the multiple levels of intervention into four-year-old Nathan's cross-gender behavior, a far less subtle expression of power is discernible in the proposals to deploy a state apparatus in the identification of potentially violent individuals. While each case has proved a rich example of different moments constituting a discursive formation, illustrative also of the distinctive kinds of power circulating within the discursive economy, a significant *complementarity* between the two—one that cannot be adequately grasped by analogy or by separate, parallel consideration—has also asserted itself.

The example of the Mama Crip demonstrates this complementarity. Underscoring the specific operation of gender at work in the production of racial difference, she is represented as a kind of "antiwoman," the very antithesis of the loving wife-and-mother figure that stands for "woman" at this time. That is to say, the conception of gender that marks the Mama Crip as a "deviant woman" is also the same that grounds the diagnosis and treatment of GID, which itself positively and implicitly casts gender in terms of the "race neutrality" that stands for whiteness. The insinuation of race in the discourse of GID is characterized, then, not by the conspicuous and, in this case, even crude sort of assessment of the racial other that we see in the case of the Mama Crip but by a more subtly advanced conception of whiteness evoked by means of certain silences or interrogatory gaps—by a failure, in other words, to see the relevance of race at all.

We find an example of this race blindness in the literature on GID in Susan Coates and Ethel Person's presentation of a study of twenty-five effeminate boys. Though this study is one of the few that specifies the racial and ethnic background of the subjects ("48% white, 40% Spanish [*sic*] and 12% black" [Coates and Person (1985) 1987, 202]), the authors nowhere analyze their findings in terms of these distinctions. The reader never learns, for example, whether a disproportionate number of children from a particular group were found to be especially deficient in "social competence" or any of the several pathological factors for which the scientists tested.

While the omission of such an analysis implies that race and ethnicity are not relevant in deriving conclusions about boys diagnosed with GID, the work of theorists such as Hortense Spillers suggests that the decision to leave out or ignore such differences demonstrates the operation of whiteness as an unmarked standard for measuring masculinity and femininity. Hence, while more specific demographic information appears in Richard Green's *"Sissy Boy Syndrome" and the Development of Homosexuality*, a fifteen-year longitudinal study that notes not only racial and ethnic factors but also religious practices and educational background (Green 1987, 14), Green's data speak to his concern only with establishing the representative nature of the sample rather than with investigating differences in gender expression as they manifest themselves across racial, ethnic, religious, or educational lines. Consistent with the findings in his 1976 paper, "One Hundred Ten Feminine and Masculine Boys: Behavioral Contrasts and Demographic Similarities" (Green 1976), which likewise ignored such differences, Green (1987) neither reports any results that might reflect such variations nor indicates that these were even noted in the study.

Furthermore, while candidly admitting that "an investigator's interest in finding out how families evolve over many years does not necessarily mean that families are equally interested in reporting their progress" (ibid., 27), Green neglects to offer any data regarding what factors might influence which families chose to or were able to continue their participation in the study.

Such analysis could have revealed something about the ways in which race and class-inflected gender norms are enforced and from what directions resistance is or could be enacted. As it is, Green's omission of these data provides a good example of how such questions are themselves preempted by the dominant discourse, thus limiting the stories the data can tell.

If the operation of race is persistently concealed and thereby present in the discourse of GID, the implication of gender norms in the kind of regulation to which African Americans are subject seem by comparison to be more readily apparent. The frequent references in the Moynihan Report to the "tangle of pathology" marking the "matriarchal" family structure of African Americans (Moynihan [1965] 1967, 30), along with Moynihan's critical assessment of the achievement of black girls in school and black women in the workforce as compared to black boys and men (ibid., 31–33), confirms the salience of gender norms in this discourse. At the same time, the assertion that, "embittered by their experiences with men, many Negro mothers often act to perpetuate the mother-centered pattern by taking a greater interest in their daughters than their sons" (quoted in ibid., 34) bears a strong resemblance to the findings of the Gender Identity Unit at Roosevelt Hospital, which highlighted the etiological significance of the "fear, anger, and devaluation of men" noted in the mothers of GID boys (Coates 1990, 423).

Ungendering Violence

What has so often been crudely represented as the "collusion" of black women in perpetuating the "pathology" of the black family is quite differently framed in the context of the discourses that purport to have the biological or genetic causes of violence at the center of their investigations. As we have seen, the use of primate research in the investigation into such causes of violence shifts the focus from behaviors that have their roots in the racist legacy of slavery, and accordingly require social remedies (Moynihan [1965] 1967, 5), to behaviors purportedly caused by biological or genetic factors such as serotonin levels and other possible matters of heritability. While the mother remains a potent figure in this latter discourse, she is not the mother we find in the Moynihan Report: It may very well make "a big difference," Stephen Suomi asserts, "what kind of mothers [monkey infants] had" (quoted in Rensberger 1992), but no one has suggested that the havoc wreaked by monkey mothers raising violent monkey children will be ameliorated with serotonin-boosting drugs or legislative intervention.

If the strategic displacement of black women and their children for monkeys and Mama Crips is one that attempts putatively to deracialize the search into the origins of violence, it could also be understood to resonate powerfully with the "ungendering" of which Spillers speaks with regard to male and female slaves in the Middle Passage (Spillers 1987, 72). As I discussed in chapter 1, Spillers argues that the conditions of capture and trade that marked enslaved bodies resulted in the loss of "gender difference in the outcome" (ibid., 67): The rules of gender that signified only with respect to white people of a particular class were deployed to "ungender" (ibid., 72) the enslaved body and thereby to make of it, in "stunning [discursive] contradiction," both a source of powerful desire and a mere thing (ibid., 67). Similarly, the conditions that mark violent individuals constitute a generalized "loss of racial difference" that converges with a contemporary ungendering. Insofar as racial difference is thus disingenuously represented as an irrelevant factor in the investigation into the source of violent behavior—violent behavior narrowly construed as "street violence"[8]—the finding that a disproportionate number of black people commit violent crimes can pass for an objective conclusion, rendering "innocent," in turn, the institutionalization of black people as individual objects of research and intervention. Taken together, deracializing and ungendering enable a contradiction articulated in the myth of a juridical equality—itself a strategic production—and satisfy the desire (Foucault [1969] 1972, 68) for a deeper inquiry into and more penetrating knowledge of the mysteries of the violent individual.

By drawing this connection between the ungendering that, Spillers contends, marked slavery in the United States and the deracializing at work in the context of the research into violence at the end of the twentieth century, I want both to illustrate the similarity between the strategic deployment demonstrated in each and to note the synergistic development that has occurred one to the other. While the work of ungendering is applied only to black women, deracializing functions by first making no one racialized and then redeploying race in a different but no less effective way. Similarly, the loss of racial difference in the context of the research on violence highlights the way in which the representation of a race-neutral science strategically functions to deflect charges of racism and to permit a racist science to continue its work. This necessity of deflecting charges of racism—charges that would have been unintelligible in the past of which Spillers speaks—is due to the location of such practices in what Foucault calls "a new discursive constellation," which is shaped by a history of strategic shifts and interventions operating at once to consolidate, destabilize, and proliferate expressions of power in which the family remains a privileged figure.[9] As a key constituent of the "whole group of relations form[ing] a principle of determination that permits or excludes, within a given discourse, a certain number of statements" (Foucault [1969] 1972, 67), the family functions as the privileged locus of the complementary deployment of race and gender.

That these deployments nevertheless appear at times to constitute mutually exclusive, even opposing categories—as we have seen with respect to the exclusion of questions relating to race in the discourse of GID, for instance, or in feminist work such as Chodorow's *Reproduction of Mothering*—is itself a discursive stratagem in which the family prominently, if sometimes silently, figures. Within the family, matters of race can be made to appear to have no relevance; similarly, while gender can be a more conspicuous factor in the discourse on violence, the identification of gender as that which is produced within the family participates in the contemporary ungendering that locates racialized violence and the welfare mothers responsible for it outside familial space, as the monstrous threat to white supremacy, the uncontrollable black body producing—and reproducing—its constituents: violent sons, wayward fathers, and the daughters who will themselves take up their mother's position. Unfettered by the responsibilities of marriage, one version of the conservative argument goes, and abetted by a state that helps "their" women "function without marriage," black men have no recourse but to "dominate as predators."[10] In short, "the crucible of crime, the source of violence ... is the utter failure of socialization of young men though marriage" (Gilder 1995). The maintenance of gender and race as opposing terms in these discourses is not only effective in concealing the productive complementary I have tried to illustrate but is also, accordingly, constitutive of it.

"Who Can Speak?": Discourse and Authority

The relationship between the analysis of discursive formations and Foucault's genealogical work, which is concerned far more explicitly with the operation of power than the archaeological works preceding it, is nonetheless anticipated at various points in *The Archaeology of Knowledge*. Consideration of power and the resistance that always attends it (Foucault [1976] 1990, 95) is perhaps especially evident in the treatment of the final direction in which Foucault indicates one must study discursive strategies, namely, the kinds of authority on which "the determination of theoretical choices" depends (Foucault [1969] 1972, 67). "This authority is characterized," he writes, "by the *function* that the discourse under study must carry out in a field of *non-discursive practices*" (ibid., 67–68; emphasis in the original). By "non-discursive," Foucault does not mean to suggest that such practices function outside of discourse; discursive practices "are not purely and simply ways of producing discourse. Rather, they are embodied in technical processes, in institutions, in patterns for general behavior, in forms for transmission and diffusion, and in pedagogical forms which, at once, impose and maintain them" (Foucault [1971] 1977, 200). Some years later Foucault portrays as unimportant the distinction between discursive and nondiscursive practices (Foucault [1977] 1980a, 198) and discusses instead the "apparatus" (*dispositif*) that combines them. However, remaining for the moment within the terms Foucault first employs may help us appreciate the reason he ultimately determines the distinction to be misleading.

What distinguishes the meaning of "strategies" in the Foucaultian sense from the traditional meaning derived from the lexicon of war is the difficulty of identifying someone like a general directing the various maneuvers. While individual players do play commanding roles or, more precisely, occupy positions of authority, the alliance of disciplinary and regulatory power revealed by an "ascending analysis of power" (Foucault [1997] 2003, 30) suggests the operation of a machinery that is considerably more complicated than the model of war can accommodate. Though the regulatory power that characterizes the management of urban Los Angeles, for example, relies on a frequently *reciprocal* visibility between surveillants and surveilled that does not accurately describe disciplinary power, such an expression of regulatory power nonetheless depends on an invisibility manifested in an *anonymity* that does in fact characterize the operation of disciplinary power (Foucault [1975] 1979, 202). Excessive visibility can accordingly become a serious liability, as Los Angeles police chief Daryl Gates found in the wake of the national media event made of the videotaped beating of Rodney King.

We find similar demonstrations of the perils of hypervisibility in the development of both GID and the Violence Initiative. In the cases of Rekers and Goodwin, the most prominent spokesman for each, the attention they drew by the revelation of the "true intentions" motivating their work finally displaced them from the influential positions they had occupied. Rekers's increasingly explicit emphasis on the prevention of homosexuality resulted in his marginalization in the field, earning him the thinly veiled scorn exemplified by his former UCLA colleague's public dismissal of him (Green 1987, 260–61).

As for Goodwin, his comments on violence in inner cities prompted his ostracism by successive presidential administrations and led eventually to his departure from public health administration. These examples might speak to the possibilities for change offered by the exposure of gross abuses of power, but in testament to Foucault's observations that "the subject of the statement is ... an empty function, that can be filled by virtually any individual" (Foucault [1969] 1972, 93), the practices associated with each have thrived in the intervening years. The continuing credibility of GID as a sound diagnosis and the fact that many people still consider the Violence Initiative to have represented a legitimate scientific investigation accordingly rest not on a "sovereign speaking subjectivity" (ibid., 122) but on the strategic assignment of subject positions. The replacement of Rekers and Goodwin with less visible figures thus not only exemplifies the kinds of strategic adaptations that occur within a discursive field but also illustrates the nature of the power that marks that field. In *Discipline and Punish*, Foucault describes the organization of disciplinary power as

> a multiple, automatic and anonymous power; for although surveillance rests on individuals, its functioning is that of a network of relations from top to bottom, but also to a certain extent from bottom to top and laterally; this network "holds" the whole together and traverses it in its entirety with effects of power that derive from one another: supervisors, perpetually supervised. The power in the hierarchized surveillance of the disciplines is not possessed as a thing, or transferred as a property; it functions like a piece of machinery. (Foucault [1975] 1979, 176–77)

The "bureaucratic concealment" (ibid., 10) that comes, on Foucault's account, to characterize punishment in the eighteenth century appears to remain a more pervasive feature of the operation of power in the late twentieth century.

Similarly and interestingly, the concealment that appears to operate at the center of Bentham's tower, maintaining the invisibility of its inhabitants, may also be discernible in the tower's periphery, where the occupants of the prison's cells—those appearing to be most visible—are located. In *City of Quartz*, Davis describes in stark terms the erection of "fortress cities" (Davis [1990] 1992, 224) that "ensure physical separation of different humanities" (ibid., 234) and mark poor urban neighborhoods as disenfranchised enemy territory. A vivid example of the way in which the function of discourse is, or must be, deployed in this particular field of nondiscursive practices may be found in this imposition of silence upon a city's poorest residents. Just as the Mama Crip story demonstrated the power of disseminating a lurid tale of moral poverty in order to garner public support for repressive law enforcement measures, the hushed counternarrative of an employed single mother highlights, in contrast, the role of a particular discursive exclusion in maintaining the nondiscursive practices that separate the inner city from us, the public. Perhaps more revealing still is the almost complete silence that issues from poor urban communities themselves, particularly the "violent youth" tellingly described by one local mayor as "the Viet Cong abroad in our society" (quoted in Davis [1990] 1992, 268):

> What would the Crips and Bloods say about the carnage if they could talk? It is, of course, a tactical absolute of "anti-terrorism"—whether practiced in Belfast, Jerusalem, or Los Angeles—to deny terrorism a public voice. Although terrorism is always portrayed precisely as inarticulate male-violence, authorities expend enormous energy to protect us from its "ravings," even at the cost of censorship and restriction of free speech. Thus the LAPD has vehemently (and usually successfully) opposed attempts by social workers and community organizers to allow gang members to tell "their side of the story." (ibid., 300)[11]

Taken with the intensified efforts to amass data, including genetic data, on inner city youth (ibid., 268), the enforcement of their silence recalls Foucault's description of "the disciplinary individual" (Foucault [1975] 1979, 227) as "the object of information, never a subject in communication" (ibid., 200).

Thinking Gender and Race Together

This question of who can speak and what can be spoken lies at the heart of Foucault's archaeological and genealogical projects. Moreover, it has been the underlying concern of this work, which has sought to respond to the difficulty of thinking gender and race together using the tools of Foucaultian method. The "rules" of a discursive formation limit the possibilities for speaking and writing—that is, for thinking—but these very limits also make thinking and its expression possible. Understandings of the operation of gender such as I discussed at the outset, for example, have become more finely tuned even as they have obscured the implication of this operation in the production of race. By thinking within the limits, observing the rules marking a historically located discursive formation, analyses such as Chodorow's have significantly clarified the nature of the production of gender while concealing the implication of the operation of race within it. In such investigations, we can see gender but not race; when we focus on race, gender recedes. If the preceding chapters demonstrate the peculiar nature of these limitations, I believe they also, much like the reversible image of the vase and faces, point to the possibilities of looking from one to the other. We cannot "see" both simultaneously, for one recedes just as the other comes to the fore, but in moving our gaze from one to the other we can nevertheless make each visible—and more: We can become aware of the ways that each shapes the other and of the way in which the evidence of this shaping itself fades away.

However, this movement must be prompted somehow, and the central aim of this text has been to demonstrate the complex ways that the figure of "the family" functions in the productions of gender and race. Examining the operation of power and its effects within the family will, I hope, provoke an examination of the operation of power outside or upon it. In so doing, we may open up new possibilities for understanding both the ways in which the production of gender and the construction of "the domestic" shapes the complex production of race and the ways the production of race, in turn, shapes gender. To the extent that our own analyses cannot themselves function outside these strictures, we must keep in mind that, as Foucault writes, "Discourse can be both an instrument and an effect of power, but also a hindrance, a stumbling-block, a point of resistance and a starting point for an opposing strategy" (Foucault [1976] 1990, 101). It is my hope that, in the stories I have recounted, we may find such a starting point.

Notes

Chapter 1

1. As Teresa de Lauretis put it, "Foucault's theory...excludes, though it does not preclude, the consideration of gender" (de Lauretis 1987, 3). See also, for example, Bordo [1985] 1988; Butler 1986; Bartky 1988; McNay 1991; Sawicki 1991. For an excellent critical analysis of feminist treatments of Foucault's work, see McLaren 2002.

2. In making this claim, I do not mean to suggest that external forces have no role to play in the enforcement of or resistance to the production of gender. I argue here only that the principal means of creating and enforcing these norms does not issue primarily from the state. While we may describe initiatives associated with the federal "Defense of Marriage Act," defining marriage as exclusively hetero-sexual, as efforts to prescribe gender roles, I would cast such initiatives as a kind of secondary enforcement of gender that is principally disciplinary in nature. Similarly, the work of the Gender Public Advocacy Coalition (GenderPAC), which "works to end discrimination and violence caused by gender stereotypes by changing public attitudes, educating elected officials and expanding legal rights" (GenderPAC 2006), suggests that some of the deleterious effects of the restrictive categories of sex and gender can be contested by particular sorts of resistance directed at the state, but GenderPAC does not—and, I would argue, rightly does not—consider the origin of these norms or their enforcement to lie in a state apparatus.

3. Two early attempts to apply Foucault's later "genealogical" analysis to the production of race include Abdul JanMohamed's "Sexuality on/of the Racial Border" and Robyn Wiegman's *American Anatomies*. JanMohamed provides a promising and provocative proposal for interrogation of a "racialized sexuality," but, working from the first volume of *The History of Sexuality*, he ultimately finds Foucault's analysis of limited use precisely because of what he describes as Foucault's "bracketing of the circuit of power at the macro...ends" (JanMohamed 1992, 97). In her otherwise excellent and ground-breaking *American Anatomies*, Wiegman forces the application of Foucault's work to race in her effort to understand Foucault's concept of "panopticism" as it could apply to the enforcement of

racial hierarchies (see Wiegman 1995, 37–42), but such an effort emphasizes the role of the "monitor" at the expense of ignoring the *internalization* of the gaze that is panopticism's central aim, a point I discuss in detail in chapter 2.

4. See, for example, Goldberg 1993, 21ff; Smedley 1993, 15–16.

5. Just as the state has some role in the enforcement of gender roles, there are certainly any number of ways that we can understand how the effects of racist exclusion have been internalized. As Linda Alcoff writes, "More than gender, race is essentially determined by history, but its historical legacy lives in our embodied selves at the deepest level of emotion, perception, imagination, and practiced movement. Race thus affects our mechanisms of perceptual attunement and the organization of our attentive senses, influencing our operations of discernment and judgment" (Alcoff 2006, 289). For a psychoanalytic account that draws similar conclusions, see Cheng 2001.

6. See also Foucault's discussion of this point in the January 15, 1975, lecture at the Collège de France, in which he criticizes the "traditional" conception of power as "outdated" and so "inadequate for the real world in which we have been living for a considerable length of time." He asks, "From where is this conception of power borrowed that sees power impinging massively from the outside, as it were, with a continuous violence that some (always the same) exercise over others (who are also always the same)? It comes from the model of, or if you like, from the historical reality of, slave society" (Foucault [1999] 2003, 50–51).

7. A notable exception is David Theo Goldberg's groundbreaking work in *Racist Culture: Philosophy and the Politics of Meaning* (1993), which could easily be characterized as an "archaeology of race." The foundation of my analysis in chapter 4 owes much to Goldberg's application of Foucault.

8. For Firestone, women's position in the family is the most salient effect of what she identifies as the "true" cause of their oppression, namely, women's disadvantaged biological role, which creates their dependence on men. In Firestone's appropriation of Marxian theory, women's bodies constitute the means of (re)production and must be seized in the revolutionary moment. For Firestone, enlistment of modern reproductive technologies to liberate women from child-bearing is the necessary condition of the possibility of breaking the "tyranny of the biological family" (Firestone [1970] 1979, 19), an institution organized wholly on the basis of a natural imperative that women need no longer tolerate. In Rubin's analysis, by contrast, it is in the historical development of kinship that the roots of women's oppression may be found, rather than the "fact" of women's biological difference. Engels's treatment of *The Origin of the Family, Private Property, and the State*, together with Levi-Strauss's postulation of the exchange of women as the structural principle of kinship settled, for Rubin, the question of the historical contingency, contra Firestone's thesis of the natural necessity, of the family. Joining these analyses with psychoanalytic accounts of the construction of desire, Rubin provides a rich descriptive treatment of the complex of woman's domestication, her use-value in a capitalist system, and compulsory heterosexuality. Rubin calls this complex the "sex-gender system," the "set of arrangements by which a society transforms biological sexuality into products of human activity, and in which these transformed needs are satisfied" (Rubin 1975, 159).

9. In making the claim that the family has been displaced by gender as the privileged object of analysis, I do not mean to suggest that consideration of the family has disappeared but rather to point out that the emphasis shifts to women's role within it. In feminist philosophy (particularly that of philosophers trained in

the analytic tradition), a good deal of important analysis of women's role and its implications for social and political thought has emerged since the publication of Chodorow's work, together with Carol Gilligan's *In a Different Voice* (1982), published four years later. Perhaps most significant among these works is *Maternal Thinking* (Ruddick 1989) and the body of work for which it has been influential, particularly the still-growing work in care ethics. For theorists trained in the continental tradition, this focus on gender has been strongly influenced by Judith Butler's work. Studies in this vein that might appear to make the institution of the family central to the analysis, however, such as Kelly Oliver's *Family Values* (1997), focus not so much on the family as on the nature of feminine subjectivity. There is, nevertheless, significant work that appeared in the late 1990s, in part a response to a growing conservative political movement in the United States that brought traditional conceptions of family to the fore (see, e.g., Fineman 1995; Young 1995, 1996; Feder and Kittay 1996; Nelson 1997; as well as Butler's 1998 Wellek Library lectures published in 2000 as *Antigone's Claim: Kinship between Life and Death*).

10. Spelman's criticism of Chodorow's analysis may be overstated to some extent. As Spelman herself notes, Chodorow grants that class difference, as well as historical changes in parenting, would most certainly result in changes to our understanding of parenting and the production of gender difference (Chodorow 1978, 215). Even so, Spelman's most significant concern is not so much with the details of Chodorow's argument as with a method that treats gender as separable from other categories of difference. Moreover, while Spelman remarks that she is concerned about the limitations of Chodorow's work, it is not entirely clear whether her reservations are owing to the analysis itself or to the problematic ways in which other thinkers have taken up the work. In a note that elaborates on this point, Spelman mentions a number of others who have extended Chodorow's analysis to make claims about the connection of sexism to other forms of domination, such as racism. This is a position Spelman attributes, not entirely fairly, to Chodorow herself (see Spelman 1988, 203n3).

11. See also, for example, Hull, Scott, and Smith, eds., *All the Women Are White, All the Blacks Are Men, but Some of Us Are Brave* (1982); hooks, *Feminist Theory: From Margin to Center* (1984); Moraga and Anzaldúa, eds., *This Bridge Called My Back* ([1981] 1983).

12. Crenshaw's analysis is itself grounded in a long tradition of critical reflection on black women's position at the "intersection" of oppression, ranging from Sojourner Truth's famous "Ain't I a Woman?" speech in 1851 (Loewenberg and Bogin 1976, 235), to Anna Julia Cooper's important *A Voice from the South* (Cooper [1892] 1998) at the end of the nineteenth century, to Patricia Hill Collins's *Black Feminist Thought* (1990).

13. I should clarify, however, that Foucault's work goes uncited in "Mama's Baby, Papa's Maybe," though his influence is everywhere evident. "Interstices: A Small Drama of Words," an earlier essay that Spillers delivered at the famous "sex-wars" conference at Barnard in 1982, anticipates this influence in both the methodology she employs and the argument Spillers will make in "Mama's Baby, Papa's Maybe." In "Interstices," Spillers explicitly draws on Foucault's *Archaeology of Knowledge* to argue that Friedrich Engels's *Origin of the Family, Private Property, and the State* and Shulamith Firestone's *Dialectic of Sex* "belong to a category of alignment that establishes a perspective between prior statements and counter-and-successive statements. That the feminist writer chal-

lenges certain symbolic formations of the past... does not destroy the previous authority, but extends its possibilities" (Spillers 1984, 88). Spillers discusses here the operation of "power that bars black women, indeed, women of color, as a proper subject of inquiry from the various topics of contemporary feminist discourse. Such exclusion is neither deliberate, perhaps, nor inevitable, for sure, but moves through phases of symbolic value that conform precisely to equations of political power." It is also in this essay that Spillers introduces the "folksay" "Mama's baby, papa's maybe" (ibid.).

14. Jacobs's narrative, *Incidents in the Life of a Slave Girl* ([1861] 1987), is one of the most important documentations of the experience of a woman in slavery.

15. For a detailed treatment of this point that beautifully complements Spillers's analysis, see Hazel Carby's discussion of the creation of the "cult of true womanhood" in the antebellum South in *Reconstructing Womanhood* (1987). True womanhood, Carby argues, was equated with motherhood, the definition of which required understanding white motherhood in opposition to the reproductive activity of the enslaved female. This understanding "necessitated the raising of protective barriers, ideological and institutional, around the form of the white mother, whose progeny were heirs to the economic, social, and political interests in the maintenance of the slave system" (ibid., 31). Such barriers were essential, in other words, for sustaining the distinction between the white mother and her heirs and the female slaves who would likewise bear the master's children.

16. While the Moynihan Report and the "culture of poverty" thesis with which it is associated appeared to lose credibility in the decade following its release—owing largely to work such as that of Joyce Ladner (1972) and Carol Stack (1974)—it was reinvigorated in the 1980s, as evidenced by Charles Murray's *Losing Ground* (1984), Bill Moyers's production of "The Vanishing Family," and the publication of Moynihan's own *Family and Nation* (Zinn [1989] 1992, 72–73). See also the special issue of *The Nation*, "Scapegoating the Family" (Gresham and Wilkerson 1989). The 1990s, marked by strident attacks on welfare, saw charges that "welfare state feminism" had displaced the "institution of slavery" as the primary causal factor of the "broken family." In 1995 George Gilder wrote in the *Wall Street Journal* that "it is an unpopular fact of life that in all societies and in all races monogamous marriage is based on patriarchal sex roles, with men the dominant provider. Welfare state feminism destroyed black families by ravaging the male role as provider" (Gilder 1995).

17. There is some variation in Foucault's discussion of the elements that make up a discursive formation and the rules that govern it. The former he enumerates as "objects, *types* of statement, concepts [and] thematic choices." The rules he refers to as "objects, *mode* of statement, concepts, [and] thematic choices" (Foucault [1969] 1972, 38; emphasis added). However, when Foucault elaborates on each of the four elements and on the rules that correspond to them, his terminology does not remain consistent. He refers to "modes of statement" as "enunciative modalities" (50) and "thematic choices" as "strategies" (64). In general I follow Gary Gutting in using the terms that appear most frequently in the text: "objects," "enunciative modalities," "concepts," and "strategies" (Gutting 1989).

18. In his excellent *Michel Foucault's Archaeology of Scientific Reason*, Gary Gutting indicates that Foucault's discussion of the levels of "spatialization" in *The Birth of the Clinic* is concerned with the description of the different levels at which classical medicine was understood, an understanding that was transformed with

the arrival of modern medicine (Gutting 1989, 112–15). In *The Archaeology of Knowledge*, however, Foucault invokes this distinction among the different levels of analysis to specify the nature of an archaeological examination and its different elements (see Foucault [1969] 1972, 44–46).

19. In this same interview, Foucault attributes his failure to see his earlier project in terms of power to the prevailing conditions of intellectual production at the time, which limited investigations of power to narrow conceptions associated with "ideology," "repression," and "the state" and which have their sources in Marxian and psychoanalytic analysis. This reflection is itself grounded in archaeological method (see Foucault [1977] 1980b, 115 ff.).

20. These lectures appeared in French for the first time in 1997 and in English in 2003. An earlier (and unauthorized) edition was published in Italian in 1990 as *Difendere la società*. The first two lectures of the series originally appeared in English in *Power/Knowledge: Selected Interviews and Other Writings* (Foucault 1980).

21. The course, titled "Abnormal," was delivered in 1974 and 1975 and was published in French for the first time in 1999 and in English in 2003.

22. Foucault describes sexuality as "an especially dense transfer point for relations of power" in the first volume of *The History of Sexuality* (Foucault [1976] 1990, 103).

Chapter 2

1. While my analysis in this chapter and throughout this book focuses on the categories of gender and race, class is certainly relevant to studies such as these. In the United States after the war, class becomes one element in the construction of "race." That is to say, socioeconomic privilege is racialized, so that privilege is marked as "white" and disadvantage as "black." Such privilege can function to "deracialize" economically advantaged people of color, just as depressed economic status can "racialize" white people. As David Theo Goldberg puts it, whiteness at this time "definitionally signifies social superiority, politically equates with control, economically equals property and privilege" (Goldberg 2002, 113). In his contribution to the collection *The Making and Unmaking of Whiteness*, John Hartigan Jr. details what he calls "the classed assumptions that contour the recognition of what counts as 'racial' in social discourse in the United States" (Hartigan 2001, 141). Here, too, Vron Ware helpfully points to the work of historians such as Alexander Saxton, David R. Roediger, Theodore W. Allan, and Grace Elizabeth Hale, "whose work has done so much to unravel, explain, and challenge the making of whiteness as an *economic*, political and social category in the U.S." (Ware 2001, 191; emphasis added). Even as I focus on the two categories of race and gender, then, we must keep in mind the prominence of class in the contemporary cultural figuration of "race."

2. Some believed that the working classes actually preferred their crowded quarters and would resist the opportunity to move outside the city even if it were possible for them to do so. Kenneth Jackson writes that *Harper's New Monthly Magazine* offered the following view in 1882: "Myriads of inmates of the squalid, distressing tenement-houses, in which morality is as impossible as happiness, would not give them up, despite their horrors, for clean, orderly, wholesome habitations in the suburbs, could they be transplanted there and back free of

charge. They are in some unaccountable way terribly in love with their own wretchedness" (quoted in Jackson 1985, 117).

3. Hayden demonstrates this possibility in the stunning juxtaposition of the stories of "Kaiserville," built at the height of the war, and Levittown just after, rendered in her *Redesigning the American Dream*. A completely integrated town built from scratch, Kaiserville was designed in order that its workers—white, black, Asian, and Latino men and women—could work shifts around the clock. Centralized child care and catering facilities provided for the shipyard workers twenty-four hours a day (Hayden 1984, 3–4). After the war, Vanport City was dismantled, and Henry Kaiser built single-family housing developments supported by the FHA. "The losers," Hayden points out, "were not the housing developers but the skilled white female and minority male and female workers who lost their wartime jobs to returning male veterans and found there were no postwar housing subsidies designed to help them find new jobs, new homes, and mortgages with easy terms" (Hayden 1984, 8–9).

4. This was a proclamation that Levitt made repeatedly as each Levittown was constructed. However, his refusal to sell houses to black families in Levittown, New Jersey, in the late 1950s despite the fact that state law by that point prohibited discrimination supported by FHA subsidies, together with Levitt's earlier efforts to discourage Jews from an upscale housing development on Long Island (Gans 1967, 372), suggests that if there was no room in his heart for prejudice, the space he found in his wallet more than sufficed.

5. We might also pose the question concerning extending mortgages to female-headed households.

6. After a Supreme Court ruling that restrictions such as these were "unenforceable" and "contrary to public policy," this clause was removed in 1948 (Lambert [1997] 1999, 495).

7. David Popenoe's discussion of Levittown, Pennsylvania, offers a more thorough inventory of rules with which residents were to comply. "Do's and don'ts" were specified in the homeowner's manual provided new buyers, which it warned, would "be strictly enforced." They included rules prohibiting fences (shrubbery—no more than three feet high—was to be installed instead of a fence) and the requirement of permission from the Levitt organization to change the color of a house. In addition to a rule forbidding clotheslines, no wash was to be hung outside on Sundays and holidays. Lawns were to be mowed and weeded weekly between April and November. The maximum number of pets (restricted to dogs and cats) was two (Popenoe 1977, 116).

8. The suit brought by the two plaintiffs here could be considered a precursor to what became known as the "Mount Laurel Decisions" rendered over the course of twenty years by New Jersey courts beginning in the 1970s. These suits challenged the right of suburban communities to pass "exclusionary zoning" that prevented people of color from residing in suburbs and enjoying the benefits that had been secured at the expense of development in poor urban neighborhoods (Haar 1996).

9. Integration of Levittown would nevertheless come. After the expiration of a court stay blocking sale to blacks in 1960, Levitt decided against bringing the case to the Supreme Court and asked clergymen from the community to announce that desegregation would begin in the new construction, meaning that current residents would be unaffected. A consultant hired by Levitt proposed further solutions in an effort to maintain the peace and stability that would ensure continued

profitability. Policies regarding the new developments provided that "Negroes should be scattered around the community (if possible, only one per block), and that under no circumstances should two Negroes be permitted to buy adjoining houses. This prevented anyone from imagining that groups of Negroes were invading the community or that a Negro subsection might develop, and made it impossible for white buyers to ask to be located in an all white section" (Gans 1967, 377). Isolation of black families was also ensured by giving them first choice of lots. "Like other purchasers," Gans writes, "Blacks chose the most private lots, backing onto open or natural areas. This not only required whites who wanted such desirable lots to choose adjacent sites, but had the effect of pushing Blacks to the edges of neighborhoods where their presence would be less conspicuous" (1967, 377). In subsequent years, Levittown, NJ, now Willingboro, would become what a 2003 article in *The Next American City* would describe as "a vibrant, diverse community. A thriving suburb with big yards, good schools, and little crime. A robustly middle class population with an African-American majority" (Pooley 2003). Willingboro's path to this remarkable result was punctuated by "white flight" and unscrupulous real estate dealings that dramatically depressed home values during a boom period, but it is a town that has been genuinely transformed. The fates of the other two Levittowns are quite different. A 1997 article in the *New York Times* marking the fiftieth anniversary of Levittown's founding reported that the town "remains overwhelmingly white—97.37 percent in the 1990 census" (Lambert 1997 [1999], 496). And the 2000 census numbers reflect that only 3 percent of Levittown, Pennsylvania, is African American (cited in Myers 2005, 4).

10. For a compelling account that situates civil rights activism in the United States and, with it, a resurgence of white racism in the context of black veterans' expectations after returning from a war—the war that had exposed and defeated the "the forces of tyranny and prejudice" in the form of Nazism—see Klinkner with Smith 1999, 202ff.

11. For a detailed treatment of these issues, see Sonya Michel's *Children's Interests/Mothers' Rights: The Shaping of America's Child Care Policy* (1999).

12. Certainly not all women occupied the class position to fulfill the normative ideal. As Hayden writes, many of the women who were laid off from their nontraditional jobs were shunted to "domestic" occupations in the public sphere—"cafeteria workers, dishwashers, maids, and supermarket clerks"—and did so without the provision of child care (Hayden 1984, 161). Nevertheless, the considerable benefits offered returning GIs meant that more women were able to give up paid employment to assume full-time responsibility for maintaining a house and raising children.

13. First-wave feminists, among them Elizabeth Cady Stanton and Charlotte Perkins Gilman, had offered scathing criticisms (and sophisticated proposals for reform) of domestic life long before. See, for example, *The Grand Domestic Revolution* (Hayden 1981) and *For Her Own Good* (Ehrenreich and English 1979).

14. While the movements of an entire family are regulated by the layout of a house, the representation of the home as the "woman's place" (Cowan 1983, 203)—the place where she nevertheless has no "room of her own," in Virginia Woolf's words (Wajcman 1991, 117)—suggests not so much that she is a privileged object of disciplinary power in the home (or in the family), so much as that "the home" is the principal site at which women are made into housewives.

15. It is perhaps especially surprising, given the frequency with which Foucault remarks upon—but did not develop—the role of the institution of the family, as I suggested in the introduction. While his parenthetical identification of the family as a disciplinary mechanism in *Discipline and Punish* (Foucault [1975] 1979, 215) might underscore how striking an omission it is, we should also consider the significance of a contradictory point Foucault made in a 1973 Collège lecture during which he remarks that "the family is a sort of cell within which the power exercised is not, as one usually says, disciplinary, but rather of the same type as the power of sovereignty" (Foucault [2003] 2006, 79). Foucault goes on to assert even more forcefully that

> it seems to me that nothing in the way the family functions enables us to see any continuity between the family and the institutions, the disciplinary apparatuses.... Instead, what do we see in the family if not a function of maximum individualization on the side of the person who exercises power, that is to say, on the father's side? The anonymity of power, the ribbon of undifferentiated power which unwinds indefinitely in a panoptic system, is utterly foreign to the constitution of the family in which the father, the bearer of the name, ... is the most intense pole of individualization, much more intense than the wife or the children. (ibid., 80)

While Foucault explains that different disciplinary systems are isotopic with one another, that is, that each must have the capacity to be linked with the others (ibid., 52–53), the family is, he explains, heterotopic with disciplinary apparatuses. And yet, despite—or because of—its distinctive operation, the family operates as "the hinge, the interlocking point, which is absolutely indispensable to the very functioning of all the disciplinary systems" (ibid., 81).

I have proposed here an alternative view of the institution of the family, one that might be read as a kind of corrective to Foucault's failure to reckon in a sustained way with the operation of gender generally, beyond his specific failure to attend to "the distinct ways in which disciplinary techniques operate on the female body," as Lois McNay has observed (McNay 1991, 132. See also, for example, Sawicki 1991, 67–68; Dean 1994, 276).

16. Bentham's interest in calculating the costs and considering the profit potential of running the Panopticon (and particularly as these related to his own gain) was considerable, his vision far exceeding in scope Levitt's two centuries later. Janet Semple, Bentham's twentieth-century champion, admits that money was a "compelling motive" for his advocacy of the Panopticon prison (Semple 1993, 7). Unpublished notes (unavailable to Foucault) reveal the Panopticon to have been only the beginning of a project Bentham called "Panopticon Town" (ibid., 284). "Panopticon Hill," as he also referred to it, would include among other inventions the "sotimion," a refuge for "fallen women" (ibid., 290), and a "paedotrophium," an orphanage of sorts, comprising children of the prisoners or the (paying) residents of the sotimion, of soldiers who died in war; they might also be the children of paupers who would "be taken by contract," their labor exchanged for the cost of the upkeep (ibid., 288). In a vision that resonates with Walt Disney's, Bentham saw Panopticon Hill as an amusement park for city dwellers, complete with rides and a "Panopticon Tavern, a place full of fantastical devices, coloured lights, mirrors, exotic scents" (ibid., 293; 295–96). "In his old age," Semple recounts, "Bentham recalled the panopticon as 'a magnificent instrument

with which I then dreamed of revolutionizing the world' " (ibid., 288). It is interesting to consider the similarities between Bentham's encompassing plan for his village with the Disney Corporation's comprehensive approach to the development of suburban towns such as "Celebration" in Florida (see Lawson 1995; Watt 1996; Ross 1999).

17. Patricia Hill Collins makes a similar point regarding what she describes as "the special role [white women play] in keeping family bloodlines pure," a role that has necessitated the management of white women's sexuality "largely through social norms that advocated pre-marital virginity" and forbade interracial marriage (Collins 2000, 163).

Chapter 3

1. Rekers writes in "Inadequate Sex Role Differentiation in Childhood: The Family and Gender Identity Disorders" that "prior to my own series of studies, no treatment procedures for Gender Identity Disorder in Childhood had been experimentally demonstrated to be effective" (Rekers 1987, 29).

2. The case study from which I am drawing here is "Self-regulation of Gender-role Behaviors: A Case Study" (Rekers and Varni 1977b). For some of the details of the therapy, I also draw from a similar case study published by Rekers and Varni the same year, "Self-monitoring and Self-reinforcement Processes in a Pre-transsexual Boy" (Rekers and Varni 1977a).

3. "Self-monitoring and Self-reinforcement Processes in a Pre-transsexual Boy" details the contents of the two tables:

> Girls' toys on one table consisted of a baby doll in a 3-foot crib, a baby bottle, baby powder, and a doll with dresses, shoes, hat and miniature clothesline; the masculine toys were a rubber knife, two dart guns with darts, a target, handcuffs, and cowboy and Indian pieces. The other table had clothing and grooming toys. The feminine articles consisted of a child-sized dress, jewelry set, and a woman's wig. The masculine apparel consisted of a sea captain's hat, a football helmet, an army helmet and army shirt, a play electric razor, and an army belt. (Rekers and Varni 1977a, 178)

4. See Ronald Bayer's *Homosexuality and American Psychiatry: The Politics of a Diagnosis* (1981) for an account of the debates within the American Psychological Association (APA) that led to the unprecedented vote by the APA membership to remove homosexuality from the *DSM* in 1973. It was not until 1986 that the compromise diagnosis "Ego-dystonic Homosexuality" was also removed.

5. See, for example, Feder 1997; Menvielle 1998; Minter 1999. See also Bradley and Zucker's reply to Menvielle (1998). Bartlett, Vasey, and Bukowski conducted empirical studies "to determine whether Gender Identity Disorder (GID) in children meets the . . . definitional criteria of mental disorder" (Bartlett, Vasey, and Bukowski 2000, 753) and concluded that GID did not in fact meet the existing criteria. Kenneth Zucker, who has emerged as the leading clinician in the area over the last twenty years, more recently collaborated on an article disputing the significance of the timing of the appearance of Gender Identity Disorder, providing a justification of the inclusion of GID in the *DSM* by what the authors characterize as an "expert consensus" (Zucker and Spitzer 2005, 31): GID is a genuine disorder, they claim, and its inclusion in the *DSM* was therefore not a

"backdoor maneuver" to pathologize homosexuality after its removal from the *DSM*. Zucker and Spitzer's anxious defense (and the misunderstanding of the critics' arguments it reveals, arguments that never disputed the "expertise" Zucker and his colleagues profess) exemplifies Foucault's understanding of the operation of power/knowledge, of the way, that is, that a prevailing organization of power shapes what counts as "true" or, in this case, what can pass muster as a "genuine pathology." The designation of "experts" is an effect of this power, and the "knowledge" they produce functions hermeneutically to consolidate the organization of power responsible for the installation of such experts in the first place.

6. I am not making the argument that sex is "simply a social construction." This is a matter that was, and to a large extent continues to be, oversimplified in feminist and nonfeminist literature. Social scientific work that considers the experience of people with intersex conditions (see, for example, Kessler 1998; Preves 2003; see also the personal narratives in Dreger 1999) suggests that individuals' own sense or understanding of their sex could be characterized as a kind of social interpretation of distinctive (and often not so distinctive) somatic impulses of various kinds, that is, that bodily feelings have, and take on, meaning that is already social. My point in this chapter, however, is not to locate some "origin" of sexual difference but to describe the mechanisms that enforce the way these differences, regardless of provenance, are supposed to manifest themselves.

7. It is this latter power that is also associated with the production of racial difference, the focus of chapter 4. The production of race is certainly operating in the discursive formation of GID, but it is well concealed, a point that I take up in the concluding chapter.

8. The term "intersex" has been controversial for some time now. It is regarded by many parents and even some clinicians as pejorative or exclusive of certain conditions that would fall under the category of a Disorder of Sex Development (DSD), that is, any congenital condition "in which development of chromosomal, gonadal or anatomical sex is atypical" (Hughes et al. 2006, 1; see also Dreger et al. 2005).

9. Biologist Anne Fausto-Sterling's "Five Sexes: Why Male and Female Are Not Enough" (1993) is the (in)famous statement of this point. She summarizes both the outrage and utopian possibilities provoked by this work in *Sexing the Body* (2000, 78–79; 295–97).

10. The very first of Rekers's published case studies, coauthored with his dissertation adviser at UCLA in 1974 (and consisting of subjects referred by Richard Green, who would later write *The "Sissy Boy Syndrome" and the Development of Homosexuality* [Green 1987]), is considerably less refined stylistically than the later case studies that form the basis of my analysis here. Nonetheless, the 1974 study's description of the interaction between the experimenters and the mother of the boy, "Kraig," is likely a fair reproduction of the interaction between Nathan's mother and the experimenters and reveals the nature of what is in effect the mother's "training":

> During the session, the mother was helped to extinguish feminine behavior (verbal and play) by instructions over the earphones such as "stop talking to him now," "pick up the book and read," "ignore him now," "look away from him." Immediately after the mother's correct response, the experimenter verbally reinforced the response, e.g. "good," "great, that's what we want," "that's right," "excellent." Similarly, if the subject picked up a

masculine toy when the mother was not watching, the experimenter instructed her, "quick, look at him now," or "talk to him now." (Rekers and Lovaas 1974, 179)

At some point during the session, the study relates, Kraig became so upset, "crying and aggressing at his mother," that the session was suspended, and Kraig's mother was "reassured . . . that she was doing the right thing and was doing it well, and that we would continue to be available in the observation room to assist her" (ibid.).

11. This work recalls similar claims advanced during the 1960s that asserted a causal relation between (primarily male) homosexuality and parents' (and particularly mothers') pathological relationships with their children. The popular *Growing Up Straight: What Every Thoughtful Parent Should Know about Homosexuality* (Wyden and Wyden 1968) summarizes these claims in chapters titled "How Mothers Raise Homosexual Sons" and "How Fathers Raise Homosexual Sons." Tellingly, daughters do not receive equal time and are afforded only one chapter, "How Parents Raise Homosexual Daughters," an asymmetry reproduced in the first two formulations of GID in *DSM-III* and *DSM-IV*.

12. Zucker and Bradley later report that

there is no consistent evidence that parents [of children diagnosed with GID] preferred a child of the opposite sex, which may have induced ambivalent feelings about the child. . . . However, there does appear to be a subgroup of these youngsters, particularly the boys, whose mothers experience what we term "pathological gender mourning," in which the wish for a child of the opposite sex remains unresolved and affects gender-related aspects of parental socialization. (Zucker and Bradley 1999a, 377)

There nevertheless remains a clear tension here between the identification of parents' tolerance or encouragement of gender nonconformity as etiologically significant (see also, e.g., Zucker 1985; Bradley 1985) and the apparent "failure" of feminists to free their children from the bonds of normative gender roles.

13. In a 1997 "Review of the Past 10 Years," Bradley and Zucker restate the claim concerning the "high levels of psychopathology observed in these mothers, especially severe depression and borderline personality disorder" but now criticize the earlier association found by Coates and Person linking GID to the "closeness" of the relationship between mothers and sons. Instead, they suggest that mothers—owing to their pathology—have insecure attachments to their sons, and although there is no work studying diagnosed girls, they recount that their clinical impressions of them are similar (Bradley and Zucker 1997, 877).

14. More recently, dissenting voices—few though they continue to be—have challenged this claim. For example, in a 1997 volume of the Jossey-Bass *Library of Current Clinical Technique*, Lock, Carrion, and Kleis write that

Our approach . . . may differ in some respects from that of other clinics because we believe that the fundamental problems that children with GID experience are for the most part due to reactions to them rather than inherent problems with them. . . . The young boys and girls with GID do not feel bad or ashamed until parents and peers make them so, or they are the focus of parental conflict that enhances gender-atypical behavior by adding an emotional valence to it. (Lock, Carrion, and Kleis 1997, 138)

In just the last few years, Children's National Medical Center has made available on the World Wide Web a pamphlet that contradicts the claims of doctors working to treat what they call "gender variance" as a disorder (see Tuerk, Menvielle, and de Jesus 2003; see also Menvielle and Tuerk 2002; Menvielle, Tuerk, and Perrin 2005).

15. While Coates's research began in the mid-1980s, examination of her work suggests that just as there may be a meaningful connection between the depathologization of homosexuality and the appearance of GID as a mental disorder, this work concerning the "pathological tendencies" of mothers may likewise be understood as a response to changes wrought by feminism's Second Wave.

16. "Early Intervention for Female Sexual Identity Disturbance: Self-monitoring of Play Behavior" (Rekers and Mead 1979) is the first "published experimental study of sexual identity disturbance in a preadolescent girl." The authors attribute the dearth of work on gender-dysphoric girls to the possibility that "early professional detection of cross-sex identification in girls is . . . hindered by parental confusion of the indicators of identity disturbance with the socially acceptable 'tomboyism' of normally identified girls" (ibid., 5). See also Zucker, Bradley, and Sanikhani (1997), in which the authors report that between 1978 and 1995 the sex ratio of referrals for treatment was 6.6:1 of boys to girls, a finding they believe could be reflective of "social factors" (ibid., 218).

17. In 2003 Dutch researchers reported success with antiteasing programs, commenting simply that, in schools that had implemented them, "children are indeed not teased." "Often," the authors write, "the reason for starting such a program is the presence of a child with GID" (Cohen-Kettenis and Pfäfflin 2003, 127). No further information or substantive research on such programs appears to be available.

18. Kenneth Zucker writes, for example, that any "clinician who is responsible for the therapeutic care of children and adolescents who have GID will be introduced quickly to complex social and ethical issues that pertain to the politics of sex and gender in postmodern Western culture" (Zucker 2004, 562).

19. In each of the texts I cite here, transsexualism is consistently specified as a risk for GID children right alongside homosexuality. More recent work on GID is much more concerned with the possibility of transsexuality, which remains, for the moment at any rate, secure as a "disorder" warranting medical treatment. For an extended discussion that considers whether the diagnosis of GID is helpful to transgender individuals in transition, see Butler 2004, 75–101.

20. Rekers went on to write *Growing Up Straight: What Families Should Know about Homosexuality* (1982a), as well as *Shaping Your Child's Sexual Identity* (1982b), manuals for parents designed to assist them in deterring their children from pursuing a "deviant" lifestyle.

21. Although the diagnosis of GID was formulated in the 1970s, a connection between early gender variance and eventual homosexuality was made much earlier. In the mid-1930s the Committee for the Study of Sex Variants (CSSV), a unique congregation of research scientists and physicians, was assembled to investigate sexual deviance in the United States (Terry 1999, 178). According to Jennifer Terry, the CSSV identified the family as a primary site for the regulation of sexual desire, following the conclusions of one of the Committee's most prominent members, that "homosexuality began to take hold in childhood. . . . Thus, adult observation and guidance of children was crucial to detecting and preventing sex variance at an early age" (ibid., 214–15). See also Jennifer Terry's historical treatment of gay men

and lesbians in recent European history, which shows the significant overlap between the enforcement of heterosexuality and the enforcement of norms of gender (Terry 1995).

22. The same can be said of some of his better-known colleagues featured intermittently in the media, such as Joseph Nicolosi, author of *Reparative Therapy for Male Homosexuality: A New Clinical Approach* (Nicolosi 1991). The National Association for the Research and Therapy of Homosexuality (NARTH), formed in 1992 to promote the cause of reparative therapy, draws extensively on the literature of GID. Zucker and Bradley, in contrast, attempt to distance themselves from such connections, disavowing Rekers's justification of treating GID as a preventive against adult homosexuality. See, for example, Zucker 1984.

23. The term "policing of gender" should of course recall Foucault's own examination of "a policing of sex," which he dates to the eighteenth century and which, he says, involves explicit state intervention in the regulation of the population: "It was necessary to analyze the birthrate, the age of marriage, the legitimate and illegitimate births, the precocity and frequency of sex relations, the ways of making them fertile or sterile [and so on]" (Foucault [1976] 1990, 25–26).

24. Citation of Rekers's work, unlike that of his more moderate peers such as Richard Green, practically disappeared in the nearly three decades since its first appearance. The last significant reference to it may be found in a 1985 article by Kenneth Zucker, "Cross-gender-identified Children" (Zucker 1985); five years later, in "Treatment of Gender Identity Disorders in Children" (Zucker 1990), largely an overview of treatments and their documented effects, Zucker mentions Rekers only in order to narrowly cast doubt on the reliability of Rekers's findings with respect to the potential of treatment of GID to prevent "transvestism, transsexualism, and some forms of homosexuality" (ibid., 33). Such a disparity could plausibly reflect a concerted distancing of the profession from Rekers as a *figure*, but Rekers's *work*, and particularly the treatment techniques he innovated, have nowhere been discredited by those advocating treatment for GID. In *The "Sissy Boy Syndrome" and the Development of Homosexuality*, Green, who referred the first patients to Rekers at UCLA, denounces the explicit moralism in Rekers's monographic work (Rekers 1982a, 1982b) and contrasts his own early work with that of Rekers (Green 1987, 260–63); he nevertheless notes that the treatment he prescribes for boys with GID conforms to Rekers's (Green 1987, 263). Susan Bradley, one of the profession's most influential figures today, offers an unacknowledged recapitulation of Rekers's work in "Gender Disorders in Childhood: A Formulation" (Bradley 1985), which appears in *Gender Dysphoria: Development, Research, Management*, a collection of essays by practitioners at the Clarke Institute. This is a chapter notable also for its early and explicit consideration of the effectiveness of treating lesbian and gay adolescents, an issue that became increasingly contested in the late nineties and continues today (see, e.g., Zucker and Spitzer 2005, 36). Interestingly, however, overviews of GID that began to appear in the late 1990s once again made frequent reference to Rekers's work (see, e.g., Bradley and Zucker 1997; Zucker and Bradley 1999b).

25. See also Zucker and Bradley's review of the literature related to "associated psychopathology" (ibid., 376).

26. I use moral legislation figuratively, but it is worth noting that Rekers has served as an "expert witness" on several occasions in precedent-setting child custody disputes involving a gay parent (see Rekers 1982b).

27. Also notable in the lengthy formulation of GID in *DSM-IV* (the first that does not include separate entries for GID in children, adolescents, and adults) is the section enumerating "Associated Features and Disorders." The juxtaposition of the different manifestations of the disorders seems calculated to identify peer teasing of children—among the first of the related features mentioned—with the assertion that "some males...resort to self treatment with hormones and may very rarely perform their own castration or penectomy. Especially in urban centers, some males...may engage in prostitution, which places them at high risk for human immunodeficiency virus (HIV) infection"; in addition, "suicide attempts and "Substance-related Disorders" are common. The description then returns to related disorders in children and adolescents, thereby framing the lurid description of the lives of "some males" with the enumeration of problems commonly associated with children, such as "isolation and ostracism" at the beginning and "Separation Anxiety" at the end (American Psychiatric Association 1994, 535).

28. See, for example, analyses such as those appearing in a special issue of *Developmental Psychology* (31:1) on "Sexual Orientation and Human Development," such as Blanchard et al. (1995), "Birth Order and Sibling Sex Ratio in Homosexual Male Adolescents and Probably Prehomosexual Feminine Boys," and Bailey and Zucker (1995), "Childhood Sex-typed Behavior and Sexual Orientation: A Conceptual Analysis and Quantitative Review."

29. See, for example, Ricks 1993; Mirken 1994; "Margie" 1994; Rafferty 1995.

30. Komiotis would become a casualty of this war. He was reported a few years later to have committed suicide (Mournian 1998).

31. Conversation with Shannon Minter, National Center for Lesbian Rights, 1994.

32. See, for example, Daphne Scholinski's account in *The Last Time I Wore a Dress* (Scholinski with Adams 1997; see also Burke 1996, 86–92), the story of Lyn Duff (ibid., 93–96), as well as the (Foucaultian) account of philosopher Ladelle McWhorter (McWhorter 1999, 25–28).

33. This matter of the true prevalence of "sexual variation," including not only variation of genitalia but also of gonads, chromosomes, or hormone levels is a vexed one. While 1 in 2,000 is a frequently cited estimate, it may occur far more frequently, in as many as 1.7 in 100 births (see Fausto-Sterling 2000, 51). It may also be fewer. The most recent publication resulting from a collaboration of the U.S. and European pediatric endocrinological societies estimates prevalence to be 1 in 4,500 (Hughes et al. 2006, 1).

34. These protocols continue to enjoy broad support, although, beginning at the turn of this century, an increasing number of voices—both those of people with intersex and doctors who have undertaken research on the deleterious effects, physical and emotional—have begun to turn the tide. See, for example, Kessler 1998; Fausto-Sterling 2000; Frader et al. 2004; as well as the essays collected in Dreger 1999 and Parens 2006.

35. "Mary's Story" is taken from the transcript of an interview I conducted in 2001. The names of the mother and daughter have been changed. This story, along with those of other parents, first appeared in "Doctors' Orders: Parents and Intersex Children" (Feder 2002).

36. Jessica was diagnosed with a form of Androgen Insensitivity Syndrome (AIS), a condition in which a fetus with a male (46XY) karyotype is unable to

respond to normal levels of circulating androgens due to an abnormal function of the androgen receptor system. In its "complete" form, AIS would result in a child with typical feminine external genitalia and undescended testes. In its "partial" form, the body can respond to some androgens, and at puberty, enlargement of the clitoris can result.

37. The use of the term "clitorectomy" is controversial. Western doctors today do not refer to "clitorectomy" but instead to "clitoral recession," apparently to distinguish current practices from those that are now decades old. Insistence on the more euphemistic term appears calculated not only to place distance between past and current practices but also to distinguish "medical" (beneficent, scientific, modern) practices from "cultural" (ignorant, primitive, uncivilized) practices that occur in "other countries." The distinction is credible neither linguistically nor practically, however. The suffix "-ectomy" simply means "to cut," not to excise completely. "Primitive" genital surgeries are not able to excise the clitoris in its entirety because the structure is too deep and therefore inaccessible to the instruments used. Philosopher Diana Meyers proposes the term "genital cutting" to circumvent the euphemistic terminology used to characterize both "medical" and "cultural" practices (see Meyers 2000, 470).

38. See, for example, the account of Catherine Tuerk, now a specialist in the treatment of GID, speaking of her son Joshua, who was subjected to treatment for gender nonconformity (Wilkinson 2001; Crawford 2003).

39. Following John Money, doctors believed (and largely continue to believe) that gender is a production of socialization, not nature. Proper gender development depends, then, on the proper appearance of genitalia; an infant's genitalia must "look like" those of their assigned sex; otherwise, doubt and confusion will disrupt this development (see, e.g., Money and Erhardt 1982, 16). For an extended treatment of Money's theory and the revelation of the falsified data that he marshaled to support it, see Colapinto 2001. Beginning in the 1960s, Money's theory was famously challenged by biologist Milton Diamond, who argued that sex hormones influence embryonic development in significant ways (see, e.g., Diamond 1976).

40. Moreover, the court's assumption that the staff of an institution can offer impartial evaluations that determine whether a child or adolescent should be admitted for treatment is in tension with the widespread employee incentive programs (involving doctors and marketing directors alike) practiced by private facilities (see, e.g., Weithorn 1988, 820; Darnton 1989, 67; Armstrong 1993, 9–10).

41. Contemporary medical ethical standards are founded on a conception of individual rights, the crowning principle of which is an individual's autonomy. It is a violation of that autonomy, for example, to withhold "informed consent," that is, full information about the nature of a procedure, together with all of its known risks and benefits. The same standards for informed consent must also extend to the consent that parents must make on behalf of their infants or underaged children. Kenneth Kipnis and Milton Diamond argue that in fact it is "not possible for a patient's parents to give informed consent to…procedures [involving corrective genital surgery], precisely because the medical profession has not systematically assessed what happens to the adults these infant patients become" (Kipnis and Diamond 1999, 187). Such an analysis might also apply to the case of Paul Komiotis; it is unlikely that his parents were informed that "reparative therapy" for a homosexual orientation has a very poor record of "success," as

the American Academy of Pediatrics stated in 1993 (American Academy of Pediatrics 1993).

42. For a subtle and compelling argument concerning the complexity of the concept of right, see Brown 1995, 96ff.

43. Indeed, the Constitutional Court of Colombia, the country's highest court, in a series of three landmark decisions in 1999, concluded that such surgeries were a violation of human rights and identified people with intersex as a protected class, concluding that children with intersex conditions could be subject to harm as a result of what was characterized as parental "intolerance." While the court had, as it affirmed, an interest in preserving family autonomy, it "found that parents are likely to make decisions based upon their own fears and concerns rather than what is best for the child, especially if they are pressed to decide quickly." In response, the court offered the basis for a new standard of consent, a " 'qualified, persistent informed consent' intended to force parental decisions to take into account only the child's interest" (Greenberg and Chase 2005). However, in this country, no such rights for children with intersex conditions—or their parents—exist. There has only recently been some movement in this direction, with activists and legal scholars beginning to outline possibilities for the assertion of some right (see, e.g., Greenberg 2003).

44. This prediction is borne out by the fact that there is no published evidence suggesting any "hazards, biological or otherwise, of having a large clitoris." While men with small penises have suffered some indignity, published studies have found that, "contrary to conventional wisdom, it is not inevitable that such [men] must 'recognize that [they] are incomplete, physically defective and...must live apart' " (Kipnis and Diamond 1999, 181).

45. I take this up in the concluding chapter.

Chapter 4

1. Letter originally published in the *Journal of the American Medical Association* 201 (1967):895; reprinted in *Biology, Crime, and Ethics: A Study of Biological Explanations for Criminal Behavior* (Marsh and Katz 1985, 123–24; emphasis in the original).

2. It should be clear that the specific expression of racism to which Foucault here refers concerns that expressed in early and mid-twentieth-century Europe. See, for example, Foucault's remarks on the origins of anti-Semitism in a 1977 interview (Foucault [1977] 1980a, 222–24). Of interest here, too, is Giorgio Agamben's application of the concept of biopower in his treatment of the National Socialist state in *Homo Sacer* ([1995] 1998). While Foucault does not himself address the racism specific to the United States—a point that Joy James wrongly, I think, takes up as an "erasure" of racism in Foucault's work (see James 1996, 24)—the analysis in this chapter demonstrates how Foucault's understanding of the operation of racism is in fact reflected in U.S. practices at the end of the twentieth century and continuing today.

3. Frederick K. Goodwin, address at the meeting of the National Mental Health Advisory Council (February 11, 1992). Quoted in Vesperi (1992), Hilts (1992), and Sellers-Diamond (1994, 426).

4. The program announcement from the National Institute of Mental Health, appearing in September 1991, titled "Research on Perpetrators of Violence," by

contrast, did not occasion dissent or controversy despite the fact that its statement of purpose closely resembles Goodwin's descriptions of the Violence Initiative. The announcement encouraged scientists to undertake "research on the etiology, course, and correlates of aggressive and violent behaviors in children, adolescents, and adults. Through this announcement, the National Institute of Mental Health (NIMH) expects to support research that will improve the scientific base for more effective and cost-efficient approaches to clinical assessment, treatment, management, and prevention" (cited in Duster 1994, 148).

5. This is an image that has its origins in the first European encounter with peoples in Africa and the Americas. See, for example, Charles Mills's discussion of Hayden White's historical treatment of the "wild man," the man who remains in the "state of nature," distinguishing the "civilized" white man from the "uncivilized" savage (Mills 1997, 43). This figure reemerges forcefully in the 1980s and 1990s in the form of what John DiIulio infamously termed "superpredators," a generation of "fatherless, Godless, jobless, and hopeless" youth whose lives are marked not by economic hardship but by "moral poverty" (see, e.g., Bennett, DiIulio, and Walters 1996).

6. Much of the debate over the Violence Initiative focused on the question of what identifying violence as a "public health" problem entails. For Goodwin and the NIH, the identification points to questions of "individual vulnerability," whereas for the Centers for Disease Control (CDC) in Atlanta, where violence was declared a national "epidemic," prevention programs target social problems: "abusive families, poor living conditions, lack of job training, easy access to handguns and racism" (Rochell 1994). For the articulation of another perspective that applies a public health model to violence, see *Violence in America: A Public Health Approach* (Rosenberg and Fenley 1991), especially the section on "Assaultive Violence" (Rosenberg and Mercy 1991). See also *Violence: Our Deadly Epidemic and Its Causes* (Gilligan 1996).

7. There is, however, some disagreement on this point. Sociologist Troy Duster, for example, commenting on the 2005 Food and Drug Administration approval of a drug to treat heart disease in African Americans—the first drug approved for the treatment of a specific racial group—believes that the move could constitute "a first step in the promotion of racialized medicine. . . . Race is too crude a measure. We should be looking at the individual and his or her biochemical makeup—not whether he or she is black or white" (quoted in Stein 2005).

8. Goodwin's appointment was of course controversial. The American Psychological Association responded to Goodwin's appointment at NIMH with a letter expressing strong opposition (Holden 1992). The American Psychiatric Association, by contrast, wrote that "it would be wrong to defend Dr. Goodwin's remark," but supported him nonetheless. The National Association of Social Workers registered its strong disapproval of Goodwin's use of research (Vesperi 1992), as did the American Orthopsychiatric Association and Blacks in Government (Shipman 1994, 238).

9. Although Goodwin advocated future exploration of family intervention, several experimental projects were already under way at the time of his presentation. See studies on "Parent Training" reported in *Understanding and Preventing Violence* (Reiss and Roth 1993, 388–90). Breggin and Breggin report that approved studies testing Ritalin for aggressive children used what the grant application described as a "substantial portion of subjects . . . from the minority community" (cited in Breggin and Breggin 1994, 107; see generally 96–114); Troy Duster cites a portion of the

research protocol for a study approved in 1991: "One hundred and twenty Black third-grade boys will be recruited from 10 classrooms in the Durham, North Carolina, school system. Dyad type will be assessed by pupil and teacher ratings of the extent to which pairs of boys in the classroom initiate aggression at one another" (Grant number R29 MH46925, cited in Duster 1994, 148). See also discussion of parent-training programs in "Changing the Rewards of Familial and Community Life" (Wilson and Herrnstein 1985, 384–89). The similarities between the intervention described here and that associated with the treatment of GID I discussed in the previous chapter are striking. The differences between them, however, are also significant. For example, while a child diagnosed with GID is treated to "restore" the gender identity of a child whose deviance has generally been picked out by his peers or even parents, the programs here bear the much more conspicuous mark of the state *seeking out* children for intervention not only for behavior modification but also for pharmaceutical treatment.

10. For a discussion of the legal concerns raised by such intervention, including issues of privacy, consent, and coercion, see Sellers-Diamond (1994). For a contemporaneous discussion of the legal concerns with respect to the genetic findings associated with the Human Genome Project, see Dreyfuss and Nelkin (1992).

11. See also Thomas Dumm's genealogy of scientific racism prompted by his reflections on the courtroom portrayal of Rodney King as one of the "gorillas in the mist" during the trial of the officers who beat him. Dumm traces the development of what he terms a "racist representational scheme," where the "body of the criminal speaks the 'truth' of the criminal's character" (Dumm 1993, 180) from nineteenth-century physician Cesare Lombroso's theory of criminal "somatotypes" to Wilson and Herrnstein's later twentieth-century postulation of "constitutional factors" determinative of blacks' criminal tendencies (ibid., 181–82). Such factors are alleged to include differences not only in physique but also in chromosomal and genetic factors (Wilson and Herrnstein 1985, 100–101; 90ff.).

12. See, for example, Herrnstein and Murray's *Bell Curve* (1994), which purports to demonstrate lower IQs in blacks, the criticisms of Gould (1996), as well as the classic refutation in Montagu ([1964] 1997).

13. See the "Symposium on Genetics and Crime," a series of short articles by participants of the conference on Politics and the Life Sciences (March 1996). See also David Wasserman and Robert Wachbroit's introduction to the collection of essays that resulted from this conference (Wasserman and Wachbroit 2001). The same year that funding was restored, Glayde Whitney, the outgoing president of the Behavior Genetics Association, told his audience in his farewell address that, "like it or not, it is reasonable scientific hypothesis that some, perhaps much, of the race difference in murder rates is caused by genetic differences in contributory variables such as low intelligence, lack of empathy, aggressive acting out and impulsive lack of foresight" (Carlier 1999, quoted by Alper and Beckwith 2002, 182).

14. Robert Wright notes that Goodwin was "the first scientist to demonstrate clinically the antidepressant effects of lithium," and he coauthored "the first paper noting the correlation between serotonin and violence" (Wright 1995, 68). In 1984 he authored a series of articles for the *Baltimore Sun*, in which he "talked about the possibility of controlling violent crime by treating criminals" with drug therapy (Bass 1993; Wright 1995, 77).

15. See Breggin and Breggin 1994. The Bregginses' concerns and those of other critics were at least partly substantiated by studies conducted at the end of the decade that demonstrated a startlingly high use of psychotropic medications among young

Medicaid recipients. A study published at the end of the decade showed that, in 1995, "stimulants were being given to more than 12 percent of 2-to-4-year-olds in one large Midwestern Medicaid program." In a Michigan study conducted in 1998, "57 percent of those under the age of 4 who were diagnosed with [Attention Deficit Hyperactivity Disorder] were being prescribed one or more psychotropic medications" (Fukuyama 2002, 51). See also Rappley et al. (1999) and Zito et al. (2000).

16. Given the amount of evidence to the contrary—before and since—this would appear to be a surprising conclusion. James Breiling of the Violence and Traumatic Stress Research Branch of NIMH has been quoted as saying that "there's no question that there's a genetic contribution [to violent behavior]" (Sipchen 1992); Markku Linnoila at NIH, famous for his work on violence and serotonin, was reported at the time to be looking for "vulnerability genes" (Stolberg 1993). The National Research Council Report *Understanding and Preventing Violence* devotes a significant portion of its speculations to what it describes as "genetic factors" in violence; in 1993 NIH researchers "revealed a faulty gene that makes certain people inherently susceptible to dropping levels of serotonin" (Rochell 1994); in November of 1995, news of a gene "linked to the control of aggression" was announced (Angier 1995).

17. Legal theorists Kimberlé Crenshaw and Gary Peller note in their contribution to *Reading Rodney King/Reading Urban Uprising* that, after the Supreme Court's 1989 ruling in *Richmond v. Croson*, the landmark affirmative action case, the meaning of "racism" for the U.S. legal system "consists of the failure to treat people on an individual basis according to terms that are neutral to race" (Crenshaw and Peller 1993, 60).

18. For more thoroughgoing discussions of "race blindness" and its implications, see Bonilla-Silva's *Racism without Racists* (2003). See also Goldberg's trenchant discussion of color blindness in *The Racial State*. "Colorblindness," Goldberg writes, is literally concerned with being blind to color. In the historical ambiguity of the failure of whiteness to recognize itself as a racial color, the implication must be that colorblindness concern itself exclusively with being blind to people of color. And through this blindness whiteness veils from itself any self-recognition in the traces of its ghostly power" (Goldberg 2002, 222–23).

19. The proposals associated with the Violence Initiative remained tainted with the charge of racism. Probably for this reason, the Clinton administration did not approve funding for the proposal (Sellers-Diamond 1994, 430). Violence research at the NIH thrived through the 1990s, however. In 1992 the budget for violence-related studies was 53.7 million dollars, and in 1993 the budget was 58 million dollars, with a panel of scientists, ethicists, and lawyers recommending a substantial increase (Williams 1994). These numbers represent a small fraction of the total budget of the NIH, of course, but the proportion devoted to biological and genetic research of violence is nonetheless considerable (Bass 1993).

20. Goldberg's use of Foucault's conception of "primitives" to describe the operation of what he calls a "racist grammar" (Goldberg 1990, 298) resonates with Hortense Spillers's (Foucaultian) deployment of the term "grammar" in "Mama's Baby, Papa's Maybe" (1987).

21. Foucault writes that the "'preconceptual level'...is not a horizon of ideality, placed, discovered, or established by a founding gesture—and one that is so original that it eludes all chronological insertion; it is not an inexhaustible a priori at the confines of history.... The 'preconceptual'...is, on the contrary, at

the most 'superficial' level (at the level of discourse), the group of rules that in fact operate within it" (Foucault [1969] 1972, 62).

22. The question of whether it is "high" or "low" levels of serotonin that make a difference in mood or aggression, interestingly, is not yet settled. That serotonin plays a significant role is not a matter of dispute; it is less clear, researchers say, whether it is the "level" of serotonin present or, instead, changes in the transmission of serotonin that are more significant. Drugs like Prozac affect not the amount but rather the "signaling" of serotonin in the brain (see, for example, Hamer and Copeland 1998, 68–73).

23. And yet, the overall crime rate—including violent crime—was decreasing during this very same period. See, for example, Butterfield (1995) and the Federal Bureau of Investigation (1998).

24. Under the 1991 Amendments to the Federal Sentencing Guidelines, "1 gm of Cocaine Base ('Crack') = 100 gm of cocaine/20 gm of heroin" (18 U.S. Code Annotated). In other words,

> defendants convicted of selling 5 grams or more of crack cocaine, worth perhaps $125, receive[d] a mandatory minimum of five years in prison. However, it [took] 500 grams of the powdered drug, nearly $50,000 worth of "yuppie cocaine," to receive an equivalent sentence. Consequently, someone caught in a drug bust with a relatively small amount of cocaine can receive a sentence that is two to three years longer than a person convicted of selling nearly 100 times that amount. (Davis [1990] 1992, 288)

It was only in 2004 that significant concerns regarding problems posed by the guidelines were raised by Supreme Court Justice Anthony Kennedy (see the report of the American Bar Association Justice Kennedy Commission 2004). A pair of Supreme Court decisions in early 2005 resulted in significant change: While the guidelines now provide recommended sentences, federal judges are no longer bound by them (see Lane 2005).

Of course, these developments in the law have a much longer history and are located within a number of overlapping social phenomena. While, as Troy Duster first showed in *The Legislation of Morality*, drug addition, once a problem of white middle-class women, was initially addressed as a private health concern, the spread of addiction to other, marginalized groups in society resulted in the recasting of addiction as a crime (Duster 1970).

25. Bayard Rustin recalls France's remark that "it is illegal for rich men and poor men alike to sleep under bridges or steal a piece of bread" (Rustin [1966] 1967, 417). See also David Goldberg's illuminating discussion of the "color blindness" advocated by the law (which historically instantiates inequalities that are then "whitewashed" and perpetuated by that same law) (Goldberg 2002, 212).

26. The growth in the prison industry during this period was unprecedented. For a forceful and compelling critique, see the series of lectures delivered by Angela Y. Davis in the mid-to-late nineties compiled in *The Prison Industrial Complex* (Davis 2000; see also Davis 2003).

27. An exception I take up in the following chapter is the account of the "Mama Crip," discussed by Mike Davis in *City of Quartz* ([1990] 1992).

28. See also Angela Y. Davis's related discussion in "Race and Criminalization: Black Americans and the Punishment Industry" (Davis 1997).

29. Here Moynihan echoes Oscar Lewis's thesis of a "culture of poverty." As Massey and Denton write, "Although Lewis explicitly connected the emergence of

these cultural patterns to structural conditions in society, he argued that once the culture of poverty was established, it became an independent cause of persistent poverty" (Massey and Denton 1993, 5).

Chapter 5

1. In fact, Levittown had been "integrated" before the arrival of the Myers family. Daisy Myers writes in her memoir (written in the early 1960s but not published until 2005) that "so many persons of varied complexions lived [in Levittown] that many of its residents assumed that the color pattern had been broken earlier—and had accepted what was a fact. Among the residents were Puerto Ricans, American Indians, and Asians. Some of the couples were a mixture of Negro and white, or white and American Indian" (Myers 2005, 25). Myers also recounts that, after her family had moved in, phone calls revealed that there were African American families living in Levittown at the time but that their light skin color had led their neighbors to perceive them as white (conversation with Daisy Myers 2006).

2. The house had just been vacated by a family relocating to Berkeley, California. It was then occupied by the "Levittown Betterment Committee," a group that formed in response to the revelation of the Myerses' move to Levittown. *Time* magazine also carried a story of the events in Levittown as they occurred and reported that the house flying the Confederate flag—"spotlighted by night"—was each evening "crowded with the members of the newly formed Dogwood Hollow Social Club who worked hard at a hard-boiled bad-neighbor policy" (quoted in Myers 2005, 69). In response to the formation of the Betterment Committee, numerous groups mobilized to create a coalition in the Citizens' Committee for Levittown (ibid., 36; Wechsler 2004, 55).

3. Bittan's account here bears an omission of its own. According to Daisy Myers, peace was finally achieved when a permanent injunction was filed by the state Justice Department and granted almost exactly a year after the Myerses' arrival (ibid., 83–86).

4. None of the accounts of Levittown emphasize this role, but in addition to the relevant points in Bittan's narrative, Daisy Myers remarks in her memoir that, among those surrounding her house that first night, the women "were the most vicious—using profanity and venting their emotions against us and whomever else they imagined was responsible for our move. They would spit and curse and urge the men to do something" (ibid., 29).

5. Stephanie Coontz reports that this measure, ratified at the state level the following year, was part of a national trend that identified "the family as the main source of morality":

> In 1991, New Hampshire decided that parents whose children produce pornography could be charged with a felony. Dermott, Arkansas, enacted an ordinance threatening parents with display in a public stockade and publication of their pictures in the local paper with the caption, "Irresponsible Parent." A law in Mississippi made parents of truants liable to a year in jail and a $1,000 fine. Some states began to experiment with ["Learnfare"] programs that denied checks to welfare families whose teenagers missed school. (Coontz 1992, 112)

6. See also Gilder's *Wealth and Poverty*, where he asserts that black marriages dissolve because "the [welfare] benefit levels destroy the father's key role and

authority" (Gilder 1981, 114). Gilder furthermore claims that children born of teenagers are "really the offspring of the welfare culture of Aid to Families with Dependent Children" (ibid., 115).

7. In "A Genealogy of 'Dependency': Tracing a Keyword of the U.S. Welfare State," Nancy Fraser and Linda Gordon detail the history of the pathologization of "dependency," culminating in the codification of "Dependent Personality Disorder" in the *DSM-III* (Fraser and Gordon 1994, 326), the same year that GID made its debut. They emphasize the gendered character of dependency and trace the development of its "feminization" to the advent of the "family wage" (as a normative ideal rather than reality) and the invention of "the housewife" in the course of the industrial era (ibid., 318). During the period of the New Deal, they recount, welfare was developed as a "two-track" system, with unemployment and old age conceived in terms of (racialized) entitlement that required no "dependency" (ibid., 321. Cf. Stack 1996, 142–56, for an account of the way such entitlements continued to exclude black people). By contrast, Aid to Dependent Children (ADC)—which was consolidated during the New Deal and later called Aid to Families with Dependent Children (AFDC)—"created the appearance that claimants were getting something for nothing" (Fraser and Gordon 1994, 321–22). Gordon's elaboration of the two-track system in *Pitied but Not Entitled* further emphasizes the way in which the differences between the tracks were grounded in and served to enforce particular visions of family: Provisions for disability and unemployment were understood to strengthen the family by maintaining the authority of the male breadwinner (Gordon 1994, 12), while ADC was intended as aid to support children who were understood, in effect, to be without "families." The mother receiving ADC was cast in the role of employee in a state-run orphanage, with concomitant state surveillance of her "job performance" (ibid., 56).

8. In *Backdoor to Eugenics*, Troy Duster discusses the dearth of material on crimes committed by the privileged classes, particularly with respect to the attribution of "genetic explanations" for such behavior (Duster 1990, 100–101). He contends that, in *Crime and Human Nature*, for instance, James Q. Wilson and Richard J. Herrnstein nowhere consider the existing data "documenting the pervasive character of crime among the most privileged strata of society... rang[ing] from criminal homicide prosecution and conviction to the knowledgeable continued pollution of workplace air with a substance known to be cancer-causing... [and including] the routinization of illegal practices among the most privileged sectors of society" (ibid., 101). What Goldberg understands as "the violence of racist expression" (Goldberg 1993, 59) is reversed in this discourse: Violence is not identified with the effects of racism but ascribed to individual, (de)racialized subjects. For a historical perspective on racial violence, see, for example, Massey and Denton for a discussion of the "wave of racial violence... that swept over northern cities in the period between 1900 and 1920," the primary tool, on Massey and Denton's reading, used by northern whites to reinforce ghetto walls (Massey and Denton 1993, 33–35).

9. This is an example of the "fourth" level of analysis to which Foucault briefly refers in *The Archaeology of Knowledge*, considering the "exchange" of one discursive formation for another (Foucault [1969] 1972, 171). While the archaeologist might note the seemingly straightforward substitution of discursive formations, Foucault explains that such substitutions constitute a "crude affirmation of discontinuity"; the transformation may not be total but involve, rather, a permutation of the previous formation (173).

10. Gilder's conviction that "Men either dominate as providers or as predators. There is hardly any other option" (Gilder 1995) finds unlikely support in the work of James Gilligan, who argues that "guilt and shame" associated with men's *dependency*—a result of pervasive race and economic injustice, not Gilder's "welfare state feminism"—motivates men to commit violence. In the chapter subtitled "We Are Not Women," Gilligan writes that "the horror of dependency is what causes violence" (Gilligan 1996, 221). However progressive in its conclusions regarding the need of the state to remedy such problems with "the equitable sharing of our collective wealth, and the creation of a classless and sexually symmetrical society" (ibid., 220), the structural similarities of Gilligan's and Gilder's arguments, together with Gilligan's conception of violence as a "public health problem" (which, as I suggest in chapter 4 does bear progressive potential), should nonetheless give one pause.

11. Davis has discussed an exception when, in 1972, the Human Relations Conference "gave a platform to sixty Black gang leaders to present their grievances. To the astonishment of officials present, the 'mad dogs' outlined an eloquent and coherent set of demands: jobs, housing, better schools, recreation facilities and community control of local institutions" (Davis [1990] 1992, 300).

After the Los Angeles riots, Davis attended a gathering of the Inglewood Crips and Bloods, who were negotiating a truce. In an interview for *Social Text*, he described the meeting as similar to the forum of 1972 but highlighted the presence of rap as a form of cultural expression—one of the few avenues, it would seem, for communicating "their side of the story." "These guys were very eloquent," Davis said, "and they spoke in a rap rhythm and with rap eloquence" (Davis, quoted in Rose 1994, 19–20). For an important contemporaneous analysis of rap and hip-hop music during this period, a field constantly marked by contests over censorship and cultural resistance, see *Black Noise: Rap Music and Black Culture in Contemporary America* (Rose 1994). The history of New York City's "cabaret laws" regulating the performance of live music generally and, throughout most of the century, jazz in particular constitutes another piece of the story of the place of music and its political suppression, which is, of course, one of the oldest cases of suppression in philosophy. See *Gigs: Jazz and the Cabaret Laws in New York City* (Chevigny [1991] 2004).

References

Agamben, Giorgio. [1995] 1998. *Homo sacer: Sovereign power and bare life*, trans. Daniel Heller-Roazen. Palo Alto, CA: Stanford University Press.

Alcoff, Linda Martín. 2006. *Visible identities: Race, gender, and the self*. New York: Oxford University Press.

Alper, Joseph S., and Jon Beckwith. 2002. Genetics, race, and ethnicity: Searching for differences. In *The double-edged helix: Social implications of genetics in a diverse society*, ed. Joseph Alper, Catherine Ard, Adrienne Asch, et al., 175–96. Baltimore: Johns Hopkins University Press.

American Academy of Pediatrics. 1993. Committee on Adolescence. Policy statement: Homosexuality and adolescence. *Pediatrics* 92, no. 4:631–34.

———. 2000. Evaluation of the newborn with developmental anomalies of the external genitalia. *Pediatrics* 106, no. 1:138–42.

American Bar Association Justice Kennedy Commission. 2004. *Report to the House of Delegates*. Washington, DC: American Bar Association.

American Psychiatric Association. 1980. *Diagnostic and statistical manual of mental disorders*, 3d ed. (*DSM-III*). Washington, DC: American Psychiatric Association.

———. 1987. *Diagnostic and statistical manual of mental disorders*, rev. 3d ed. (*DSM-III-R*). Washington, DC: American Psychiatric Association.

———. 1994. *Diagnostic and statistical manual of mental disorders*, 4th ed. (*DSM-IV*). Washington, DC: American Psychiatric Association.

Angier, Natalie. 1995. Gene may help allay aggression, study finds. *San Jose Mercury News* (November 24).

Armstrong, Louise. 1993. *And they call it help: The psychiatric policing of America's children*. Reading, MA: Addison-Wesley.

Bailey, Michael J., and Kenneth J. Zucker. 1995. Childhood sex-typed behavior and sexual orientation: A conceptual analysis and quantitative review. *Developmental Psychology* 31, no. 1:43–55.

Barrett, Michèle, and Mary McIntosh. [1982] 1990. *The anti-social family*, 2d ed. London: Verso.

Bartky, Sandra. 1988. Foucault, femininity, and the modernization of patriarchal power. In *Feminism and Foucault: Reflections on resistance*, ed. Irene Diamond and Lee Quinby, 61–86. Boston: Northeastern University Press.

Bartlett, Nancy H., Paul L. Vasey, and William M. Bukowski. 2000. Is Gender Identity Disorder in children a mental disorder? *Sex Roles* 43, nos. 11–12:753–85.

Bass, Alison. 1993. Controversy places research in peril. *Boston Globe* (February 8).

Bayer, Ronald. 1981. *Homosexuality and American psychiatry: The politics of diagnosis*. Princeton, NJ: Princeton University Press.

Beauvoir, Simone de. [1949] 1989. *The second sex*, trans. H. M. Parshley. New York: Vintage.

Bennett, William J., John J. DiIulio Jr., and John P. Walters. 1996. *Body count: Moral poverty and how to win America's war against crime and drugs*. New York: Simon & Schuster.

Bentham, Jeremy. [1787] 1962. *Panopticon, or, the inspection-house, &c.*, in *The works of Jeremy Bentham*, vol. IV, ed. John Bowring, 39–66. Edinburgh: Tait.

Bittan, David B. 1958. Ordeal in Levittown. *Look* 22 (August 18).

Blanchard, Ray, Kenneth J. Zucker, Susan J. Bradley, and Caitlin S. Hume. 1995. Birth order and sibling sex ratio in homosexual male adolescents and probably prehomosexual boys. *Developmental Psychology* 31, no. 1:22–30.

Bonilla-Silva, Eduardo. 2003. *Racism without racists: Color-blind racism and the persistence of inequality in the United States*. Lanham, MD: Rowman and Littlefield.

Bordo, Susan. [1985] 1988. Anorexia nervosa: Psychopathology as the crystallization of culture. In *Feminism and Foucault: Reflections on resistance*, ed. Irene Diamond and Lee Quinby, 87–117. Boston: Northeastern University Press.

——. 1993. *Unbearable weight: Feminism, Western culture, and the body*. Berkeley: University of California Press.

Bradley, Susan J. 1985. Gender disorders in childhood: A formulation. In *Gender dysphoria: Development, research, management*, ed. Betty W. Steiner, 175–88. New York: Plenum.

——. 1997. Gender Identity Disorder: A review of the past 10 years. *Journal of the American Academy of Child and Adolescent Psychiatry* 36, no. 7:872–80.

——. 1998. Gender Identity Disorder: Reply. *Journal of the American Academy of Child and Adolescent Psychiatry* 37, no. 7:244–45.

Bradley, Susan J., and Kenneth J. Zucker. 1990. Gender Identity Disorder and psychosexual problems in children and adolescents. *Canadian Journal of Psychiatry* 35:477–86.

Breggin, Peter R., and Ginger Ross Breggin. 1994. *The war against children: How the drugs, programs, and theories of the psychiatric establishment are threatening America's children with a medical "cure" for violence*. New York: St. Martin's Press.

Brown, Wendy. 1995. *States of injury: Power and freedom in late modernity*. Princeton, NJ: Princeton University Press.

Burke, Phyllis. 1996. *Gender shock: Exploding the myths of male and female*. New York: Anchor.

Butler, Judith. 1986. Variations on sex and gender: Beauvoir, Wittig, and Foucault. *Praxis International* 5, no. 4:505–16.

——. 2000. *Antigone's claim: Kinship between life and death*. New York: Columbia University Press.

——. 2004. *Undoing gender*. New York: Routledge.

Butterfield, Fox. 1995. Grim forecast is offered on rising juvenile crime: New study challenges prevention programs. *New York Times* (September 8).

——. 1996. Study finds disparity in justice for blacks. *New York Times* (February 13).

Canguilhem, Georges. [1943] 1989. *The normal and the pathological*, trans. Carolyn R. Fawcett. New York: Zone.

Carby, Hazel V. 1987. *Reconstructing womanhood: The emergence of the Afro-American woman novelist*. New York: Oxford University Press.

Carlier, M. 1999. Le contexte actuel des controverses sur les différences entre races: Analyse de quelques évènements récents. *Psychologie Française* 44:107–11.

Caro, Robert A. 1974. *The power broker: Robert Moses and the fall of New York*. New York: Knopf.

Cheng, Anne Anlin. 2001. *The melancholy of race: Psychoanalysis, assimilation, and hidden grief*. New York: Oxford University Press.

Chevigny, Paul. [1991] 2004. *Gigs: Jazz and the cabaret laws in New York City*. New York: Routledge.

Chodorow, Nancy. [1978] 1999. *The reproduction of mothering: Psychoanalysis and the sociology of gender*. Berkeley: University of California Press.

Coates, Susan. 1990. Ontogenesis of boyhood Gender Identity Disorder. *Journal of American Academy of Psychoanalysis* 18, no. 3:414–38.

Coates, Susan, and Ethel Spector Person. [1985] 1987. Extreme boyhood femininity: Isolated behavior or pervasive disorder? In *Annual progress in child psychiatry and child development 1986*, ed. Stella Chess and Alexander Thomas, 197–213. New York: Brunner/Mazel.

Cohen-Kettenis, Peggy T., and Friedemann Pfäfflin. 2003. *Transgenderism and intersexuality in childhood and adolescence: Making choices*. Thousand Oaks, CA: Sage.

Colapinto, John. 2001. *As nature made him: The boy who was raised as a girl*. New York: Perennial.

Collins, Patricia Hill. 1990. *Black feminist thought: Knowledge, consciousness, and the politics of empowerment*. Boston: Unwin Hyman.

——. 2000. It's all in the family: Intersections of gender, race, and nation. In *Decentering the center: Philosophy for a multicultural, postcolonial, and feminist world*, ed. Uma Narayan and Sandra Harding, 156–76. Bloomington: Indiana University Press.

Combahee River Collective. [1979] 1982. A black feminist statement. In *All the women are white, all the blacks are men, but some of us are brave: Black women's studies*, ed. Gloria T. Hull, Patricia Bell Scott, and Barbara Smith, 13–22. Old Westbury, NY: Feminist Press.

Coontz, Stephanie. 1988. *The social origins of private life: A history of American families 1600–1900*. New York: Verso.

——. 1992. *The way we never were: American families and the nostalgia trap*. New York: Basic.

Cooper, Anna Julia. [1892] 1998. *A voice from the South: By a black woman of the South*, ed. Charles Lemert. Lanham, MD: Rowman and Littlefield.

Corbett, Ken. 1998. Cross-gendered identification and homosexual boyhood: Toward a more complex theory of gender. *American Journal of Orthopsychiatry* 68:352–60.

Cowan, Ruth Schwartz. 1979. From Virginia Dare to Virginia Slims: Women and technology in American life. *Technology and Culture* 20, no. 1:51–63.

——. 1983. *More work for mother: The ironies of household technology from the open hearth to the microwave*. New York: Basic.

Crawford, Nicole. 2003. Understanding children's atypical gender behavior. *Monitor on Psychology* 34, no. 8:40.

Crenshaw, Kimberlé Williams. 1991. Mapping the margins: Intersectionality, identity politics, and violence against women of color. *Stanford Law Review* 43, no. 6:1241–99.

Crenshaw, Kimberlé Williams, and Gary Peller. 1993. Reel time/real justice. In *Reading Rodney King/reading urban uprising*, ed. Robert Gooding-Williams, 56–72. New York: Routledge.

Darnton, Nina. 1989. Committed youth. *Newsweek* (July 31).

Davis, Angela Y. 1997. Race and criminalization: Black Americans and the punishment industry. In *The house that race built: Black Americans, U.S. terrain*, ed. Wahneema Lubiano, 26–279. New York: Pantheon.

——. 2000. *The prison industrial complex* (audio CD). Oakland, CA: AK Press.

——. 2003. *Are prisons obsolete?* New York: Seven Stories.

Davis, Mike. [1990] 1992. *City of quartz: Excavating the future in Los Angeles*. New York: Vintage.

Dean, Carolyn J. 1994. The productive hypothesis: Gender and the history of sexuality. *History and Theory* 33, no. 3:271–96.

de Lauretis, Teresa. 1987. *Technologies of gender: Essays in theory, film, and fiction*. Bloomington: Indiana University Press.

Diamond, Milton. 1976. Human sexual development: Biological foundation for social development. In *Human sexuality in four perspectives*, ed. Frank. A. Beach, 22–61. Baltimore: Johns Hopkins University Press.

Dreger, Alice Domurat, ed. 1999. *Intersex in the age of ethics*. Hagerstown, MD: University Publishing Group.

Dreger, Alice Domurat, Cheryl Chase, Aron Sousa, et al. 2005. Changing the nomenclature/taxonomy for intersex: A scientific and clinical rationale. *Journal of Pediatric Endocrinology and Metabolism* 18, no. 8:729–33.

Dreyfuss, Rochelle Cooper, and Dorothy Nelkin. 1992. The jurisprudence of genetics. *Vanderbilt Law Review* 45, no. 2:313–48.

Dumm, Thomas. 1993. The new enclosures: Racism in the normalized community. In *Reading Rodney King/reading urban uprising*, ed. Robert Goodin-Williams, 78–195. New York: Routledge.

Duster, Troy. 1970. *The legislation of morality: Law, drugs, and moral judgment*. New York: Free Press.

——. 1990. *Backdoor to eugenics*. New York: Routledge.

——. 1994. Human genetics, evolutionary theory, and social stratification. In *The genetic frontier: Ethics, law, and policy*, ed. Mark S. Frankel and Albert Teich, 131–53. Washington, DC: American Association for the Advancement of Science.

Echols, Alice. 1989. *Daring to be bad: Radical feminism in America, 1967–1975*. Minneapolis: University of Minnesota Press.

Ehrenreich, Barbara, and Deirdre English. 1979. *For her own good*. Garden City, NY: Doubleday.

Eze, Emmanuel Chukwudi, ed. 1997. *Race and the enlightenment: A reader*. New York: Blackwell.

Fausto-Sterling, Anne. 1993. The five sexes: Why male and female are not enough. *The Sciences* (March–April):20–24.

——. 2000. *Sexing the body: Gender politics and the construction of sexuality*. New York: Basic Books.

Feder, Ellen K. 1997. Disciplining the family: The case of Gender Identity Disorder. *Philosophical Studies* 85, nos. 2/3:195–211.

———. 2002. Doctors' orders: Parents and intersex children. In *The subject of care: Feminist perspectives on dependency*, ed. Eva Feder Kittay and Ellen K. Feder, 294–320. Lanham, MD: Rowman and Littlefield.

Feder, Ellen K., and Eva Feder Kittay, eds. 1996. *Hypatia: A Journal of Feminist Philosophy* (special issue, The Family and Feminist Theory) 11, no. 1.

Federal Bureau of Investigation. 1998. *FBI Law Enforcement Bulletin* 67, no. 3 (March 1).

Fineman, Martha Albertson. 1995. *The neutered mother, the sexual family, and other twentieth-century tragedies*. New York: Routledge.

Firestone, Shulamith. [1970] 1979. *The dialectic of sex: The case for feminist revolution*. London: Women's Press.

Foucault, Michel. [1961] 1988. *Madness and civilization: A history of insanity in the Age of Reason*, trans. Richard Howard. New York: Vintage.

———. [1963] 1975. *The birth of the clinic: An archaeology of medical perception*, trans. A. M. Sheridan Smith. New York: Vintage.

———. [1966] 1973. *The order of things: An archaeology of the human sciences*. New York: Vintage.

———. [1969; 1971] 1972. *The archaeology of knowledge and the discourse on language*, trans. A. M. Sheridan Smith. New York: Pantheon.

———. [1971] 1977. Nietzsche, genealogy, history. In *Language, counter-memory, practice: Selected essays and interviews*, ed. Donald F. Bouchard, 139–64. Ithaca, NY: Cornell University Press.

———. [1975] 1979. *Discipline and punish: The birth of the prison*, trans. Alan Sheridan. New York: Vintage.

———. [1975] 1980. Prison talk. In *Power/knowledge: Selected interviews and other writings 1972–1977*, ed. Colin Gordon, 37–54. New York: Pantheon.

———. [1976] 1980. The politics of health in the eighteenth century. In *Power/knowledge: Selected interviews and other writings, 1972–1977*, ed. Colin Gordon, 166–82. New York: Pantheon.

———. [1976] 1990. *The history of sexuality*, vol. 1: *An introduction*, trans. Robert Hurley. New York: Vintage.

———. [1977] 1980a. The confession of the flesh. In *Power/knowledge: Selected interviews and other writings, 1972–1977*, ed. Colin Gordon, 194–228. New York: Pantheon.

———. [1977] 1980b. Truth and power. In *Power/knowledge: Selected interviews and other writings, 1972–1977*, ed. Colin Gordon, 109–33. New York: Pantheon.

———. 1980. *Power/knowledge: Selected interviews and other writings, 1972–1977*, ed. Colin Gordon. New York: Pantheon.

———. [1982] 1983. The subject and power. In *Michel Foucault: Beyond structuralism and hermeneutics*, ed. Hubert L. Dreyfus and Paul Rabinow, 145–62. Chicago: University of Chicago Press.

———. [1997] 2003. *Society must be defended: Lectures at the Collège de France, 1975–76*, ed. Mauro Bertani and Allessandro Fontana; trans. David Macey. New York: Picador.

———. [1999] 2003. *Abnormal: Lectures at the Collège de France, 1974–75*, ed. Valerio Marchetti and Antonella Salomoni; trans. Graham Burchell. New York: Picador.

Foucault, Michel. [2003] 2006. *Psychiatric power: Lectures at the Collège de France, 1973–74,* ed. Jacques Lagrange; trans. Graham Burchell. New York: Palgrave Macmillan.

Frader, Joel, Priscilla Alderson, Adrienne Asch, et al. 2004. Health care professionals and intersex conditions. *Archives of Pediatric and Adolescent Medicine* 158, no. 4:426–28.

Fraser, Nancy, and Linda Gordon. 1994. A genealogy of "dependency": Tracing a keywork of the U.S. Welfare State. *Signs: Journal of Women in Culture and Society* 19, no. 2:309–36.

Friedan, Betty. 1963. *The feminine mystique.* New York: Norton.

Fukuyama, Francis. 2002. *Our posthuman future: Consequences of the biotechnology revolution.* New York: Farrar, Straus, & Giroux.

Gans, Herbert J. 1967. *The Levittowners: Ways of life and politics in a new suburban community.* New York: Pantheon.

GenderPAC. 2006. Mission statement. http://www.gpac.org/gpac/index.html.

Gilder, George. 1981. *Wealth and poverty.* New York: Basic Books.

———. 1995. The roots of black poverty. *Wall Street Journal* (October 30).

Gilligan, Carol. 1982. *In a different voice: Psychological theory and women's development.* Cambridge, MA: Harvard University Press.

Gilligan, James. 1996. *Violence: Our deadly epidemic and its causes.* New York: Putnam.

Glassner, Barry. 1999. *The culture of fear: Why Americans are afraid of the wrong things.* New York: Basic Books.

Goffman, Erving. 1961. On the characteristics of total institutions. In *Asylums: Essays on the social situation of mental patients and other inmates,* 1–124. Garden City, NY: Anchor.

Goldberg, David Theo. 1990. The social formation of racist discourse. In *Anatomy of racism,* ed. David Theo Goldberg, 295–318. Minneapolis: University of Minnesota Press.

———. 1993. *Racist culture: Philosophy and the politics of meaning.* Oxford: Blackwell.

———. 2002. *The racial state.* Oxford: Blackwell.

Goodwin, Frederick K. 1992a. Address at the National Mental Health Advisory Council, Bethesda, MD, February 11.

———. 1992b. Conduct disorder as a precursor to adult violence and substance abuse: Can the progression be halted? Address to the American Psychiatric Association Annual Convention, Washington, DC, May 5.

Gordon, Linda. 1994. *Pitied but not entitled: Single mothers and the history of welfare, 1890–1935.* New York: Free Press.

Gould, Stephen Jay. 1996. *The mismeasure of man,* 2d ed. New York: Norton.

Green, Richard. 1976. One hundred ten feminine and masculine boys: Behavioral contrasts and demographic similarities. *Archives of Sexual Behavior* 5, no. 5:425–46.

———. 1987. *The "sissy boy syndrome" and the development of homosexuality.* New Haven, CT: Yale University Press.

Greenberg, Julie A. 2003. Legal aspects of gender assignment. *Endocrinologist* 13, no. 3:277–86.

Greenberg, Julie A., and Cheryl Chase. 2005. Background of Colombia decisions. http://www.isna.org/node/21.

Gresham, Jewell Handy, and Margaret B. Wilkerson, eds. 1989. *The nation: Scapegoating the black family* (July 24–31):110–47.

Gutting, Gary. 1989. *Michel Foucault's archaeology of scientific reason.* New York: Cambridge University Press.

———. 1994. Foucault and the history of madness. In *The Cambridge companion to Foucault*, ed. Gary Gutting, 47–70. New York: Cambridge University Press.

Haar, Charles M. 1996. *Suburbs under siege: Race, space, and audacious judges.* Princeton, NJ: Princeton University Press.

Hamer, Dean H., and Peter Copeland. 1998. *Living with our genes: Why they matter more than you think.* New York: Doubleday.

Haraway, Donna J. 1989. *Primate visions: Gender, race, and nature in the world of modern science.* New York: Routledge.

Harris, Cheryl I. 1993. Whiteness as property. *Harvard Law Review* 106, no. 8:1707–91.

Hartigan, John, Jr. 2001. "White devils" talk back: What antiracists can learn from whites in Detroit. In *The making and unmaking of whiteness*, ed. Birgit Brander Rasmussen, Eric Klinenberg, Irene J. Nexica, and Matt Wray, 138–66. Durham, NC: Duke University Press.

Hartmann, Heidi I. 1981. The family as the locus of gender, class, and political struggle: The example of housework. *Signs: Journal of Culture and Society* 6, no. 3:366–94.

Hayden, Dolores. 1981. *The grand domestic revolution: A history of feminist designs for American homes, neighborhoods, and cities.* Cambridge, MA: MIT Press.

———. 1984. *Redesigning the American dream: The future of housing, work, and family life.* New York: Norton.

Herrnstein, Richard J., and Charles A. Murray. 1994. *The bell curve: Intelligence and class struggle in America.* New York: Free Press.

Higley, J. D., and Stephen Suomi. 1996. Reactivity and social competence affect individual difference in reaction to severe stress in children: Investigations using nonhuman primates. In *Intense stress and mental disturbance in children*, ed. C. R. Pfeffer, 1–69. Washington, DC: American Psychiatric Press.

Hilts, Philip J. 1992. Federal official apologizes for remarks on inner cities. *New York Times* (February 22).

Holden, Constance. 1992. Health official falls, lands in NIMH; Frederick K. Goodwin's remarks about inner-city anger congressmen; he resigned as head of the Alcohol, Drug Abuse, and Mental Health Administration and was appointed director of the National Institute of Mental Health. *Science* (March 6).

hooks, bell. 1984. *Feminist theory: From margin to center.* Boston: South End Press.

Hughes, Ieuan A., Chris Houk, S. Faisal Ahmed, and Peter A. Lee. 2006. Consensus statement on management of intersex conditions. *Archives of Disease in Childhood* 14, no. 15:1–10.

Hull, Gloria T., Patricia Bell Scott, and Barbara Smith, eds. 1982. *All the women are white, all the blacks are men, but some of us are brave: Black women's studies.* Old Westbury, NY: Feminist Press.

Jackson, Kenneth T. 1985. *The crabgrass frontier: The suburbanization of the United States.* New York: Oxford University Press.

Jacobs, Harriet. [1861] 1987. *Incidents in the life of a slave girl.* In *The classic slave narratives*, ed. Henry Louis Gates Jr., 333–515. New York: Signet.

James, Joy. 1996. *Resisting state violence: Radicalism, gender, and race in U.S. culture*. Minneapolis: University of Minnesota Press.

JanMohamed, Abdul. 1992. Sexuality on/of the racial border: Foucault, Wright, and the articulation of a "racialized sexuality." In *Discourses of sexuality: From Aristotle to AIDS*, ed. Domna Stanton, 94–116. Ann Arbor: University of Michigan Press.

Kessler, Suzanne. 1998. *Lessons from the intersexed*. New Brunswick, NJ: Rutgers University Press.

Kipnis, Kenneth, and Milton Diamond. 1999. Pediatric ethics and the surgical assignment of sex. In *Intersex in the age of ethics*, ed. Alice Domerat Dreger, 173–93. Hagerstown, MD: University Publishing Group.

Klinkner, Philip A., with Rogers M. Smith. 1999. *The unsteady march: The rise and decline of racial equality in America*. Chicago: University of Chicago Press.

Ladner, Joyce. 1972. *Tomorrow's tomorrow: The black woman*. New York: Doubleday.

Lambert, Bruce. [1997] 1999. At 50, Levittown contends with legacy of racial bias. In *Strangers & neighbors: Relations between blacks & Jews in the United States*, ed. Maurianne Adams and John Bracey, 495–99. Amherst: University of Massachusetts Press.

Lane, Charles. 2005. Sentencing guidelines no longer mandatory: Federal judges may deviate, court rules. *Washington Post* (January 13).

Langdon, Philip. 1994. *A better place to live: Reshaping the American suburb*. Amherst: University of Massachusetts Press.

Lawson, Carol. 1995. Disney's newest show is a town. *New York Times* (November 16).

Lipsitz, George. 1995. The possessive investment in whiteness: Racialized social democracy and the "white" problem in American studies. *American Quarterly* 47, no. 3:369–87.

Lock, James, Victor G. Carrion, and Brian N. Kleis. 1997. Gender issues. In *Treating preschool children*, ed. Hans Steiner, 137–58. San Francisco: Jossey-Bass.

Loewenberg, Bert J., and Ruth Bogin, eds. 1976. *Black women in nineteenth-century American life*. University Park: Pennsylvania State University Press.

Lubiano, Wahneema. 1992. Black ladies, welfare queens, and state minstrels: Ideological warfare by narrative means. In *Race-ing justice, en-gendering power: Essays on Anita Hill, Clarence Thomas, and the construction of social reality*, ed. Toni Morrison, 323–63. New York: Pantheon.

Maguire, Kathleen, and Ann L. Pastore, eds. 1998. *Sourcebook of criminal justice statistics, 1997*. Washington, DC: Bureau of Justice Statistics.

Mainardi, Pat. 1970. The politics of housework. In *Sisterhood is powerful*, ed. Robin Morgan, 447–54. New York: Vintage.

Marantz, Sonia A. 1984. Mothers of extremely feminine boys: Child-rearing practices and psychopathology. PhD diss., New York University.

Margie. 1994. Notes from the inside. *Sassy* (June):52–53, 66.

Mark, Vernon, William Sweet, and Frank Ervin. [1967] 1985. Role of brain disease in riots and urban violence. In *Biology, crime, and ethics: A study of biological explanations for criminal behavior*, ed. Frank H. Marsh and Janet Katz, 123–25. Cincinnati: Anderson.

Marsh, Frank H., and Janet Katz, eds. 1985. *Biology, crime, and ethics: A study of biological explanations for criminal behavior*. Cincinnati: Anderson.

Massey, Douglas S., and Nancy A. Denton. 1993. *American apartheid: Segregation and the making of the underclass.* Cambridge: Harvard University Press.

McLaren, Margaret A. 2002. *Feminism, Foucault, and embodied subjectivity.* Albany: SUNY Press.

McNay, Lois. 1991. The Foucauldian body and the exclusion of experience. *Hypatia* 6, no. 3:125–39.

McWhorter, Ladelle. 1999. *Bodies and pleasures: Foucault and the politics of sexual normalization.* Indianapolis: Indiana University Press.

Menvielle, Edgardo J. 1998. Gender Identity Disorder [letter to the editor]. *Journal of the American Academy of Child and Adolescent Psychiatry* 37, no. 3:243–44.

Menvielle, Edgardo J., and Catherine Tuerk. 2002. A support group for parents of gender-nonconforming boys. *Journal of the American Academy of Child and Adolescent Psychiatry* 41, no. 8:1010–13.

Menvielle, Edgardo J., Catherine Tuerk, and Ellen C. Perrin. 2005. To the beat of a different drummer: The gender-variant child. *Contemporary Pediatrics* 22, no. 2:38–39; 41–45.

Mestel, Rosie. 1994. What triggers the violence within? *New Scientist* (February 26):31–34.

Meyers, Diana Tietjens. 2000. Feminism and women's autonomy: The challenge of female genital cutting. *Metaphilosophy* 31, no. 5:469–91.

Michel, Sonya. 1999. *Children's interests/mothers' rights: The shaping of America's child care policy.* New Haven, CT: Yale University Press.

Mills, Charles. 1997. *The racial contract.* Ithaca, NY: Cornell University Press.

Minter, Shannon. 1999. Diagnosis and treatment of Gender Identity Disorder in children. In *Sissies and tomboys,* ed. Matthew Rottnek, 9–33. New York: New York University Press.

Mirken, Bruce. 1994. Setting them straight. *Ten Percent* (June):55–59, 84.

Money, John, and Anke A. Ehrhardt. 1982. *Man and woman, boy and girl.* Baltimore: Johns Hopkins University Press.

Montagu, Ashley. [1964] 1997. *Man's most dangerous myth: The fallacy of race,* 6th ed. Walnut Creek, CA: Alma Mira.

Moraga, Cherríe, and Gloria Anzaldúa. [1981] 1983. *This bridge called my back: Writings by radical women of color.* New York: Kitchen Table, Women of Color Press.

Morgan, Kathryn Pauly. 2005. Gender police. In *Foucault and the government of disability,* ed. Shelley Tremain, 298–328. Ann Arbor: University of Michigan Press.

Mournian, Thomas. 1998. Hiding out. *San Francisco Bay Guardian* (April 18).

Moynihan, Daniel Patrick. [1965] 1967. The Negro family: The case for national action. In *The Moynihan Report and the politics of controversy: A transaction social science and public policy report,* ed. Lee Rainwater and William L. Yancey, 39–124. Cambridge, MA: MIT Press.

Murray, Charles. 1984. *Losing ground.* New York: Basic Books.

Myers, Daisy D. 2005. *Sticks 'n stones: The Myers family in Levittown.* York, PA: York County Heritage Trust.

Nelson, Hilde Lindemann, ed. 1997. *Stories and their limits: Narrative approaches to bioethics.* New York: Routledge.

Nicholson, Linda J. 1986. *Gender and history: The limits of social theory in the age of the family.* New York: Columbia University Press.

Nicolosi, Joseph. 1991. *Reparative therapy of male homosexuality: A new clinical approach.* Northvale, NJ: Aronson.

Oakley, Ann. 1974a. *Housewife.* New York: Penguin.

———. 1974b. *The sociology of housework.* New York: Pantheon.

Oliver, Kelly. 1997. *Family values: Subjects between nature and culture.* New York: Routledge.

Painter, Nell Irvin. 1992. Hill, Thomas, and the use of racial stereotype. In *Racing justice, en-gendering power: Essays on Anita Hill, Clarence Thomas, and the construction of social reality,* ed. Toni Morrison, 200–14. New York: Pantheon.

Palen, John J. 1995. *The suburbs.* New York: McGraw-Hill.

Parens, Erik, ed. 2006. *Surgically shaping children.* Baltimore: Johns Hopkins University Press.

Politics and the life sciences. 1996. Symposium: Genetics and crime. *Politics and the Life Sciences* 15, no. 1 (March):83–110.

Pooley, Karen Beck. 2003. The other Levittown: Race and place in Willingboro, NJ. *The Next American City* 2:8–11.

Popenoe, David. 1977. *The suburban environment: Sweden and the United States.* Chicago: University of Chicago Press.

Preves, Sharon. 2003. *Intersex and identity: The contested self.* New Brunswick, NJ: Rutgers University Press.

Rafferty, Carole. 1995. Mistaken identities. *San Jose Mercury News* (July 18).

Rappley, Marsha, Patricia B. Mullan, Francisco J. Alvarez, et al. 1999. Diagnosis of attention-deficit/hyperactivity disorder and use of psychotropic medication in very young children. *Archives of Pediatrics and Adolescent Medicine* 153, no. 10:1039–45.

Rawlinson, Mary C. 1987. Foucault's strategy: Knowledge, power, and the specificity of truth. *Journal of Medicine and Philosophy* 12, no. 4:371–95.

Reiman, Jeffrey. [1979] 2004. *The rich get richer and the poor get prison: Ideology, class, and criminal justice.* Boston: Allyn and Bacon.

Reiss, Albert J., Jr., and Jeffrey A. Roth, eds. 1993. *Understanding and preventing violence.* Washington, DC: National Academy Press.

Rekers, George A. 1982a. *Growing up straight: What families should know about homosexuality.* Chicago: Moody.

———. 1982b. *Shaping your child's sexual identity.* Grand Rapids, MI: Baker Book House.

———. 1987. Inadequate sex role differentiation in childhood: The family and Gender Identity Disorders. *Journal of Family and Culture* 2, no. 7:8–37.

Rekers, George A., P. M. Bentler, A. C. Rosen, and O. Ivar Lovaas. 1977. Child gender disturbances: A clinical rationale for intervention. *Psychotherapy: Theory, Research, and Practice* 14, no. 1:2–11.

Rekers, George A., and O. Ivar Lovaas. 1974. Behavioral treatment of deviant sex-role behaviors in a male child. *Journal of Applied Behavior Analysis* 7, no. 2:173–90.

Rekers, George A., and Shasta Mead. 1979. Early intervention for female sexual identity disturbance: Self-monitoring of play behavior. *Journal of Abnormal Child Psychology* 7, no. 4:405–23.

Rekers, George A., and James Varni. 1977a. Self-monitoring and self-reinforcement processes in a pre-transsexual boy. *Journal of Behavior Therapy and Experimental Psychiatry* 10, no. 2:177–80.

———. 1977b. Self-regulation of gender-role behaviors: A case study. *Journal of Behavior Therapy and Experimental Psychiatry* 8, no. 4:427–32.

Rensberger, Boyce. 1992. Science and sensitivity: Primates, politics, and the sudden debate over the origins of human violence. *Washington Post* (March 1).

Reuters. 1995. Nearly 7% of adult black males were inmates in '94, study says. *New York Times* (December 4).

Ricks, Ingrid. 1993. Mind games. *The Advocate* (December 28):38–40.

Ricoeur, Paul. [1983] 1984. *Time and narrative*, vol. 1, trans. Kathleen Blamey and David Pellauer. Chicago: University of Chicago Press.

Roberts, Dorothy. 1997. *Killing the black body: Race, reproduction, and the meaning of liberty*. New York: Pantheon.

Rochell, Anne. 1994. Atlanta's killing ground: Scientists probe the violent mind; chemicals in brain a link, researchers say. *Atlanta Journal and Constitution* (June 20).

Rose, Tricia. 1994. *Black noise: Rap music and black culture in contemporary America*. Middletown, CT: Wesleyan University Press.

Rosenberg, Mark L., and Mary Ann Fenley, eds. 1991. *Violence in America: A public health approach*. New York: Oxford University Press.

Rosenberg, Mark L., and James A. Mercy. 1991. Assaultive violence. In *Violence in America: A public health approach*, ed. Mark L. Rosenberg and Mary Ann Fenley, 14–50. New York: Oxford University Press.

Rosenberg, Miriam. 2001. Children with gender identity issues and their parents in individual and group treatment. *Journal of the American Academy of Child and Adolescent Psychiatry* 41, no. 5:619–21.

Ross, Andrew. 1999. *The Celebration chronicles: Life, liberty, and the pursuit of property values*. New York: Ballantine.

Rubin, Gayle. 1975. The traffic in women: Notes on the "political economy" of sex. In *Toward an anthropology of women*, ed. Rayna Reiter, 157–210. New York: Monthly Review Press.

Ruddick, Sara. 1989. *Maternal thinking: Toward a politics of peace*. New York: Ballantine.

Rustin, Bayard. [1966] 1967. Why don't Negroes...In *The Moynihan Report and the politics of controversy: A transaction social science and public policy report*, ed. Lee Rainwater and William L. Yancey, 417–26. Cambridge, MA: MIT Press.

Sánchez, George J. 1995. Reading Reginald Denny: The politics of whiteness in the late twentieth century. *American Quarterly* 47, no. 3:388–94.

Sawicki, Jana. 1991. *Disciplining Foucault: Feminism, power, and the body*. New York: Routledge.

Scheman, Naomi. 1999. Queering the center by centering the queer: Reflections on transsexuals and secular Jews. In *Sissies and tomboys*, ed. Matthew Rottnek, 58–103. New York: New York University Press.

Scholinski, Daphne, with Jane Meredith Adams. 1997. *The last time I wore a dress*. New York: Riverhead.

Schwartz, Ira M., Marilyn Jackson-Beeck, and Roger Anderson. 1984. The "hidden" system of juvenile control. *Crime and Delinquency* 30, no. 3:371–85.

Sedgwick, Eve Kosofsky. 1991. How to bring your kids up gay. *Social Text* 29:18–27.

Sellers-Diamond, Alfreda. 1994. Disposable children in black faces: The violence initiative as inner-city containment policy. *UMKC Law Review* 62, no. 3:423–69.

Semple, Janet. 1993. *Bentham's prison: A study of the Panopticon penitentiary.* New York: Clarendon.

Shipman, Pat. 1994. *The evolution of racism: Human differences and the use and abuse of science.* New York: Simon & Schuster.

Sipchen, Bob. 1992. The U.S. wants to use its public health know-how to treat the plague of violence, but critics fear that would erode civil liberties: A cure for violence? *Los Angeles Times* (April 24).

Smedley, Audrey. 1993. *Race in North America: Origin and evolution of a worldview.* Boulder, CO: Westview.

Solinger, Rickie. 1992. *Wake up little Susie: Single pregnancy and race before* Roe v. Wade. New York: Routledge.

Spelman, Elizabeth V. 1988. *Inessential woman: Problems of exclusion in feminist thought.* Boston: Beacon.

Spillers, Hortense. 1984. Interstices: A small drama of words. In *Pleasure and danger: Exploring female sexuality*, ed. Carol S. Vance, 73–100. New York: Routledge.

———. 1987. Mama's baby, papa's maybe: An American grammar book. *Diacritics* 17, no. 2:64–81.

Spivak, Gayatri Chakravorty. 1993. More on power/knowledge. In *Outside in the teaching machine*, 25–52. New York: Routledge.

Stack, Carol B. 1974. *All our kin: Strategies for survival in a black community.* New York: Harper Torchbooks.

———. 1996. *Call to home: African Americans reclaim the rural South.* New York: Basic Books.

Stampp, Kenneth M. 1956. *The peculiar institution: Slavery in the ante-bellum South.* New York: Knopf.

Stein, Rob. 2005. Heart drug for blacks endorsed: Racial tailoring would be a first; idea stirs debate. *Washington Post* (June 17).

Stilgoe, John R. 1988. *Borderland: Origins of the American suburb, 1820–1939.* New Haven, CT: Yale University Press.

Stolberg, Sheryl. 1993. Fear clouds search for genetic roots of violence; many say studies could open the door to abuses and racism. *Los Angeles Times* (December 30).

Stoler, Ann Laura. 1995. *Race and the education of desire: Foucault's* History of sexuality *and the colonial order of things.* Durham, NC: Duke University Press.

Stone-Mediatore, Shari. 2003. *Reading across borders: Storytelling and knowledges of resistance.* New York: Palgrave.

Suomi, Stephen J. 2002. Parents, peers, and the process of socialization in primates. In *Parenting and the child's world: Influences on academic, intellectual, and social-emotional development*, ed. John G. Borkowski, Sharon Landesman Ramey, and Marie Bristol-Power, 265–82. Mahwah, NJ: Erlbaum.

———. 2003. Gene-environment interactions and the neurobiology of social conflict. *Annals of the New York Academy of Sciences* 1008:132–39.

Terry, Jennifer. 1995. Anxious slippages between "us" and "them": A brief history of the scientific search for homosexual bodies. In *Deviant bodies: Critical perspectives on difference in science and popular culture*, ed. Jennifer Terry and Jacqueline Urla, 129–69. Indianapolis: Indiana University Press.

———. 1999. *An American obsession: Science, medicine, and homosexuality in modern society.* Chicago: University of Chicago Press.

Touchette, Nancy. 1994. Biochemical factors in impulsive and violent behavior. *Journal of NIH Research* 6:27–29.

Tuerk, Catherine, Edgardo Menvielle, and James de Jesús. 2003. *If you are concerned about your child's gender behaviors: A guide for parents*. Pamphlet. Children's National Medical Center Outreach Program for Children with Gender-variant Behaviors and Their Families.

U.S. Congress. *Disapproval of certain sentencing guideline amendments*, HR 237, 104th Cong., 1st sess., *Congressional Record* 141 (October 18, 1995): H 10259, H 10275.

Vesperi, Maria D. 1992. The politics of nature vs. nurture. *Saint Petersburg Times* (March 15).

Wajcman, Judy. 1991. *Feminism confronts technology*. University Park: Pennsylvania State University Press.

Ware, Vron. 2001. Perfidious Albion: Whiteness and the international imagination. In *The making and unmaking of whiteness*, ed. Birgit Brander Rasmussen, Eric Klinenberg, Irene J. Nexica, and Matt Wray, 184–213. Durham, NC: Duke University Press.

Wasserman, David, and Robert Wachbroit, eds. 2001. *Genetics and criminal behavior*. New York: Cambridge University Press.

Watt, Sally. 1996. Disney Corp. unveils Celebration, a more civic suburb. *All Things Considered* (July 26).

Wechsler, Lewis. 2004. *The first stone: A memoir of the racial integration of Levittown, Pennsylvania*. Chicago: Grounds for Growth Press.

Weithorn, Lois. 1988. Mental hospitalization of troublesome youth: An analysis of skyrocketing admission rates. *Stanford Law Review* 40, no. 3:773–838.

Wiegman, Robyn. 1995. *American anatomies: Theorizing race and gender*. Durham, NC: Duke University Press.

Wilkinson, Stephanie. 2001. Drop the Barbie! *Brain, Child* 2, no. 4:32–41.

Williams, Juan. 1994. Violence, genes, and prejudice. *Discover* (November): 92–102.

Williams, Patricia J. 1995. *The rooster's egg: On the persistence of prejudice*. Cambridge, MA: Harvard University Press.

Wilson, James Q., and Richard J. Herrnstein. 1985. *Crime and human nature*. New York: Simon & Schuster.

Winner, Langdon. 1980. Do artifacts have politics? *Daedalus* 109, no. 1: 121–36.

Wright, Robert. 1995. The biology of violence. *New Yorker* (March 13):67–77.

Wyden, Peter, and Barbara Wyden. 1968. *Growing up straight: What every thoughtful parent should know about homosexuality*. New York: Stein and Day.

Young, Iris Marion. 1995. Mothers, citizenship, and independence: A critique of pure family values. *Ethics: A Journal of Political, Legal, and Moral Philosophy* 105, no. 3:535–56.

———. 1996. Reflections on families in the age of Murphy Brown: On justice, gender, and sexuality. In *Revisioning the political: Feminist reconstructions of traditional concepts in Western political theory*, ed. Nancy J. Hirschmann and Christine Di Stefano, 251–70. Boulder, CO: Westview.

Zinn, Maxine Baca. [1989] 1992. Family, race, and poverty in the eighties. In *Rethinking the family: Some feminist questions*, rev. ed., ed. Barrie Thorne and Marilyn Yalom, 71–90. Boston: Northeastern University Press.

Zito, Julie Magno, Daniel J. Safer, Susan dosReis, et al. 2000. Trends in the prescribing of psychotropic medications to preschoolers. *Journal of the American Medical Association* 283, no. 8:1025–60.

Zucker, Kenneth J. 1984. Review of *Growing up straight: What every family should know about homosexuality* and *shaping your child's sexual identity*, by G. A. Rekers. *Archives of Sexual Behavior* 13, no. 4:387–90.

———. 1985. Cross-gender-identified children. In *Gender dysphoria: Development, research, management*, ed. Betty W. Steiner, 75–174. New York: Plenum.

———. 1990. Treatment of Gender Identity Disorders in children. In *Clinical management of Gender Identity Disorders in children and adults*, ed. Ray Blanchard and Betty W. Steiner, 25–46. Washington, DC: American Psychiatric Press.

———. 2004. Gender identity development and issues. *Child and Adolescent Psychiatric Clinics of North America* 13, no. 3:551–68.

Zucker, Kenneth J., and Susan J. Bradley. 1999a. *Gender Identity Disorder and psychosexual problems in children and adolescents*. New York: Guilford.

———. 1999b. Gender Identity Disorder and transvestic fetishism. In *Child and adolescent psychological disorders: A comprehensive textbook*, ed. S. D. Netherton, Deborah Holmes, and C. Eugene Walker, 367–96. New York: Oxford University Press.

Zucker, Kenneth J., Susan J. Bradley, and Mohammad Sanikhani. 1997. Sex differences in referral rates of children with Gender Identity Disorder: Some hypotheses. *Journal of Abnormal Child Psychology* 25, no. 3:217–27.

Zucker, Kenneth J., and Moshe Ipp. 1993. Delayed naming of a newborn boy: Relationship to the mother's wish for a girl and subsequent cross-gender identity in the child by the age of two. *Journal of Psychology and Human Sexuality* 6, no. 1:57–68.

Zucker, Kenneth J., and Robert L. Spitzer. 2005. Was the gender-identity disorder of childhood diagnosis introduced into *DSM-III* as a backdoor maneuver to replace homosexuality? A historical note. *Journal of Sex and Marital Therapy* 31, no. 1:31–42.

Index